Let's Keep

Follow Us Online

Visit US at

www.EffortlessMath.com

Call

https://goo.gl/2B6qWW

1-469-230-3605

Online Math Lessons

It's easy! Here's how it works.

1- Request a FREE introductory session.

2- Meet a Math tutor online.

3- Start Learning Math in Minutes.

Send Email to: **info@EffortlessMath.com**

Or Call: **+1-469-230-3605**

Basic Math Operations Workbook

Addition, Subtraction Multiplication, and Division

Fun Daily Math Worksheets for Grade 1 – 3

By

Reza Nazari

&

Ava Ross

All inquiries should be addressed to:

info@effortlessMath.com

www.EffortlessMath.com

ISBN–13: 978–1986356176

ISBN–10: 1986356175

Published by: Effortless Math Education

www.EffortlessMath.com

Description

Learning the basic math operations facilitates the learning of advanced math topics. Therefore, mastering basic math skills is among the most important things in a child's learning journey from 6 to 10 years old. It opens doors and brings out their full potential in many ways. But often children can need a helping hand when it comes to understanding the concepts mathematics.

In this Math Workbook, students can learn the basic math operations in a structured manner. In the book, you will find a complete home–study program to help children practice the essential math skills.

The book is in–depth and carries many great features, including:

- Lively layout and easy–to–follow explanations
- Fun, interactive and concrete
- Targeted, skill–building practice
- About 200 ready–to–reproduce practice pages
- Easy–to–follow directions and fun exercises

Designed for after school study and self–study, this book is ideal for homeschoolers, special needs and gifted children alike. You can also use the worksheets during the summer to get your children ready for the upcoming school term.

The engaging questions in this book provide students with the repeated practice they need to help them master basic Math skills. Each page features several basic Math problems.

This engaging format motivates students to improve their knowledge of Math.

About the Author

Reza Nazari is the author of more than 100 Math learning books including:

– **Math for Super Smart Students:** Fifth Graders and Older by Reza Nazari

– **Math and Critical Thinking Challenges:** For the Middle and High School Student

– **Effortless Math Education Workbooks**

Reza is also an experienced Math instructor and a test–prep expert who has been tutoring students since 2008. Reza is the founder of Effortless Math Education, a tutoring company that has helped many students raise their Math knowledge—and succeed in their studies. Reza provides an individualized custom learning plan and the personalized attention that makes a difference in how students view math.

You can contact Reza via email at:
Reza@EffortlessMath.com

Find Reza's professional profile at:
goo.gl/zoC9rJ

Contents

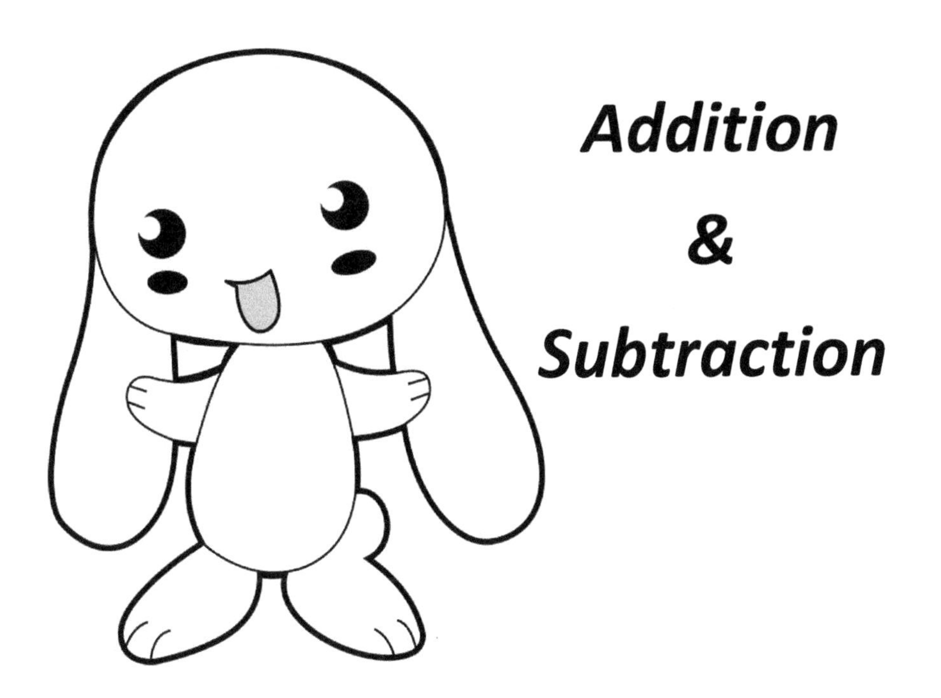

Addition & Subtraction

Adding by 1, 2 and 3

Write an addition fact for the following pictures.

☺☺	+	☺☺	=	☺☺ ☺☺	___ + ___ = ___
☺	+	☺☺	=	☺☺☺	___ + ___ = ___
☺☺☺	+	☺☺☺☺	=	☺☺☺ ☺☺☺☺	___ + ___ = ___
☺☺	+	☺☺☺ ☺☺	=	☺☺☺☺ ☺☺☺	___ + ___ = ___
☺☺☺	+	☺☺☺ ☺☺☺	=	☺☺☺☺ ☺☺☺☺☺	___ + ___ = ___
☺	+	☺☺☺ ☺☺☺☺	=	☺☺☺☺ ☺☺☺☺	___ + ___ = ___
☺☺☺	+	☺☺☺☺ ☺☺☺☺	=	☺☺☺☺☺☺ ☺☺☺☺☺	___ + ___ = ___
☺☺	+	☺☺☺ ☺☺☺ ☺☺☺	=	☺☺☺☺☺☺ ☺☺☺☺☺	___ + ___ = ___

Add each number in the top row by 1, 2 and 3.

+	0	1	2	3	4	5	6	7	8	9	10	11	12
1													
2													
3													

Match.

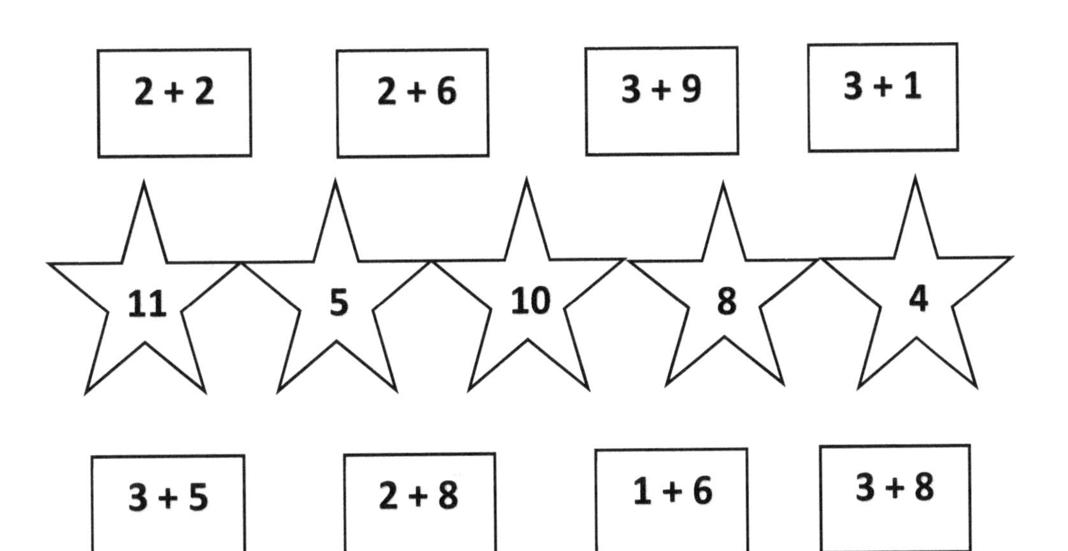

Write the answers in the boxes.

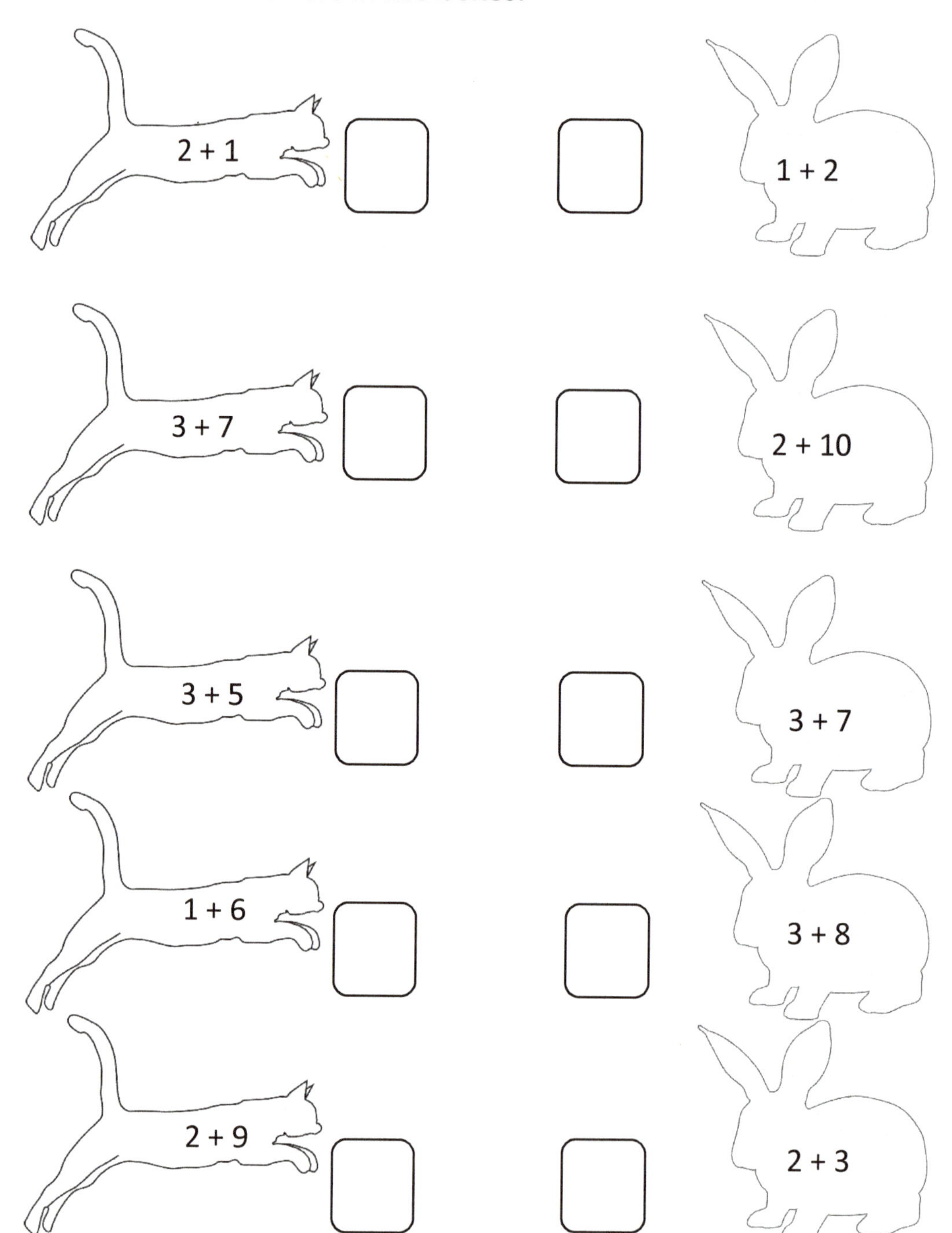

Find each sum.

$2 + 9 =$ ____	$3 + 8 =$ ____	$3 + 5 =$ ____
$3 + 9 =$ ____	$2 + 10 =$ ____	$1 + 6 =$ ____
$3 + 4 =$ ____	$2 + 4 =$ ____	$3 + 1 =$ ____

Sara had 2 oranges. She gets 3 more from her friend Wanda. How many oranges does Sara have now?

_____ oranges

Find each missing number.

2 + ___ = 3

3 + 0 = ___

___ + 4 = 7

3 + ___ = 13

3 + ___ = 6

___ + 12 = 15

___ + 1 = 4

3 + 11 = ___

3 + 9 = ___

___ + 2 = 5

___ + 7 = 10

3 + ___ = 9

3 + 8 = ___

3 + 13 = ___

Olivia has 6 candies. She was given 9 more candies. How many candies does Olivia have now?

_____ candies

Adding by 4 and 5

Write an addition fact for the following pictures.

☺☺
☺☺☺ + ☺ = ☺☺☺
☺☺☺ ___ + ___ = ___

☺☺
☺☺ + ☺☺ = ☺☺☺
☺☺☺ ___ + ___ = ___

☺☺
☺☺ + ☺☺☺
☺☺ = ☺☺☺☺☺
☺☺☺☺ ___ + ___ = ___

☺☺
☺☺☺ + ☺☺☺
☺☺☺☺ = ☺☺☺☺☺☺
☺☺☺☺☺☺ ___ + ___ = ___

☺☺
☺☺☺ + ☺☺☺
☺☺☺
☺☺☺ = ☺☺☺☺☺☺☺
☺☺☺☺☺☺☺ ___ + ___ = ___

Add each number in the top row by 4 and 5 .

+	0	1	2	3	4	5	6	7	8	9	10	11	12
4													
5													

Match.

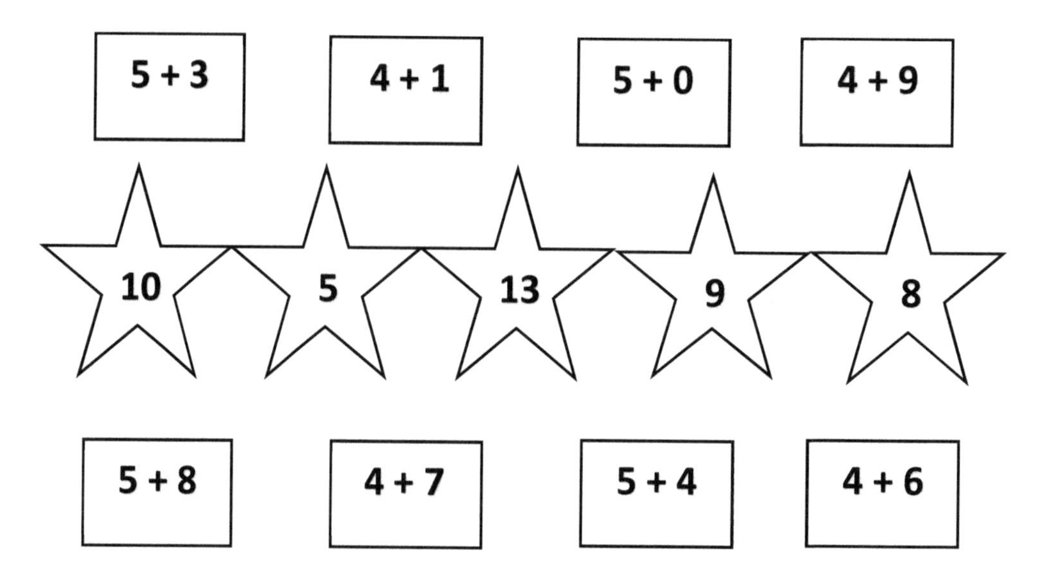

Write the answers in the boxes.

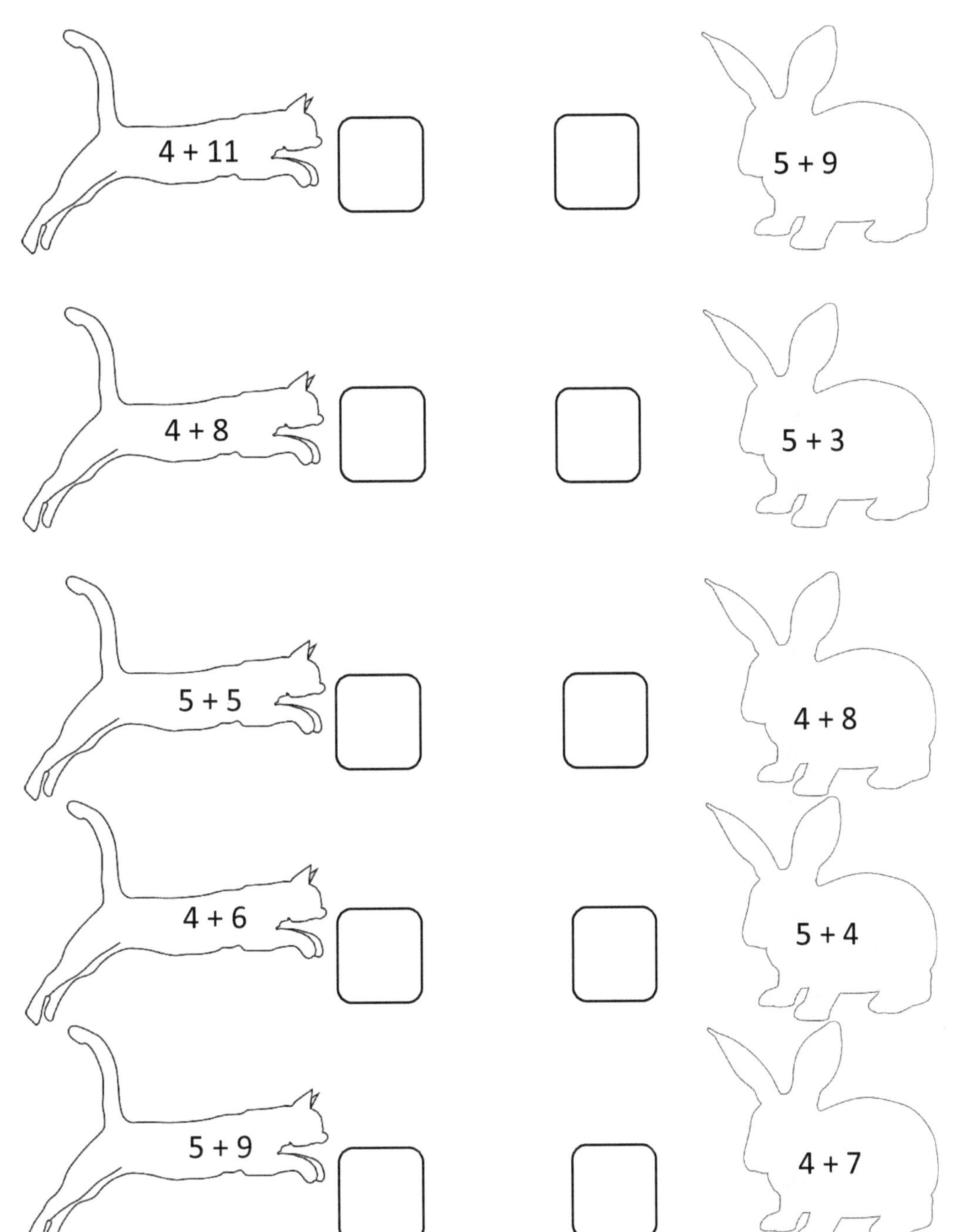

Find each sum.

$5 + 5 =$ ____	$4 + 3 =$ ____	$5 + 7 =$ ____
$4 + 8 =$ ____	$5 + 3 =$ ____	$4 + 5 =$ ____
$5 + 7 =$ ____	$5 + 9 =$ ____	$4 + 1 =$ ____

If there are 5 balls in a box and Jackson puts 8 more balls inside, how many balls are in the box?

_____ balls

Find each missing number.

4 + ___ = 7

___ + 3 = 8

4 + ___ = 6

___ + 3 = 7

5 + 4 = ___

___ + 1 = 5

5 + 7 = ___

5 + 1 = ___

5 + ___ = 9

___ + 4 = 8

5 + 10 = ___

___ + 11 = 15

5 + ___ = 10

5 + 12 = ___

Sophia has 4 apples. Emma gives Sophia 9 more. How many apples does Sophia have in all?

_____ apples

Subtraction by 1

Write a subtraction fact for the following pictures.

☺ − ☺ =   ___ - ___ = ___

☺☺ − ☺ = ☺   ___ - ___ = ___

☺☺
☺☺☺ − ☺ = ☺☺☺☺   ___ - ___ = ___

☺☺
☺☺ − ☺ = ☺☺☺   ___ - ___ = ___

☺☺☺
☺☺☺ − ☺ = ☺☺☺
☺☺   ___ - ___ = ___

☺☺☺
☺☺☺☺ − ☺ = ☺☺☺
☺☺☺   ___ - ___ = ___

☺☺☺☺
☺☺☺☺ − ☺ = ☺☺☺☺
☺☺☺   ___ - ___ = ___

☺☺☺
☺☺☺
☺☺☺ − ☺ = ☺☺☺☺
☺☺☺☺   ___ - ___ = ___

Subtract 1 from each number in the top.

—	1	2	3	4	5	6	7	8	9	10	11	12
1												

Match the values of the boxes and stars.

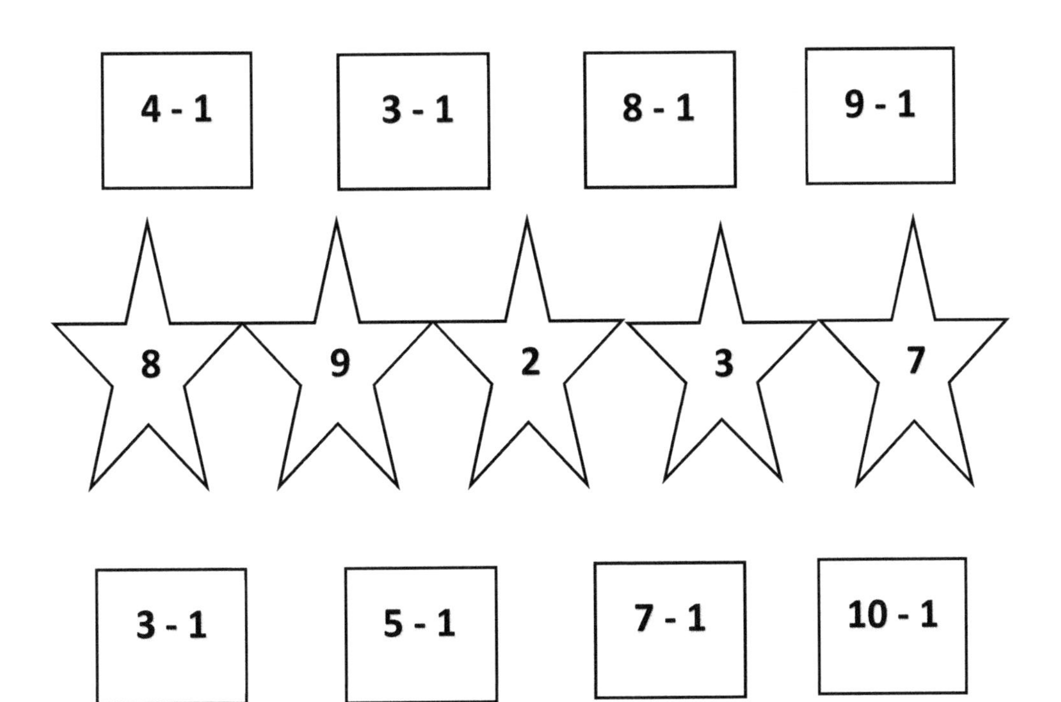

Write the answers in the boxes.

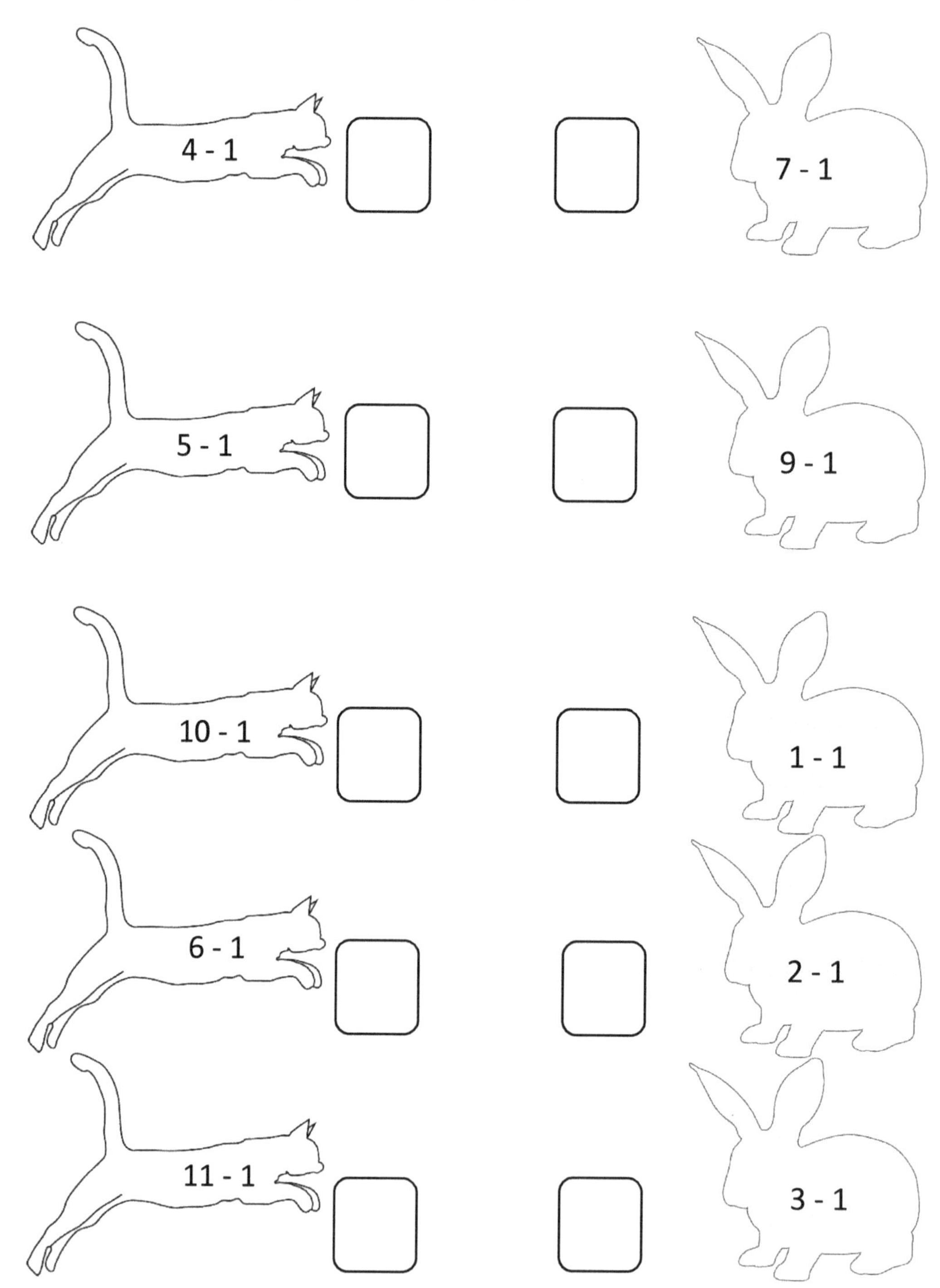

Find each difference.

$$\begin{array}{r} 5 \\ -\ 1 \\ \hline \underline{\qquad} \end{array} \qquad \begin{array}{r} 10 \\ -\ 1 \\ \hline \underline{\qquad} \end{array} \qquad \begin{array}{r} 9 \\ -\ 1 \\ \hline \underline{\qquad} \end{array}$$

$$\begin{array}{r} 8 \\ -\ 1 \\ \hline \underline{\qquad} \end{array} \qquad \begin{array}{r} 6 \\ -\ 1 \\ \hline \underline{\qquad} \end{array} \qquad \begin{array}{r} 3 \\ -\ 1 \\ \hline \underline{\qquad} \end{array}$$

$$\begin{array}{r} 7 \\ -\ 1 \\ \hline \underline{\qquad} \end{array} \qquad \begin{array}{r} 2 \\ -\ 1 \\ \hline \underline{\qquad} \end{array} \qquad \begin{array}{r} 4 \\ -\ 1 \\ \hline \underline{\qquad} \end{array}$$

Lily picked 9 apples from the orchard, and gave 1 apple to her friend Aria. How many apples does Lily have now ?

______ apples

Find each missing number.

1 – ___ = 0

1– 0 = ___

___ – 1 = 3

2 – ___ = 1

7 – ___ = 6

___ – 1 = 2

___ – 1 = 4

11 – 1 = ___

6 – 1 = ___

___ – 1 = 7

___ – 1 = 8

12 – ___ = 11

10 – 1 = ___

13 – 1 = ___

There are 12 cards in the drawer. Mia took 1 cards from the drawer. How many cards are now in the drawer?

_____ cards

Subtraction by 2

Write a subtraction fact for the following pictures.

☺☺ – ☺☺ =   __ - __ = __

☺☺☺ ☺☺☺ – ☺☺ = ☺☺ ☺☺   __ - __ = __

☺☺☺ ☺☺☺☺ – ☺☺ = ☺☺☺ ☺☺   __ - __ = __

☺☺☺ ☺☺☺ ☺☺☺ – ☺☺ = ☺☺☺☺ ☺☺☺   __ - __ = __

Subtract each number in the top row by 2.

—	2	3	4	5	6	7	8	9	10	11	12
2											

Match.

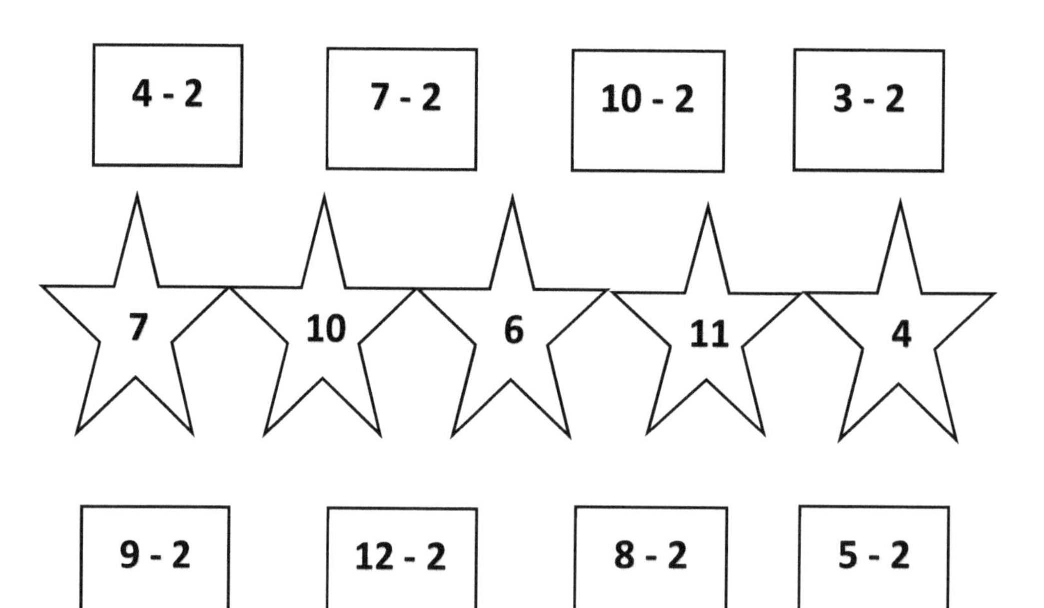

Write the answers in the boxes.

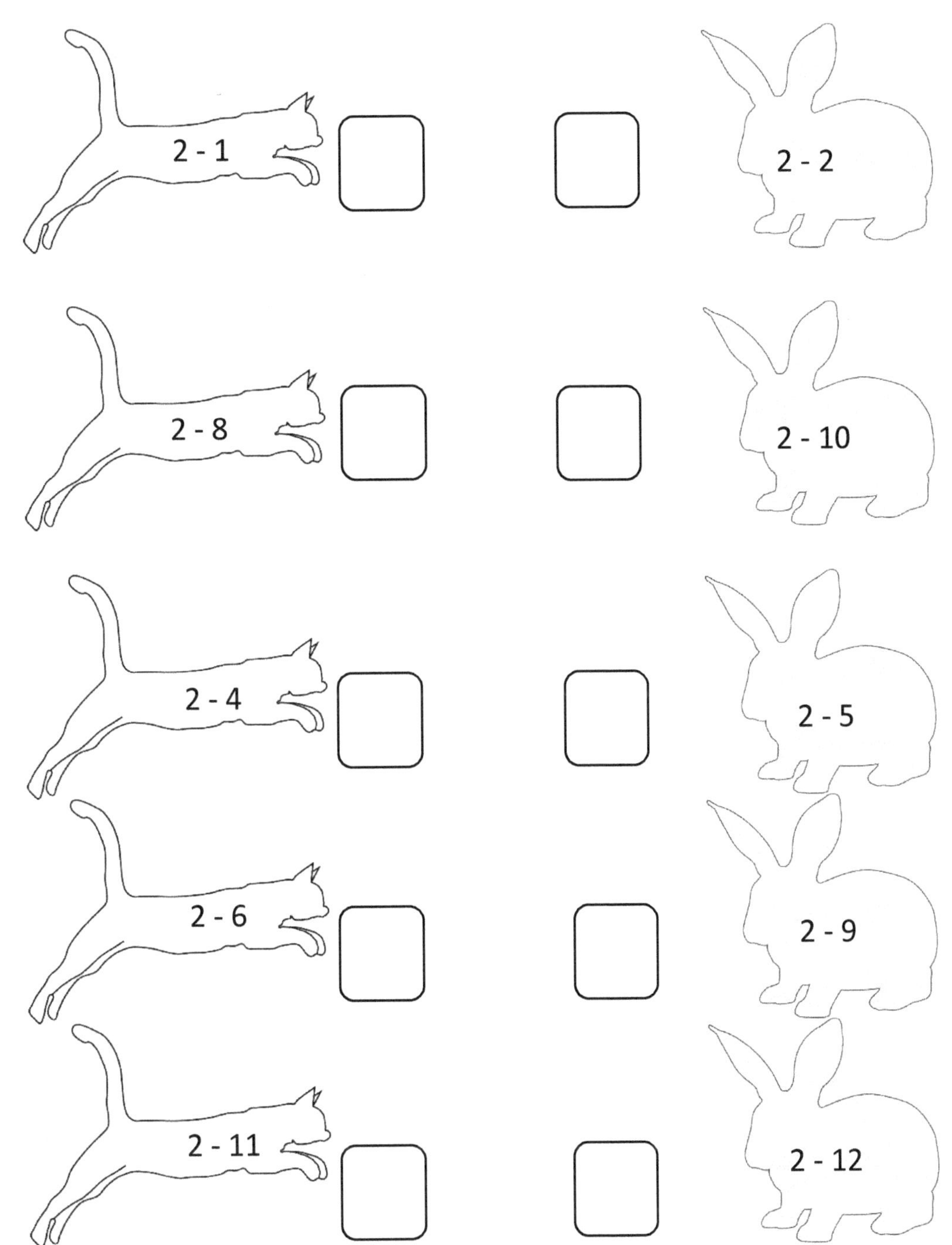

Find each difference.

$\begin{array}{r} 6 \\ -\ 2 \\ \hline \end{array}$ ______	$\begin{array}{r} 9 \\ -\ 2 \\ \hline \end{array}$ ______	$\begin{array}{r} 12 \\ -\ 2 \\ \hline \end{array}$ ______
$\begin{array}{r} 11 \\ -\ 2 \\ \hline \end{array}$ ______	$\begin{array}{r} 8 \\ -\ 2 \\ \hline \end{array}$ ______	$\begin{array}{r} 5 \\ -\ 2 \\ \hline \end{array}$ ______
$\begin{array}{r} 3 \\ -\ 2 \\ \hline \end{array}$ ______	$\begin{array}{r} 4 \\ -\ 2 \\ \hline \end{array}$ ______	$\begin{array}{r} 7 \\ -\ 2 \\ \hline \end{array}$ ______

Zoe has 9 marbles, she gave Olivia 2 of the marbles. How many marbles does she now have ?

______ marbles

Find each missing number.

$12 - \_\_\_ = 10$

$11 - 2 = \_\_\_$

$\_\_\_ - 2 = 5$

$9 - \_\_\_ = 7$

$5 - \_\_\_ = 3$

$\_\_\_ - 2 = 0$

$\_\_\_ - 2 = 2$

$2 - 1 = \_\_\_$

$9 - 2 = \_\_\_$

$\_\_\_ - 2 = 1$

$\_\_\_ - 2 = 6$

$6 - \_\_\_ = 4$

$10 - 2 = \_\_\_$

$13 - 2 = \_\_\_$

Emily grew 13 pumpkins, but the rabbits ate 2 of them. How many pumpkins does Emily have left?

_____ pumpkins

Subtraction by 3

Write a subtraction fact for the following pictures.

☺☺
☺☺☺ − ☺☺☺ = ☺☺ ___ - ___ = ___

☺☺☺
☺☺ − ☺☺☺ = ☺☺ ___ - ___ = ___

☺☺☺
☺☺☺ − ☺☺☺ = ☺☺☺ ___ - ___ = ___

☺☺☺☺
☺☺☺☺ − ☺☺☺ = ☺☺☺
☺☺ ___ - ___ = ___

☺☺☺
☺☺☺☺ − ☺☺☺ = ☺☺
☺☺ ___ - ___ = ___

Subtract each number in the top row by 3.

—	3	4	5	6	7	8	9	10	11	12
3										

Match.

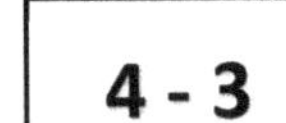

7 - 3 9 - 3 6 - 3

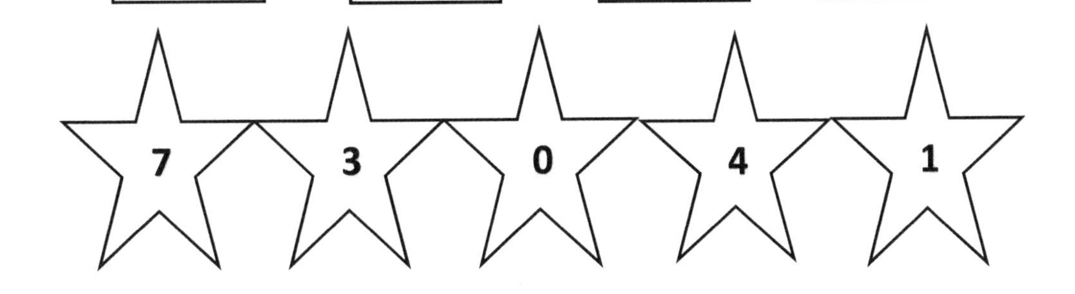

3 - 3 8 - 3 5 - 3 10 - 3

Write the answers in the boxes.

Find each difference.

$$\begin{array}{r} 5 \\ - \quad 3 \\ \hline \end{array}$$

$$\begin{array}{r} 6 \\ - \quad 3 \\ \hline \end{array}$$

$$\begin{array}{r} 8 \\ - \quad 3 \\ \hline \end{array}$$

$$\begin{array}{r} 4 \\ - \quad 3 \\ \hline \end{array}$$

$$\begin{array}{r} 7 \\ - \quad 3 \\ \hline \end{array}$$

$$\begin{array}{r} 10 \\ - \quad 3 \\ \hline \end{array}$$

$$\begin{array}{r} 11 \\ - \quad 3 \\ \hline \end{array}$$

$$\begin{array}{r} 9 \\ - \quad 3 \\ \hline \end{array}$$

$$\begin{array}{r} 12 \\ - \quad 3 \\ \hline \end{array}$$

Richard found 11 seashells on the beach, he gave Aria 3 of the seashells. How many seashells does he now have?

_____ seashells

Find each missing number.

10 – ___ = 7

5 – 3 = ___

___ – 3 = 3

13 – ___ = 10

3 – ___ = 0

___ – 3 = 9

___ – 3 = 1

14 – 3 = ___

9 – 3 = ___

___ – 3 = 12

___ – 3 = 5

16 – ___ = 13

11 – 3 = ___

17 – 3 = ___

Ella's high school played 12 basketball games last year. She attended 3 games. How many basketball games did Ella miss?

_____ basketball games

Subtraction and adding by 1, 2 and 3

Match.

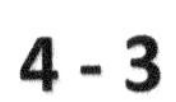

4 - 3	4 + 2	9 - 1	6 + 3

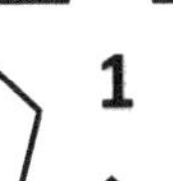

8 7 6 9 1

10 - 1	3 - 2	3 + 5	8 - 2

Solve.

2 + 3 = 5	5 – 3 = 2
8 + 3 = ___	___ – 3 = ___
5 + 2 = ___	___ – 2 = ___
7 + 3 = ___	___ – 3 = ___
4 + 1 = ___	___ – 1 = ___
9 + 3 = ___	___ – 3 = ___
7 + 1 = ___	___ – 1 = ___

Write the answers in the boxes.

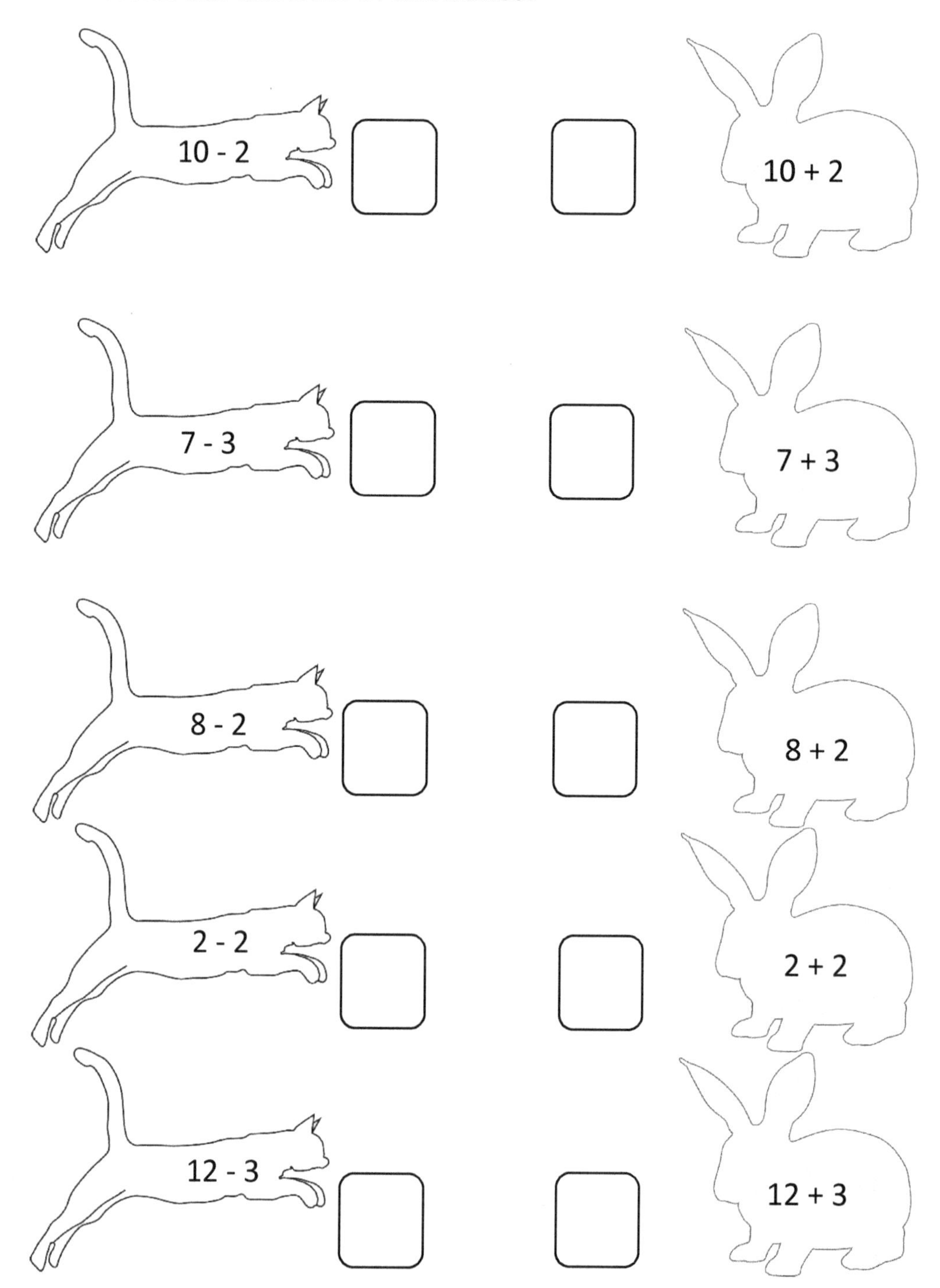

Find each difference.

13 − 2 = ___	10 − 4 = ___	3 − 3 = ___
12 + 4 = ___	13 − 3 = ___	14 + 2 = ___
9 − 3 = ___	10 + 3 = ___	6 − 2 = ___

Jacob collects 13 oranges. Jacob's mother gives him 3 more. How many oranges does Jacob have? _____ oranges

Eliana had 13 old books. She sold 3 books. How many books does Eliana now have? ______ books

Adding by 6

Write a fact for the following pictures.

☺☺☺
☺☺☺ + ☺ = ☺☺☺
☺☺☺☺ ___ + ___ = ___

☺☺☺
☺☺☺ + ☺☺☺☺ = ☺☺☺☺
☺☺☺☺ ___ + ___ = ___

☺☺☺
☺☺☺ + ☺☺☺
☺☺ = ☺☺☺☺☺☺
☺☺☺☺☺ ___ + ___ = ___

☺☺☺
☺☺☺ + ☺☺☺
☺☺☺☺ = ☺☺☺☺☺☺
☺☺☺☺☺☺ ___ + ___ = ___

☺☺☺
☺☺☺ + ☺☺☺☺
☺☺☺☺ = ☺☺☺☺☺☺☺
☺☺☺☺☺☺☺ ___ + ___ = ___

Add each number in the top row by 6.

+	0	1	2	3	4	5	6	7	8	9	10	11	12
6													

Match.

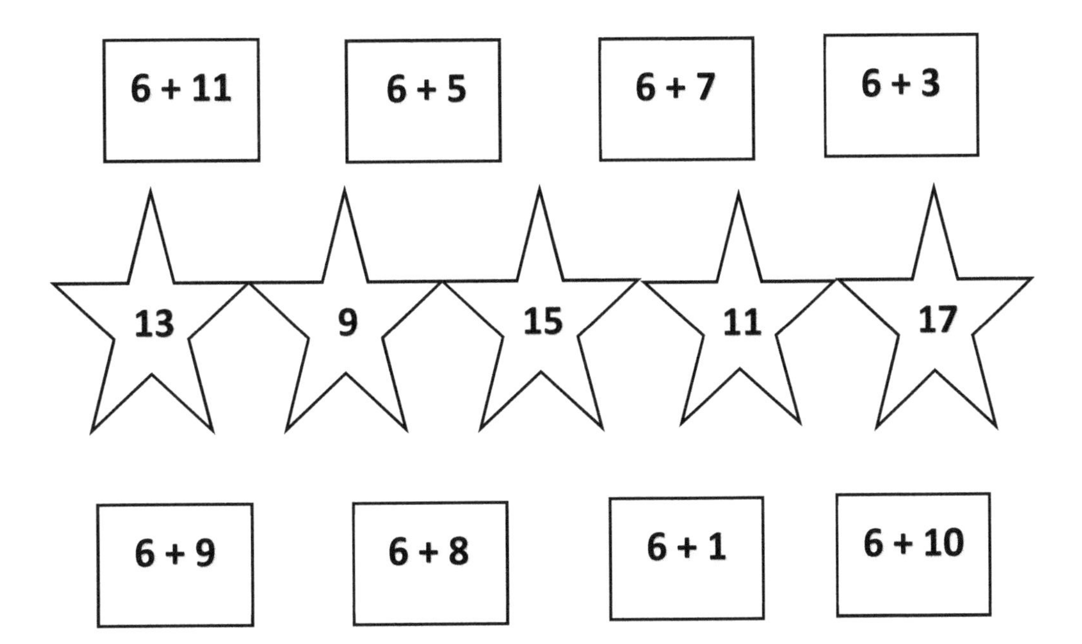

Write the answers in the boxes.

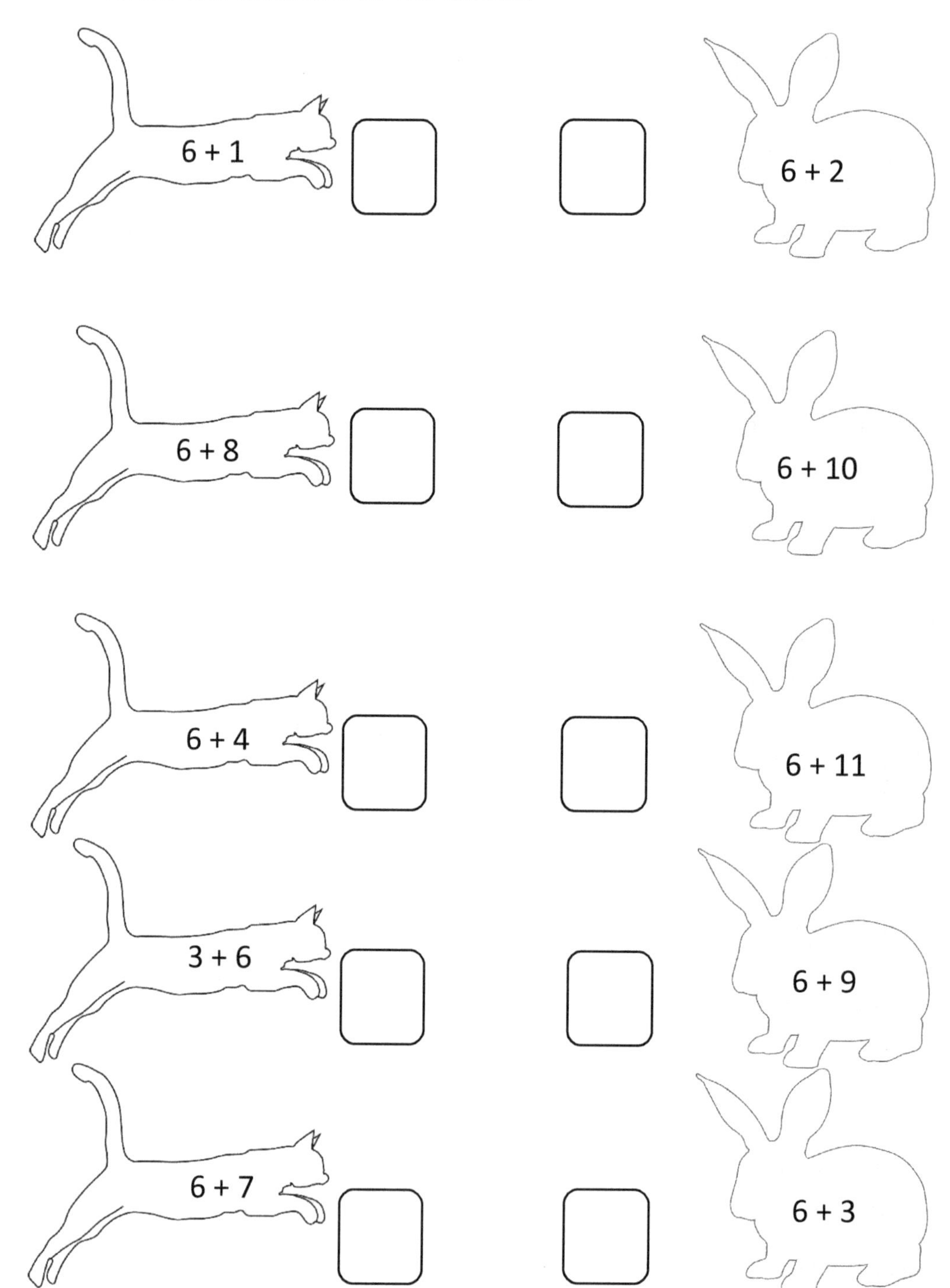

Find each sum.

$$\begin{array}{r} 6 \\ +5 \\ \hline \end{array}$$ ______

$$\begin{array}{r} 6 \\ +7 \\ \hline \end{array}$$ ______

$$\begin{array}{r} 6 \\ +3 \\ \hline \end{array}$$ ______

$$\begin{array}{r} 6 \\ +8 \\ \hline \end{array}$$ ______

$$\begin{array}{r} 6 \\ +10 \\ \hline \end{array}$$ ______

$$\begin{array}{r} 6 \\ +6 \\ \hline \end{array}$$ ______

$$\begin{array}{r} 6 \\ +2 \\ \hline \end{array}$$ ______

$$\begin{array}{r} 6 \\ +4 \\ \hline \end{array}$$ ______

$$\begin{array}{r} 6 \\ +11 \\ \hline \end{array}$$ ______

Jacob collects 6 oranges. Jacob's mother gives him 5 more. How many oranges does Jacob have?

_____ oranges

Find each missing number.

6 + ___ = 8

6 + 4 = ___

___ + 6 = 12

6 + ___ = 9

6 + ___ = 15

___ + 11 = 17

___ + 1 = 7

6 + 12 = ___

6 + 10 = ___

___ + 0 = 6

___ + 7 = 13

6 + ___ = 11

6 + 8 = ___

6 + 13 = ___

Ella has 6 pens. She buys 6 more. How many pens does Ella have in all?

_____ pens

Adding by 7

Write a fact for the following pictures.

☺☺☺☺ ☺☺☺ + ☺☺ = ☺☺ ☺☺☺ ___ + ___ = ___

☺☺☺☺ ☺☺☺ + ☺☺☺ ☺☺ = ☺☺☺☺ ☺☺☺☺ ___ + ___ = ___

☺☺☺☺ ☺☺☺ + ☺☺☺ ☺☺☺☺ = ☺☺☺☺☺☺☺ ☺☺☺☺☺☺☺ ___ + ___ = ___

☺☺☺☺ ☺☺☺ + ☺☺☺☺ ☺☺☺☺ = ☺☺☺☺☺ ☺☺☺☺ ☺☺☺☺☺☺ ___ + ___ = ___

Add each number in the top row by 7.

+	0	1	2	3	4	5	6	7	8	9	10	11	12
7													

Match.

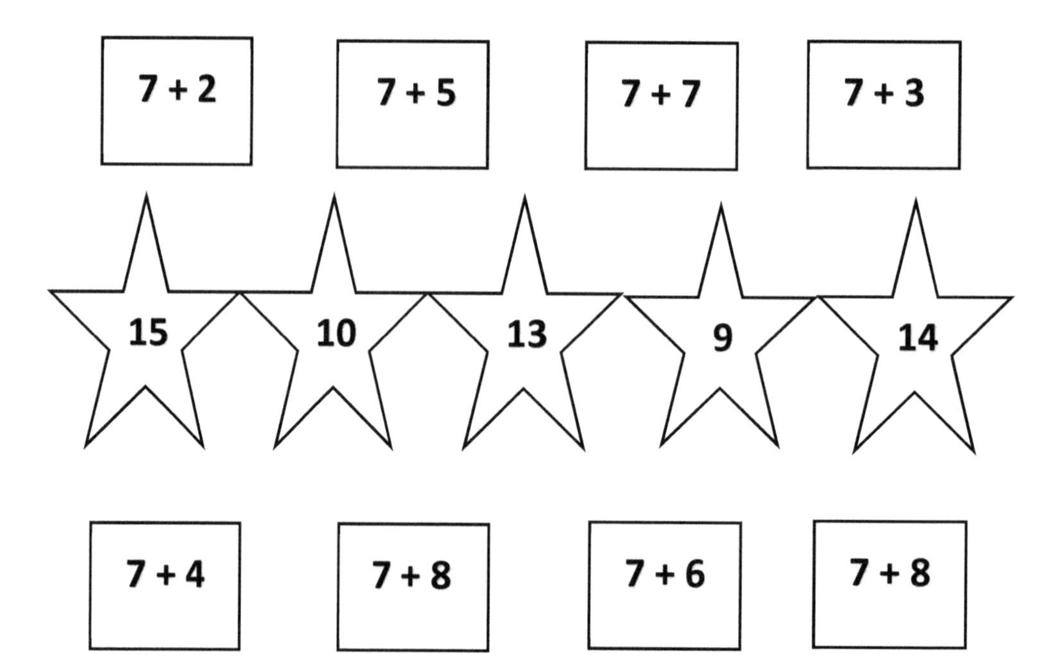

Write the answers in the boxes.

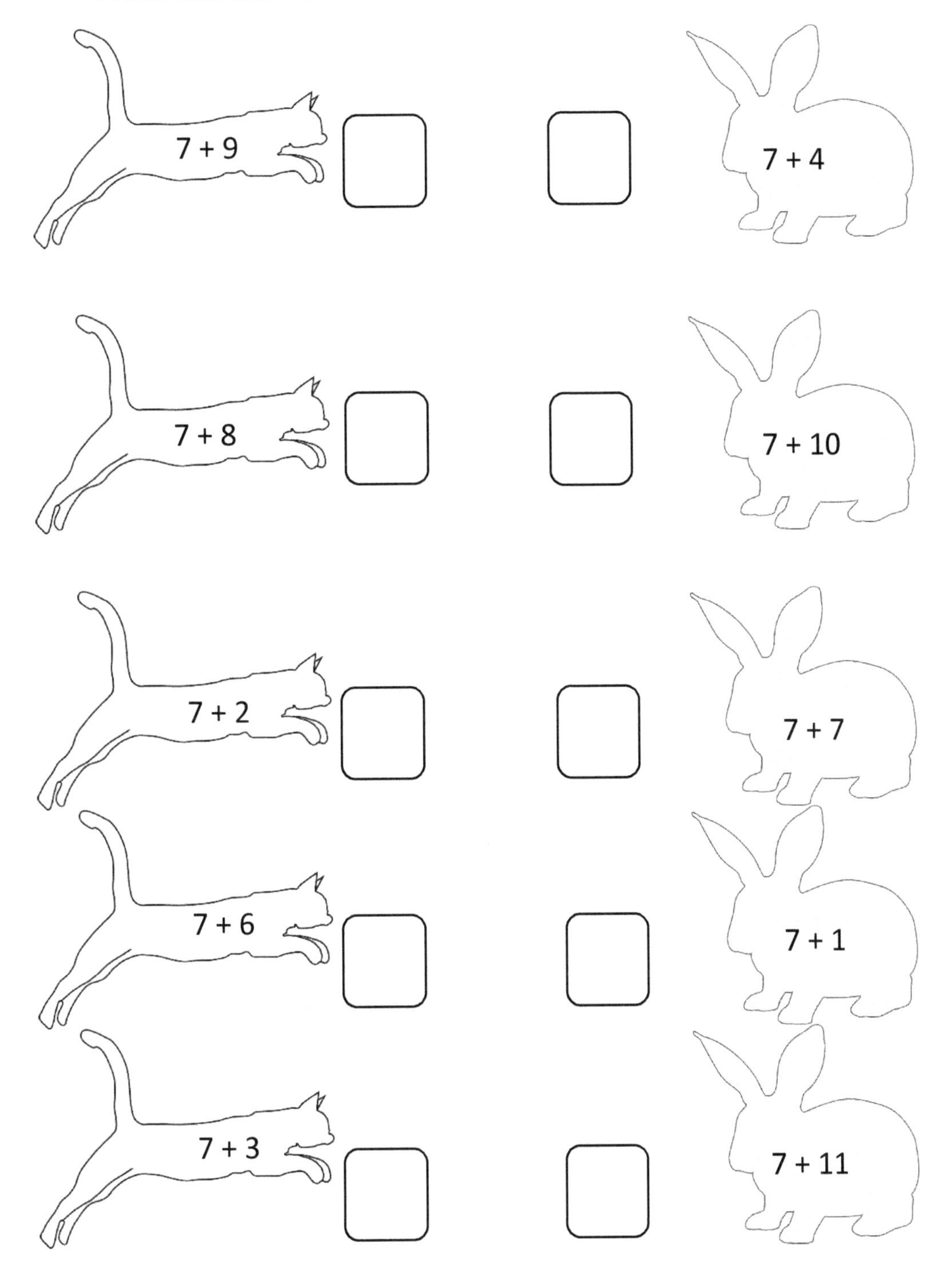

Find each sum.

$$\begin{array}{r} 7 \\ +\ 6 \\ \hline \end{array}$$ ______

$$\begin{array}{r} 7 \\ +\ 11 \\ \hline \end{array}$$ ______

$$\begin{array}{r} 7 \\ +\ 3 \\ \hline \end{array}$$ ______

$$\begin{array}{r} 7 \\ +\ 8 \\ \hline \end{array}$$ ______

$$\begin{array}{r} 7 \\ +\ 10 \\ \hline \end{array}$$ ______

$$\begin{array}{r} 7 \\ +\ 5 \\ \hline \end{array}$$ ______

$$\begin{array}{r} 7 \\ +\ 2 \\ \hline \end{array}$$ ______

$$\begin{array}{r} 7 \\ +\ 4 \\ \hline \end{array}$$ ______

$$\begin{array}{r} 7 \\ +\ 12 \\ \hline \end{array}$$ ______

There are 7 marbles. 4 marbles more are added. How many marbles are there in total?

______ marbles

Find each missing number.

7 + ___ = 10

7 + 0 = ___

___ + 5 = 12

7 + ___ = 13

7 + ___ = 9

___ + 12 = 19

___ + 1 = 8

7 + 10 = ___

7 + 9 = ___

___ + 4 = 11

___ + 7 = 14

7 + ___ = 20

7 + 8 = ___

7 + 11 = ___

John has 7 stickers. Joe has 13 stickers. How many stickers do they have in all?

_____ stickers

Adding by 8

Write a fact for the following pictures.

☺☺☺☺
☺☺☺☺ + ☺☺☺☺ = ☺☺☺
☺☺☺
☺☺☺
☺☺☺

__ + __ = __

☺☺☺☺
☺☺☺☺ + ☺☺☺
☺☺☺ = ☺☺☺☺☺
☺☺☺☺
☺☺☺☺☺

__ + __ = __

☺☺☺☺
☺☺☺☺ + ☺☺☺☺
☺☺☺☺ = ☺☺☺☺☺
☺☺☺☺☺
☺☺☺☺☺☺

__ + __ = __

☺☺☺☺
☺☺☺☺ + ☺☺☺☺
☺☺☺ = ☺☺☺☺☺
☺☺☺☺☺
☺☺☺☺☺

__ + __ = __

Add each number in the top row by 8.

+	0	1	2	3	4	5	6	7	8	9	10	11	12
8													

Match.

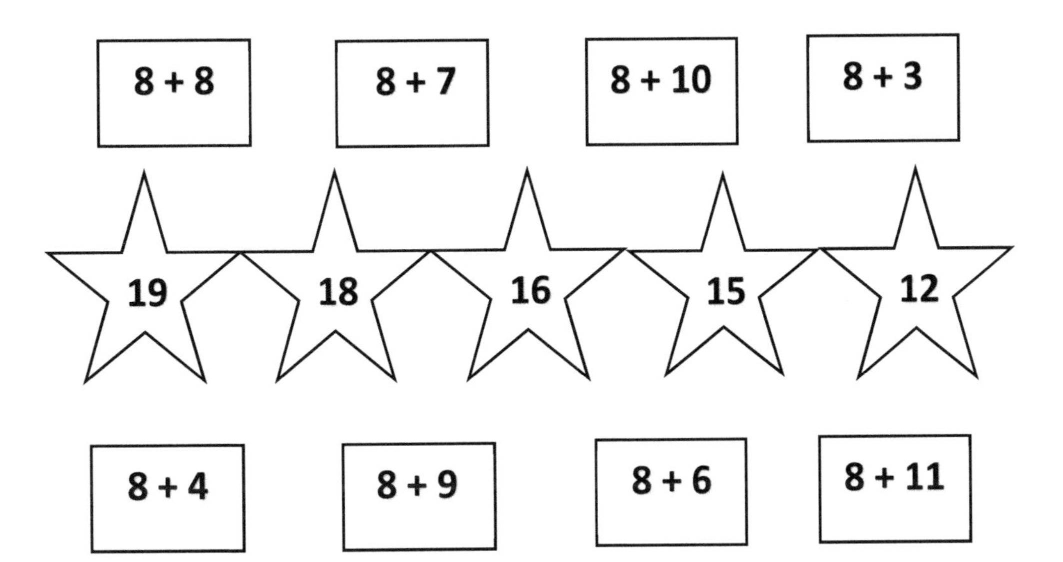

Write the answers in the boxes.

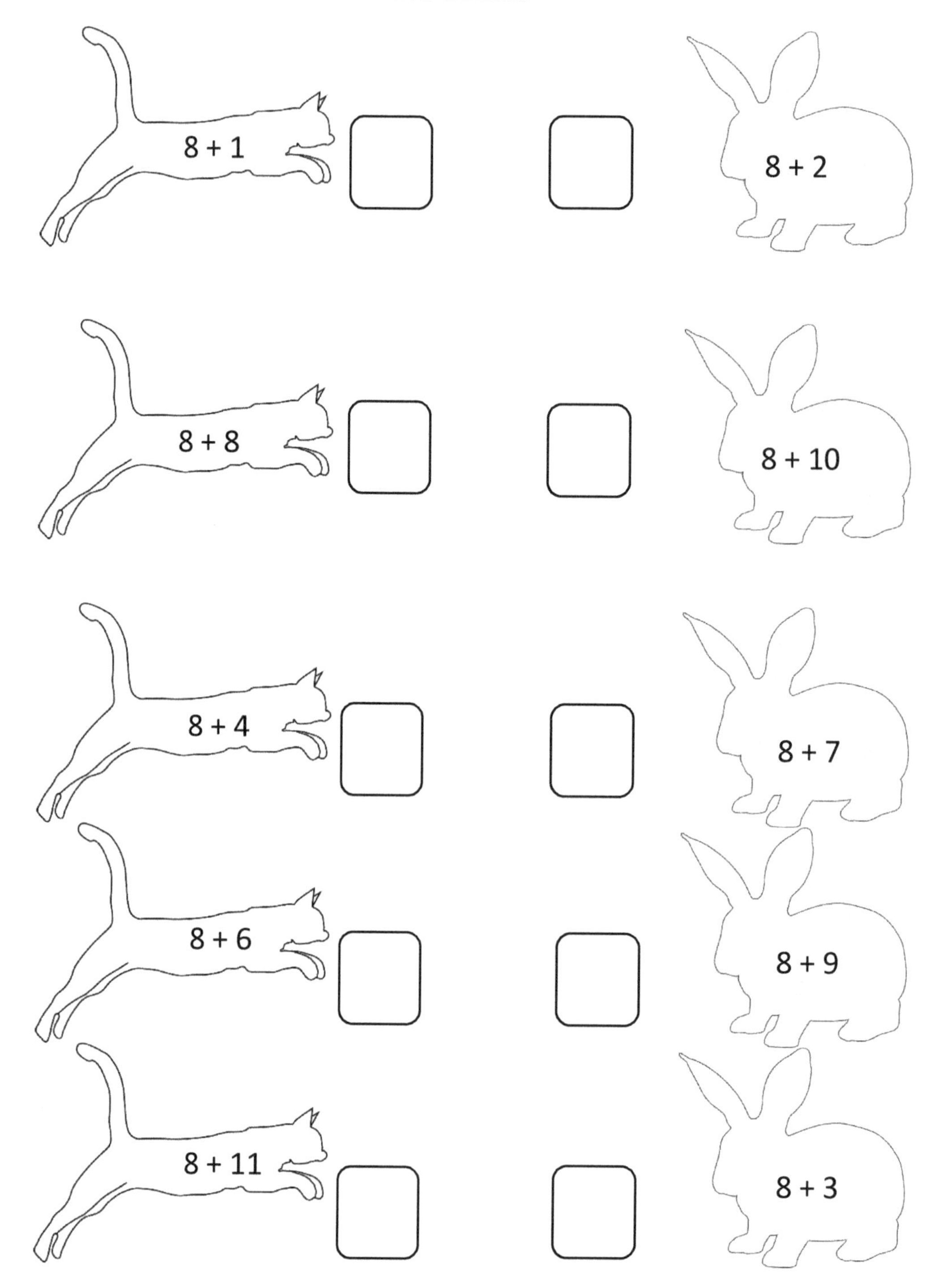

Find each sum.

$8 + 2 = $ ___	$8 + 8 = $ ___	$8 + 3 = $ ___
$8 + 4 = $ ___	$8 + 11 = $ ___	$8 + 12 = $ ___
$8 + 2 = $ ___	$8 + 5 = $ ___	$8 + 1 = $ ___

Ali has 8 blocks. Shawn has 11 blocks. How many blocks do they have in all?

_____ blocks

Find each missing number.

8 + ___ = 11

8 + 9 = ___

___ + 6 = 14

8 + ___ = 19

8 + ___ = 10

___ + 12 = 20

___ + 1 = 9

8 + 10 = ___

8 + 9 = ___

___ + 4 = 12

___ + 7 = 15

8 + ___ = 0

8 + 8 = ___

8 + 13 = ___

If there are 8 cards in a box and Ava puts 14 more cards inside, how many marbles are in the box?

_____ cards

Subtraction by 4

Write a subtraction fact for the following pictures.

☺☺☺ ☺☺☺ – ☺☺ ☺☺ = __ - __ = __

☺☺☺☺☺ ☺☺☺☺ – ☺☺ ☺☺ = __ - __ = __

☺☺☺☺☺ ☺☺☺☺☺ – ☺☺ ☺☺ = __ - __ = __

☺☺☺ ☺☺☺ ☺☺☺ ☺☺☺ – ☺☺ ☺☺ = __ - __ = __

☺☺☺☺☺ ☺☺☺☺ – ☺☺ ☺☺ = __ - __ = __

Subtract each number in the top row by 4.

—	4	5	6	7	8	9	10	11	12	13	14	15
4												

Match.

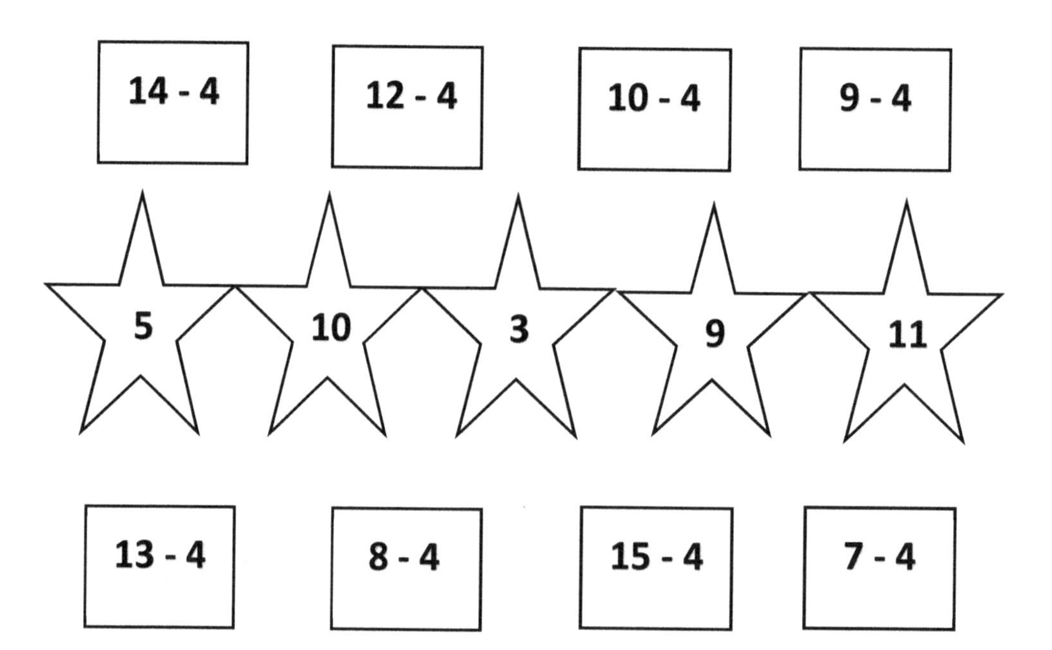

Write the answers in the boxes.

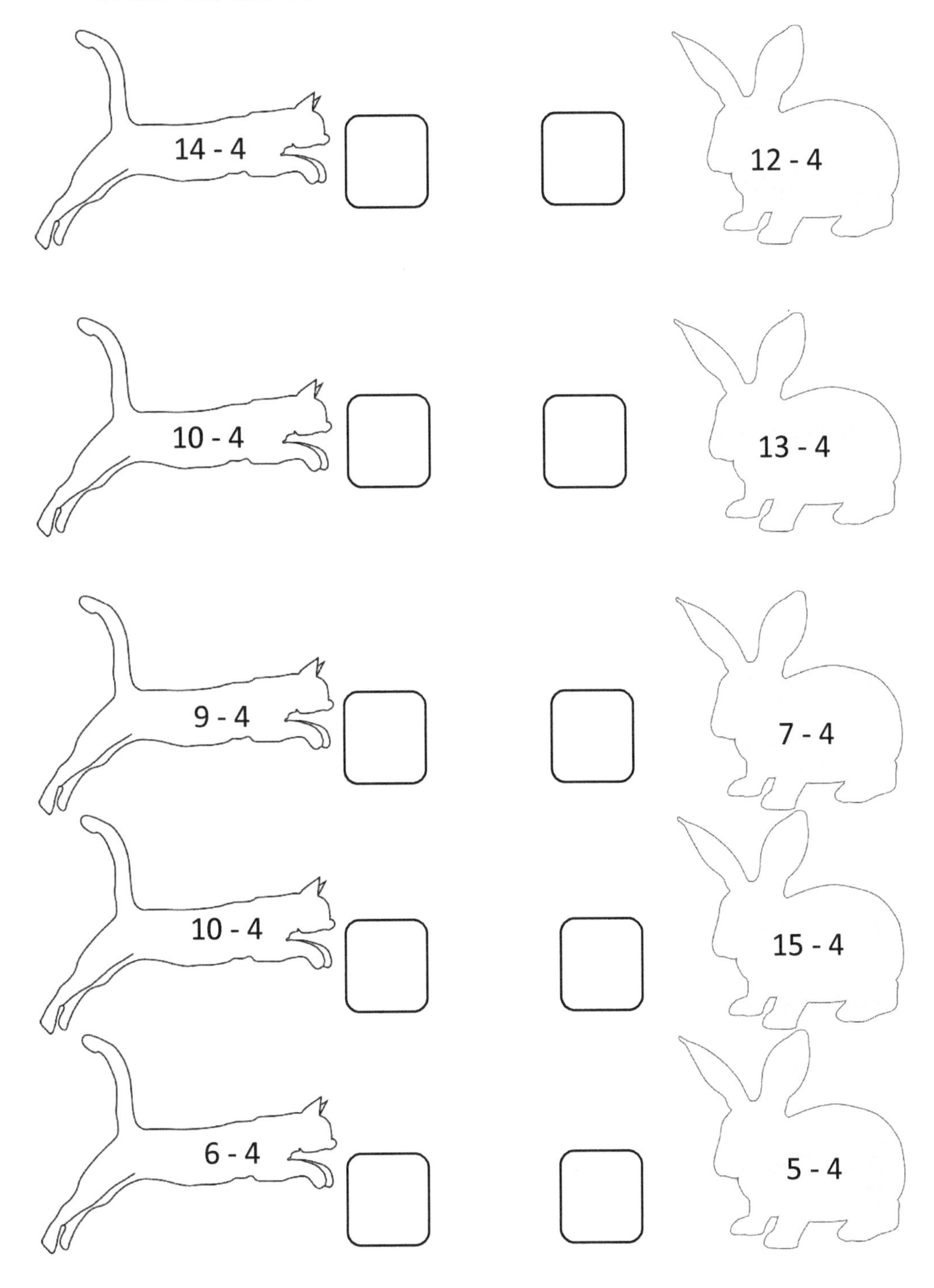

Find each difference.

$$\begin{array}{r} 14 \\ -\ 4 \\ \hline \_\_\_\_ \end{array} \quad \begin{array}{r} 16 \\ -\ 4 \\ \hline \_\_\_\_ \end{array} \quad \begin{array}{r} 12 \\ -\ 4 \\ \hline \_\_\_\_ \end{array}$$

$$\begin{array}{r} 9 \\ -\ 4 \\ \hline \_\_\_\_ \end{array} \quad \begin{array}{r} 15 \\ -\ 4 \\ \hline \_\_\_\_ \end{array} \quad \begin{array}{r} 19 \\ -\ 4 \\ \hline \_\_\_\_ \end{array}$$

$$\begin{array}{r} 17 \\ -\ 4 \\ \hline \_\_\_\_ \end{array} \quad \begin{array}{r} 13 \\ -\ 4 \\ \hline \_\_\_\_ \end{array} \quad \begin{array}{r} 18 \\ -\ 4 \\ \hline \_\_\_\_ \end{array}$$

Maria had 12 coins in his bank. She spent 4 of her coins. How many coins does she have now?

_____ coins

Find each missing number.

18 – ___ = 4

14 – 4 = ___

___ – 4 = 6

18 – ___ = 14

17 – ___ = 13

___ – 0 = 4

___ – 4 = 3

19 – 4 = ___

12 – 4 = ___

___ – 4 = 12

___ – 4 = 7

20 – ___ = 16

4 – 4 = ___

13 – 4 = ___

Eliana had 7 old books. She sold 4 books. How many books does Eliana now have?

_____ books

Subtraction by 5

Write a subtraction fact for the following pictures.

☺☺
☺☺☺ – ☺☺
☺☺☺ = ___ - ___ = ___

☺☺☺
☺☺☺ – ☺☺☺
☺☺ = ___ - ___ = ___

☺☺☺☺
☺☺☺ – ☺☺
☺☺☺ = ___ - ___ = ___

☺☺☺☺
☺☺☺☺ – ☺☺
☺☺☺ = ___ - ___ = ___

Eliana had 9 old books. She sold 5 books. How many books does Eliana now have?

_____ books

Subtract each number in the top row by 5.

—	5	6	7	8	9	10	11	12	13	14	15	16
5												

Match.

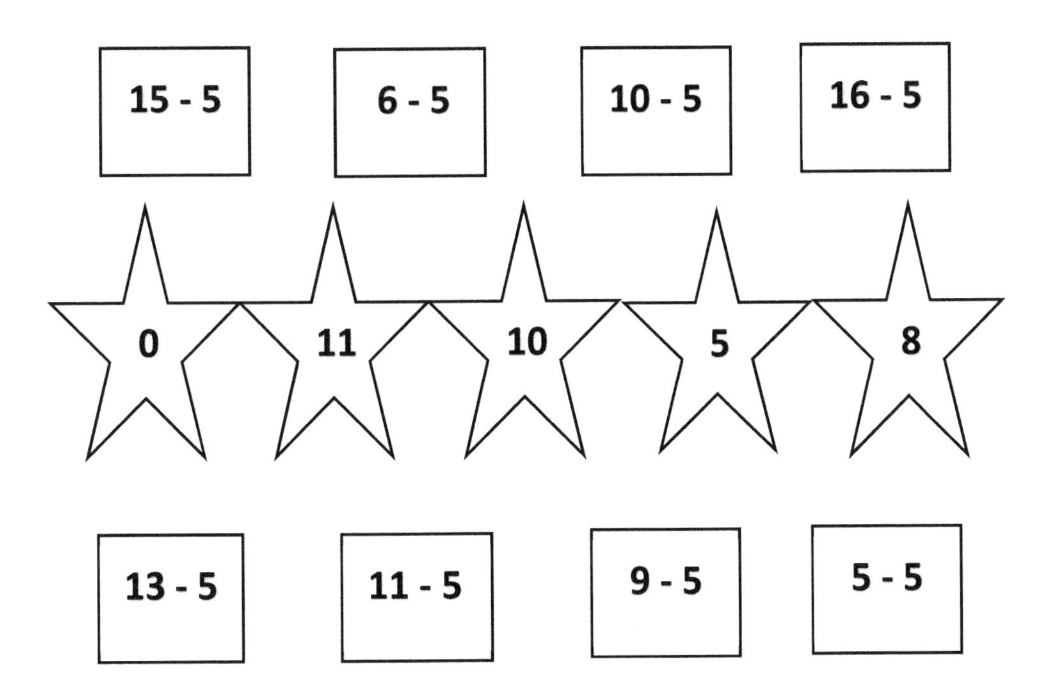

Write the answers in the boxes.

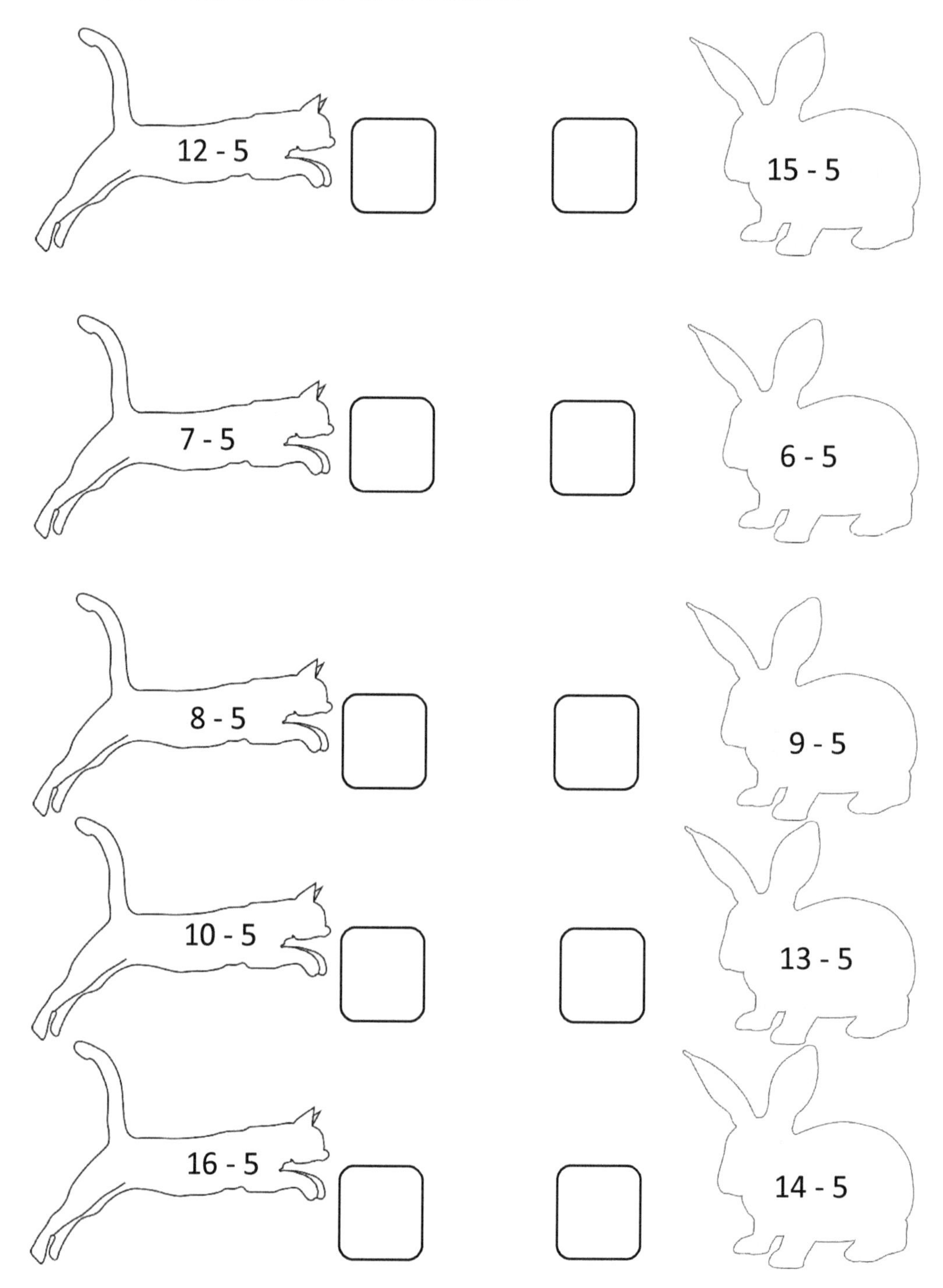

Find each difference.

$$\begin{array}{r} 15 \\ -\ 5 \\ \hline \end{array}$$ ______

$$\begin{array}{r} 11 \\ -\ 5 \\ \hline \end{array}$$ ______

$$\begin{array}{r} 5 \\ -\ 5 \\ \hline \end{array}$$ ______

$$\begin{array}{r} 17 \\ -\ 5 \\ \hline \end{array}$$ ______

$$\begin{array}{r} 16 \\ -\ 5 \\ \hline \end{array}$$ ______

$$\begin{array}{r} 19 \\ -\ 5 \\ \hline \end{array}$$ ______

$$\begin{array}{r} 13 \\ -\ 5 \\ \hline \end{array}$$ ______

$$\begin{array}{r} 10 \\ -\ 5 \\ \hline \end{array}$$ ______

$$\begin{array}{r} 14 \\ -\ 5 \\ \hline \end{array}$$ ______

Taylor picked 15 apples from the orchard, and gave 5 apples to his friend Aria. How many apples does Taylor have now ?

______ apples

Find each missing number.

15 – ___ = 10

9 – 5 = ___

___ – 5 = 5

12 – ___ = 7

5 – ___ = 0

___ – 5 = 8

___ – 5 = 1

19 – 5 = ___

11 – 5 = ___

___ – 5 = 2

___ – 5 = 15

8 – ___ = 3

16 – 5 = ___

14 – 5 = ___

There are 17 cards in the drawer. Mia took 5 cards from the drawer. How many cards are now in the drawer?

_____ cards

Subtraction by 6

Write a subtraction fact for the following pictures.

☺☺☺
☺☺☺
☺☺☺ – ☺☺☺
☺☺☺ = ___ - ___ = ___

☺☺☺☺
☺☺☺ – ☺☺☺
☺☺☺ = ___ - ___ = ___

☺☺☺
☺☺☺☺ – ☺☺☺
☺☺☺ = ___ - ___ = ___

☺☺☺☺
☺☺☺☺ – ☺☺☺
☺☺☺ = ___ - ___ = ___

There are 14 trees currently in the park. Park workers cut down 6 trees that were damaged. How many trees will be in the park?

_____ trees

Subtract each number in the top row by 6.

—	6	7	8	9	10	11	12	13	14	15	16	17	18
6													

Match.

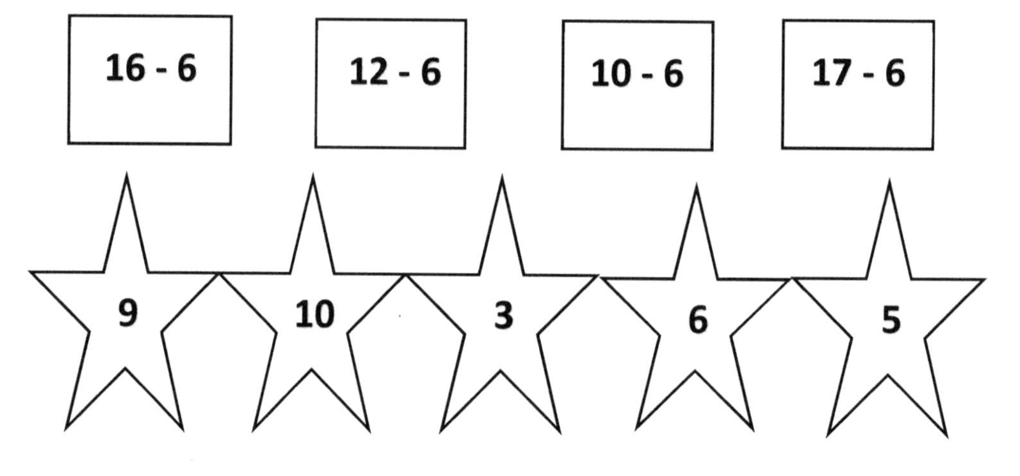

9 - 6

11 - 6

13 - 6

15 - 6

Write the answers in the boxes.

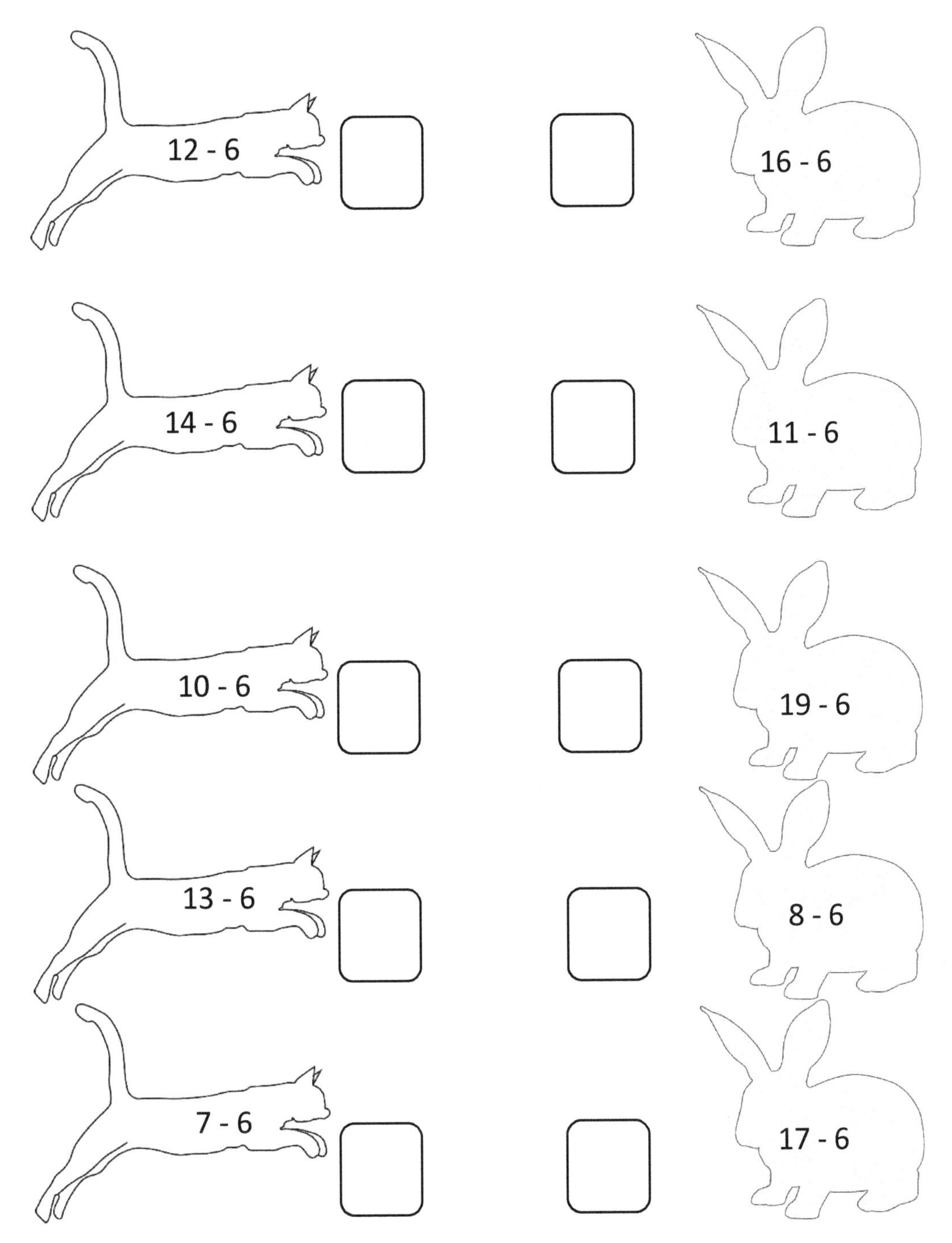

Find each difference.

$$\begin{array}{r} 19 \\ -\ \ 6 \\ \hline \end{array}$$

$$\begin{array}{r} 20 \\ -\ \ 6 \\ \hline \end{array}$$

$$\begin{array}{r} 14 \\ -\ \ 6 \\ \hline \end{array}$$

$$\begin{array}{r} 12 \\ -\ \ 6 \\ \hline \end{array}$$

$$\begin{array}{r} 13 \\ -\ \ 6 \\ \hline \end{array}$$

$$\begin{array}{r} 16 \\ -\ \ 6 \\ \hline \end{array}$$

$$\begin{array}{r} 14 \\ -\ \ 6 \\ \hline \end{array}$$

$$\begin{array}{r} 11 \\ -\ \ 6 \\ \hline \end{array}$$

$$\begin{array}{r} 10 \\ -\ \ 6 \\ \hline \end{array}$$

Allen had 67 coins in his bank. He spent 26 of his coins. How many coins does he have now?

_____ coins

Find each missing number.

12 – ___ = 6

___ – 6 = 5

14 – ___ = 8

___ – 6 = 11

13 – 6 = ___

___ – 6 = 9

8 – 6 = ___

18 – 6 = ___

20 – ___ = 14

___ – 6 = 13

7 – 6 = ___

___ – 6 = 0

16 – ___ = 10

9 – 6 = ___

Scott found 12 seashells on the beach, he gave Aria 6 of the seashells. How many seashells does he now have?

______ seashells

Subtraction and adding by 4, 5 and 6

Match.

14 - 4	12 - 5	12 - 6	15 - 6

8 7 6 9 10

11 - 4	5 + 1	4 + 6	6 + 3

Solve.

6 + 3 = 9	9 – 3 = 6
7 + 6 = ___	___ – 6 = ___
10 + 5 = ___	___ – 5 = ___
8 + 6 = ___	___ – 6 = ___
9 + 4 = ___	___ – 4 = ___
10 + 6 = ___	___ – 6 = ___
5 + 5 = ___	___ – 5 = ___

Write the answers in the boxes.

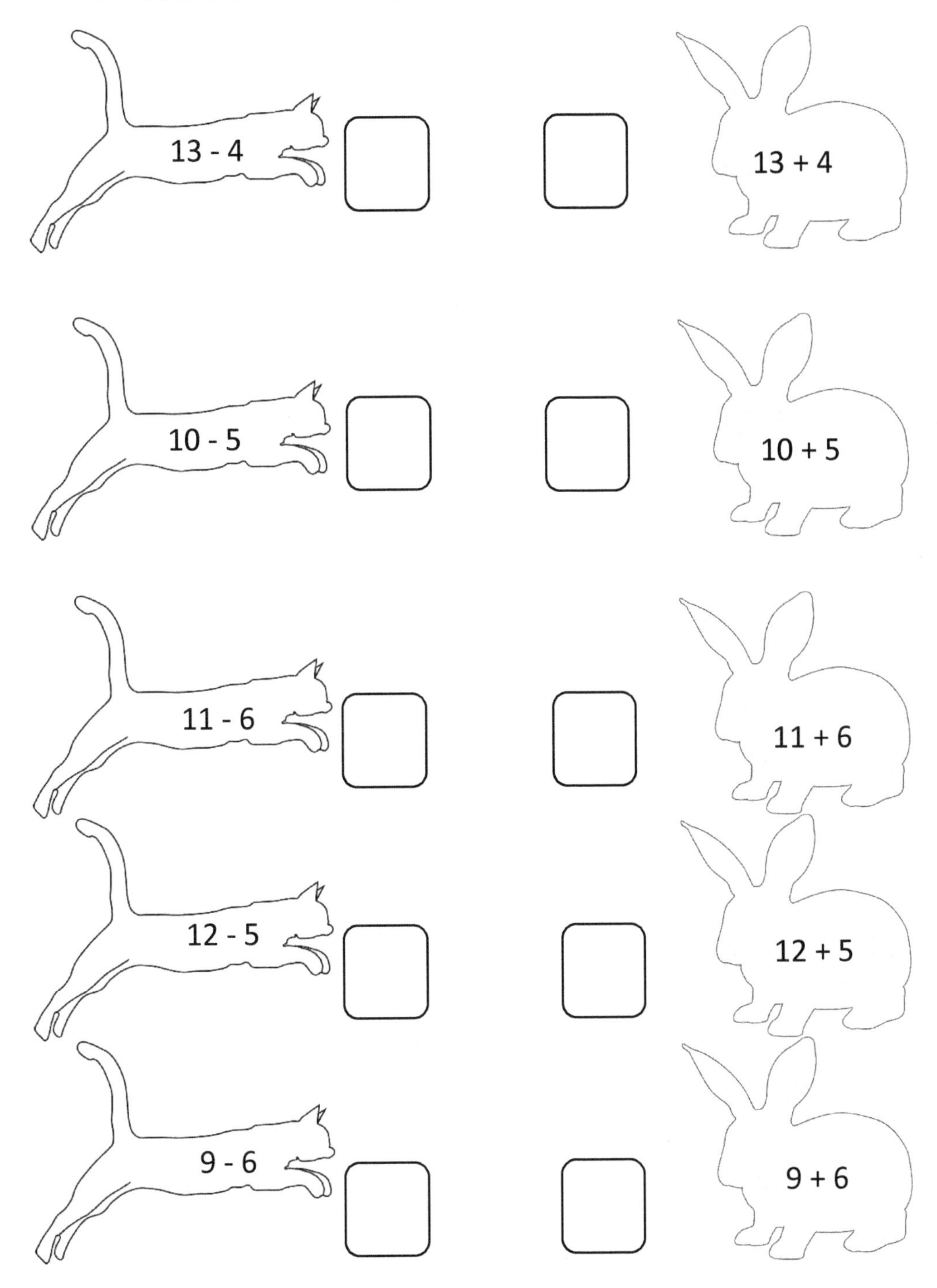

Find each difference.

15 − 6 _____	14 − 4 _____	13 + 6 _____
15 + 5 _____	14 − 5 _____	16 + 6 _____
16 − 5 _____	13 − 6 _____	11 − 4 _____

Connor collects 20 candies. Connor's friend gives him 6 more. How many candies does Connor have?

______ candies

Richard found 20 seashells on the beach, he gave Aria 6 of the seashells. How many seashells does he now have?

______ seashells

Adding by 9

Write a fact for the following pictures.

☺☺☺☺
☺☺☺☺☺ + ☺☺ = ☺☺☺☺☺☺
☺☺☺☺☺

__ + __ = __

☺☺☺☺
☺☺☺☺☺ + ☺☺☺
☺☺ = ☺☺☺☺☺
☺☺☺☺☺
☺☺☺☺

__ + __ = __

☺☺☺☺
☺☺☺
☺☺ + ☺☺☺
☺☺☺ = ☺☺☺☺☺
☺☺☺☺☺
☺☺☺☺☺

__ + __ = __

☺☺☺☺
☺☺☺☺☺ + ☺☺☺☺
☺☺☺☺ = ☺☺☺☺☺☺
☺☺☺☺☺☺
☺☺☺☺☺

__ + __ = __

☺☺☺☺
☺☺☺
☺☺ + ☺☺☺
☺☺☺
☺☺☺ = ☺☺☺☺☺☺☺
☺☺☺☺☺☺☺
☺☺☺☺☺☺☺

__ + __ = __

Add each number in the top row by 9.

+	0	1	2	3	4	5	6	7	8	9	10	11	12
9													

Match.

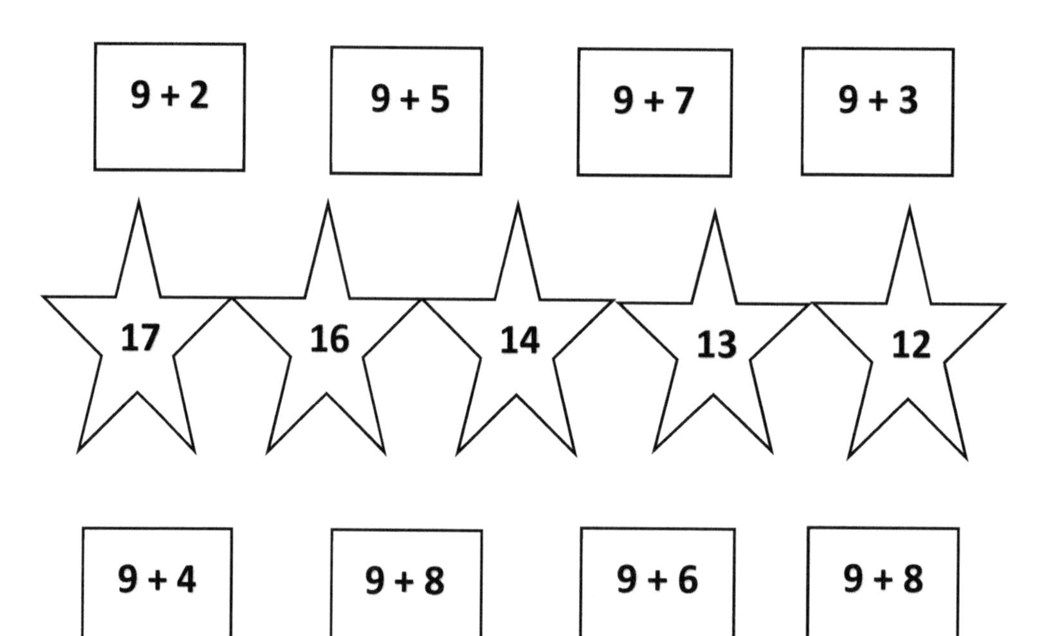

Write the answers in the boxes.

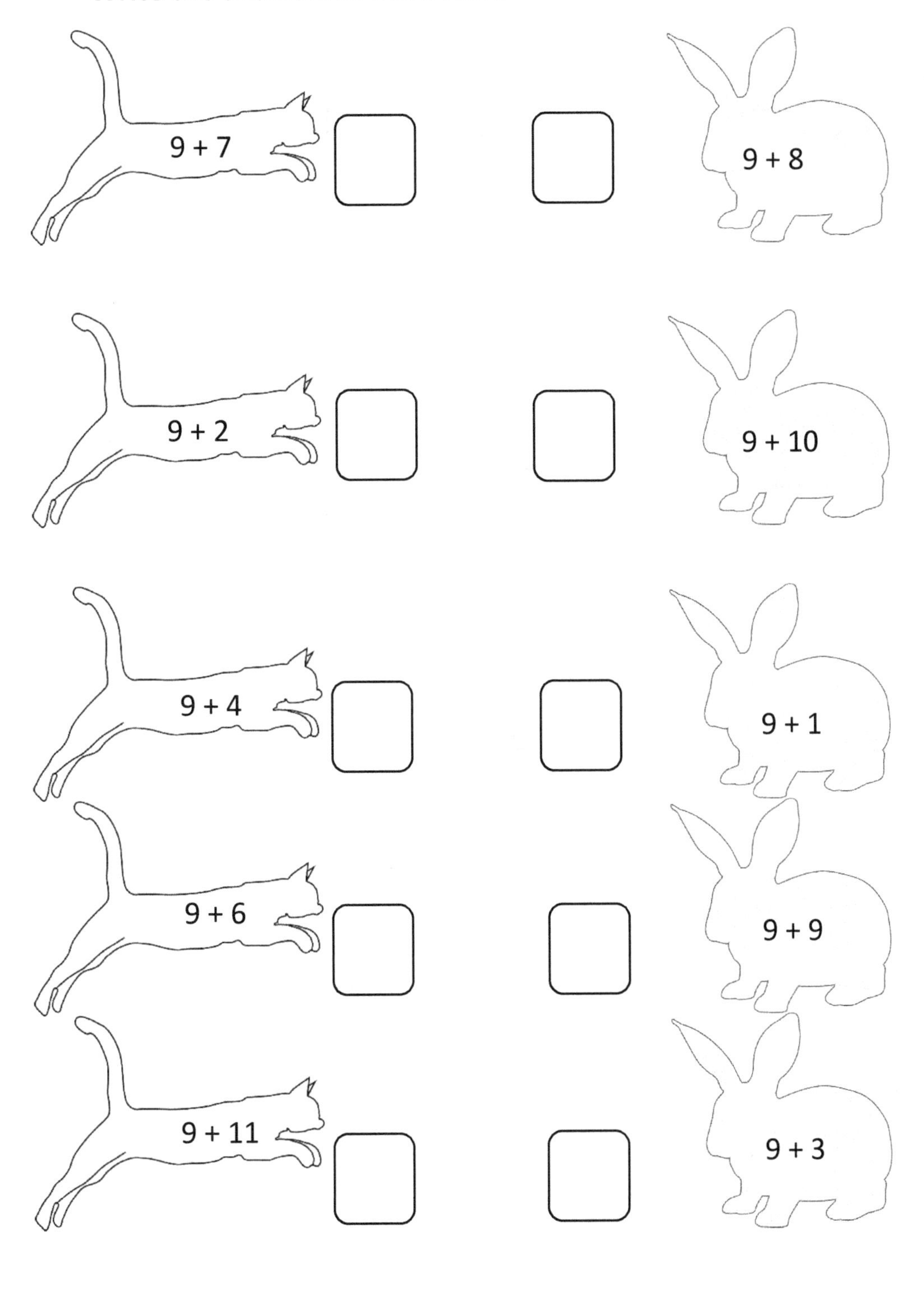

Find each sum.

9 + 6 = ____	9 + 7 = ____	9 + 4 = ____
9 + 8 = ____	9 + 11 = ____	9 + 5 = ____
9 + 5 = ____	9 + 4 = ____	9 + 1 = ____

Avery collects 9 cards. Avery's friend gives her 11 more. How many cards does Avery have?

_____ cards

Find each missing number.

9 + ___ = 10

9 + 10 = ___

___ + 5 = 14

9 + ___ = 12

9 + ___ = 11

___ + 11 = 20

___ + 5 = 14

9 + 13 = ___

9 + 8 = ___

___ + 4 = 13

___ + 9 = 18

9 + ___ = 9

9 + 6 = ___

9 + 12 = ___

Mila starts with 9 stamps. She buys 13 more. How many stamps does Mila have now?

______ stamps

Adding by 10

Write a fact for the following pictures.

☺☺☺☺☺
☺☺☺☺☺ + ☺☺☺ = ☺☺☺☺☺☺
☺☺☺☺☺☺   __ + __ = __

☺☺☺☺☺
☺☺☺☺☺ + ☺☺☺
☺☺ = ☺☺☺☺☺
☺☺☺☺☺
☺☺☺☺☺   __ + __ = __

☺☺☺☺☺
☺☺☺☺☺ + ☺☺☺
☺☺☺☺ = ☺☺☺☺☺
☺☺☺☺☺
☺☺☺☺☺
☺☺   __ + __ = __

☺☺☺☺☺
☺☺☺☺☺ + ☺☺☺☺
☺☺☺☺ = ☺☺☺☺☺
☺☺☺☺☺
☺☺☺☺☺
☺☺☺   __ + __ = __

Add each number in the top row by 10.

+	0	1	2	3	4	5	6	7	8	9	10	11	12
10													

Match.

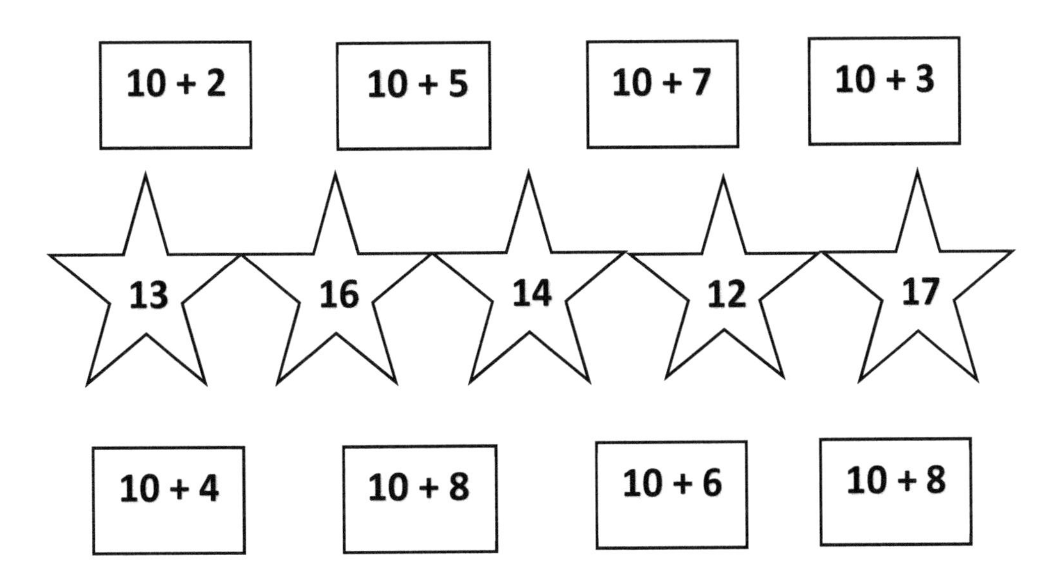

Write the answers in the boxes.

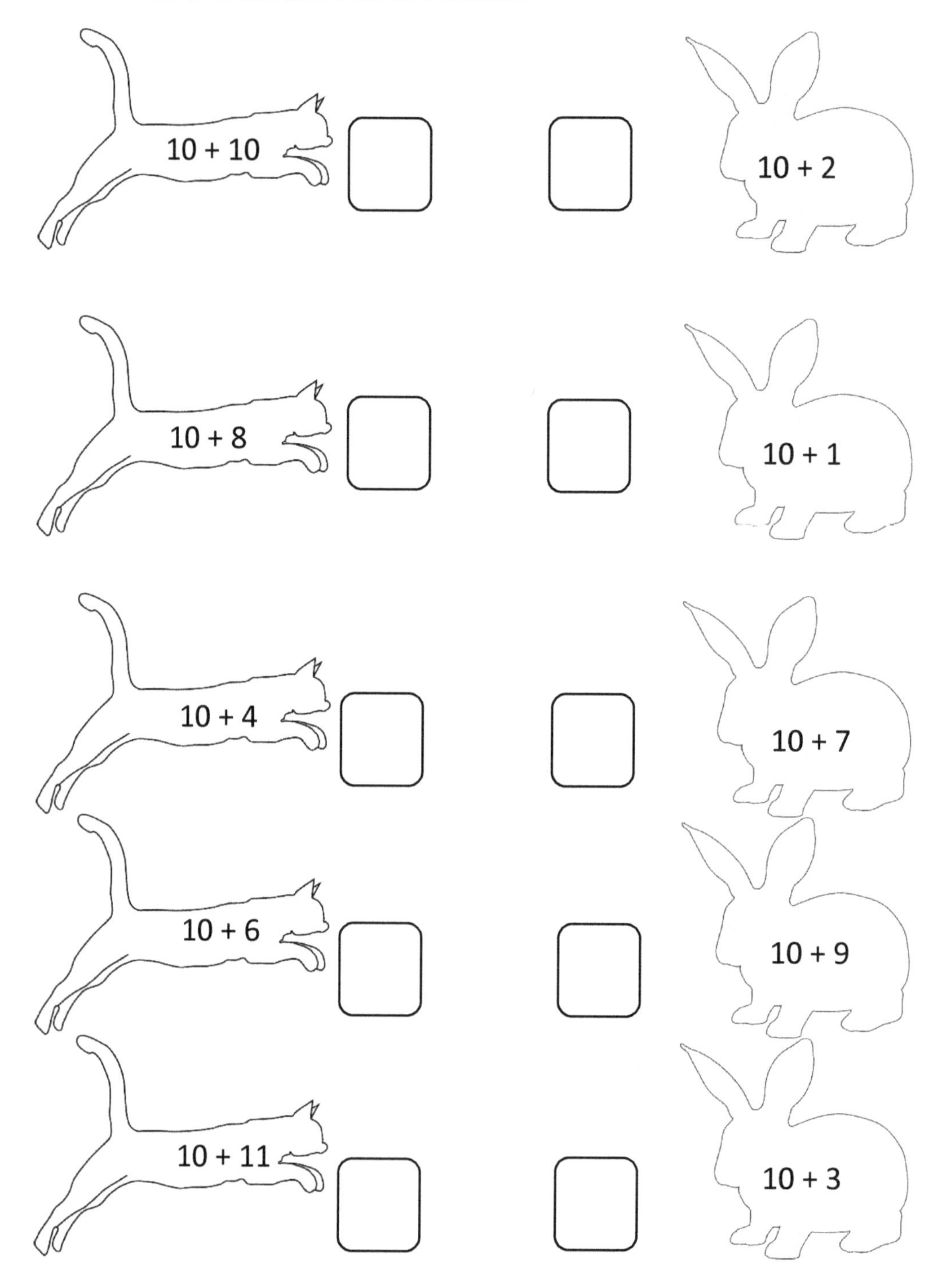

Find each sum.

$10 + 5 =$ ____	$10 + 7 =$ ____	$10 + 3 =$ ____
$10 + 8 =$ ____	$10 + 10 =$ ____	$10 + 6 =$ ____
$10 + 2 =$ ____	$10 + 4 =$ ____	$10 + 1 =$ ____

If there are 10 peanuts in a box and John puts 10 more peanuts inside, how many peanuts are in the box?

_____ peanuts

Find each missing number.

10 + ___ = 15

10 + 0 = ___

___ + 7 = 17

10 + ___ = 12

10 + ___ = 19

___ + 4 = 14

___ + 1 = 11

10 + 11 = ___

10 + 3 = ___

___ + 13 = 23

___ + 6 = 16

10 + ___ = 19

10 + 8 = ___

10 + 12 = ___

There are 10 pencils. 14 pencils more are added. How many are there in total?

_____ pencils

Subtraction by 7

Write a subtraction fact for the following pictures.

☺☺☺☺ – ☺☺☺☺ = ___ - ___ = ___
☺☺☺☺ ☺☺☺

☺☺☺☺ – ☺☺☺☺ = ___ - ___ = ___
☺☺☺☺ ☺☺☺
☺☺☺☺

☺☺☺ – ☺☺☺ = ___ - ___ = ___
☺☺☺ ☺☺☺☺
☺☺☺

☺☺☺☺☺ – ☺☺☺☺ = ___ - ___ = ___
☺☺☺☺☺ ☺☺☺

Subtract each number in the top row by 7.

—	7	8	9	10	11	12	13	14	15	16	17	18
7												

Match.

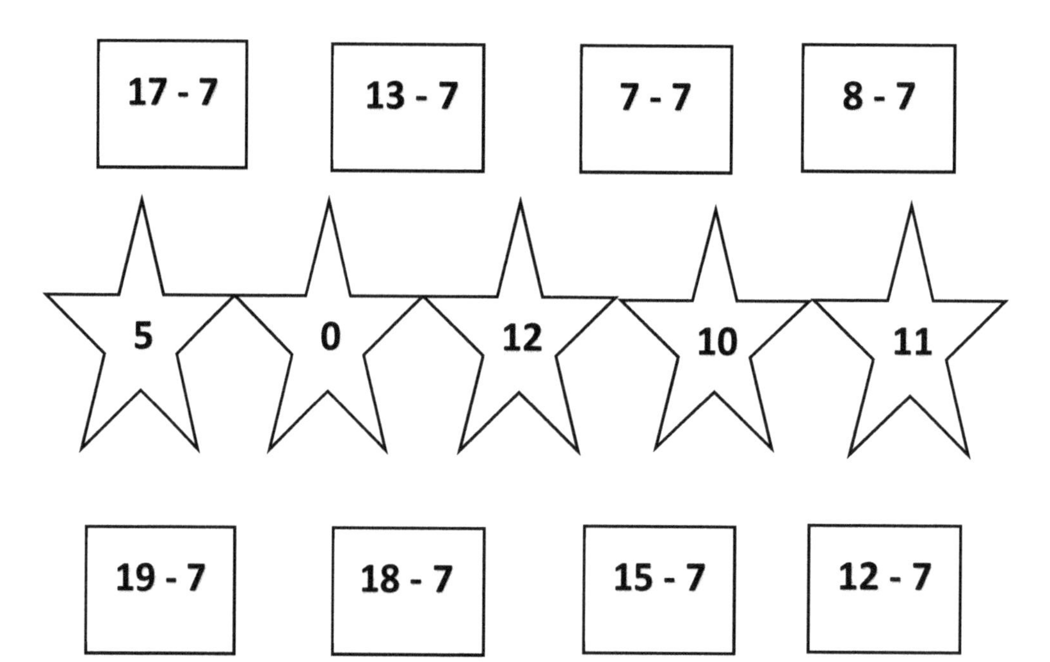

Write the answers in the boxes.

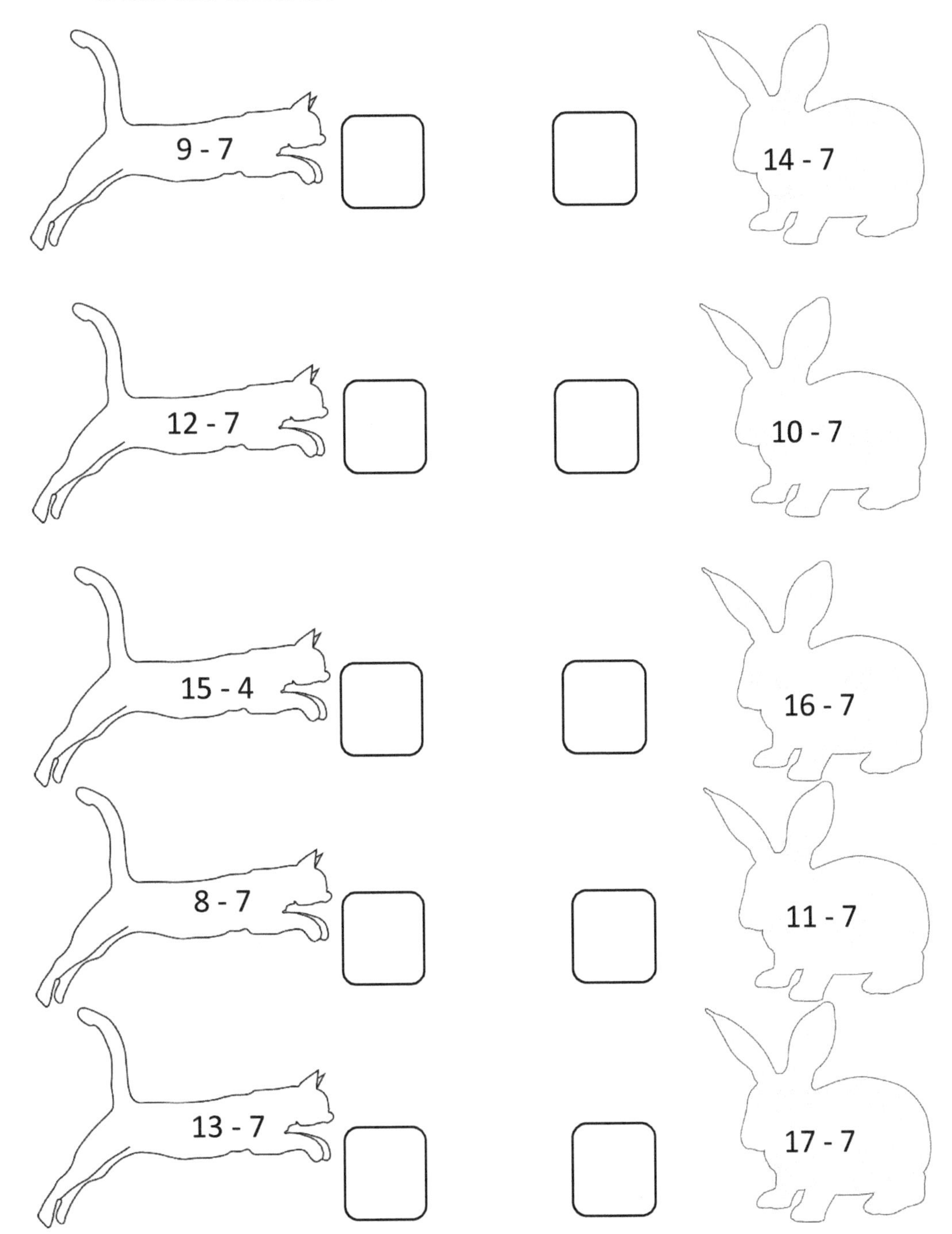

Find each difference.

$$\begin{array}{r} 20 \\ -\ 7 \\ \hline \end{array}$$ ______

$$\begin{array}{r} 13 \\ -\ 7 \\ \hline \end{array}$$ ______

$$\begin{array}{r} 9 \\ -\ 7 \\ \hline \end{array}$$ ______

$$\begin{array}{r} 17 \\ -\ 7 \\ \hline \end{array}$$ ______

$$\begin{array}{r} 19 \\ -\ 7 \\ \hline \end{array}$$ ______

$$\begin{array}{r} 12 \\ -\ 7 \\ \hline \end{array}$$ ______

$$\begin{array}{r} 16 \\ -\ 4 \\ \hline \end{array}$$ ______

$$\begin{array}{r} 15 \\ -\ 7 \\ \hline \end{array}$$ ______

$$\begin{array}{r} 18 \\ -\ 7 \\ \hline \end{array}$$ ______

Smith has 20 marbles, he gave Olivia 7 of the marbles. How many marbles does he now have ?

_____ marbles

Find each missing number.

20 – ___ = 13

15 – 7 = ___

___ – 7 = 9

7 – ___ = 0

11 – ___ = 4

___ – 7 = 2

___ – 7 = 8

10 – 7 = ___

9 – 7 = ___

___ – 7 = 5

___ – 7 = 7

22 – ___ = 15

21 – 7 = ___

24 – 7 = ___

John picked 23 apples from the orchard and gave 7 apples to his friend Aria. How many apples does John have now?

_____ apples

Subtraction by 8

Write a subtraction fact for the following pictures.

☺☺☺☺
☺☺☺☺
☺☺☺☺ – ☺☺☺☺
☺☺☺☺ = ___ - ___ = ___

☺☺☺
☺☺☺
☺☺☺ – ☺☺☺☺
☺☺☺☺ = ___ - ___ = ___

☺☺☺☺
☺☺☺☺
☺☺☺☺
☺☺☺☺ – ☺☺☺☺
☺☺☺☺ = ___ - ___ = ___

☺☺☺
☺☺☺
☺☺☺
☺☺☺ – ☺☺☺☺
☺☺☺☺ = ___ - ___ = ___

Subtract each number in the top row by 8.

—	8	9	10	11	12	13	14	15	16	17	18	19	20
8													

Match.

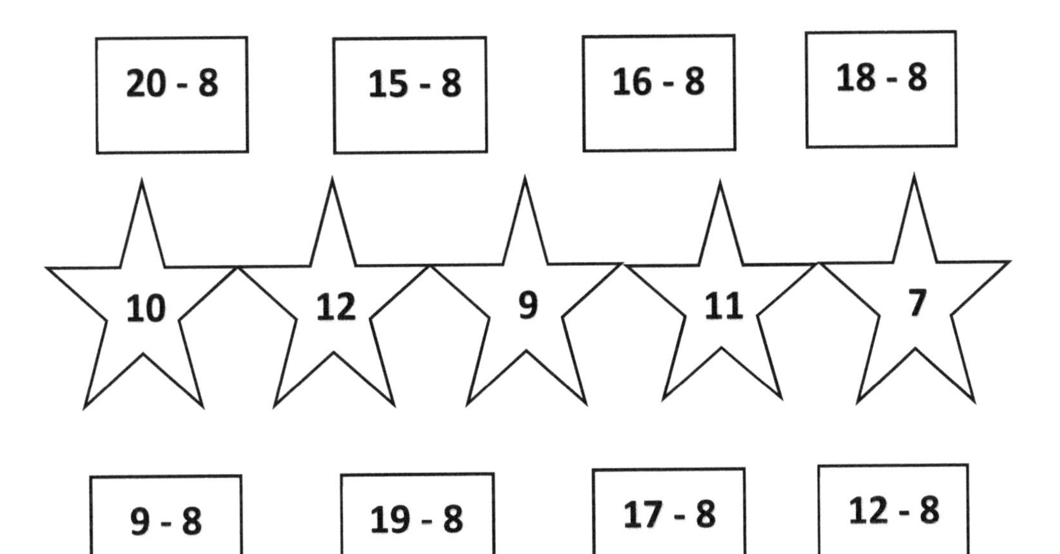

Write the answers in the boxes.

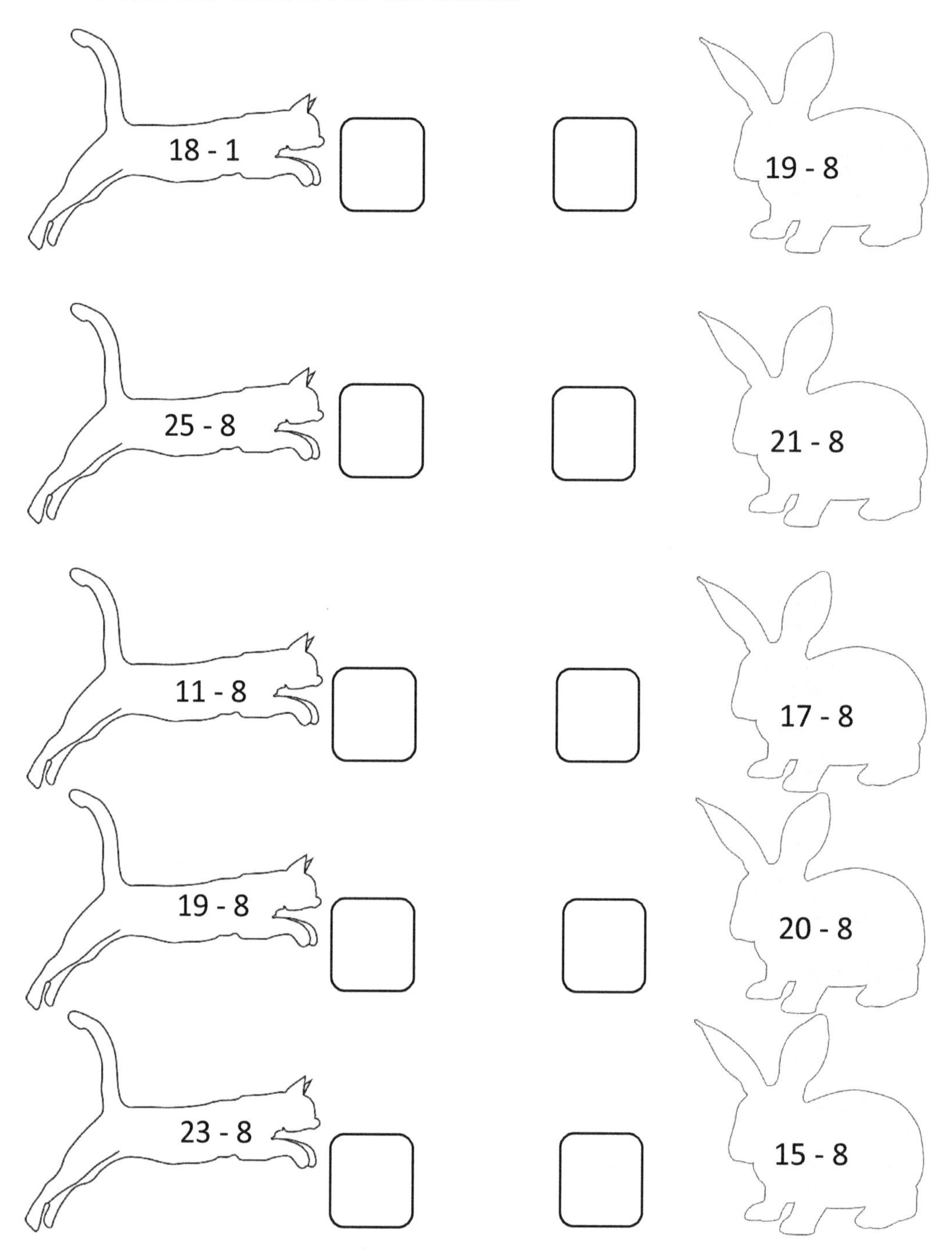

Find each difference.

$$\begin{array}{r} 12 \\ -\ 8 \\ \hline \underline{} \end{array}$$

$$\begin{array}{r} 18 \\ -\ 8 \\ \hline \underline{} \end{array}$$

$$\begin{array}{r} 28 \\ -\ 8 \\ \hline \underline{} \end{array}$$

$$\begin{array}{r} 25 \\ -\ 8 \\ \hline \underline{} \end{array}$$

$$\begin{array}{r} 26 \\ -\ 8 \\ \hline \underline{} \end{array}$$

$$\begin{array}{r} 20 \\ -\ 8 \\ \hline \underline{} \end{array}$$

$$\begin{array}{r} 29 \\ -\ 8 \\ \hline \underline{} \end{array}$$

$$\begin{array}{r} 30 \\ -\ 8 \\ \hline \underline{} \end{array}$$

$$\begin{array}{r} 23 \\ -\ 8 \\ \hline \underline{} \end{array}$$

There are 30 cards in the drawer. Mia took 8 cards from the drawer. How many cards are now in the drawer?

_____ cards

Find each missing number.

$23 - \_\_\_ = 15$

$20 - 8 = \_\_\_$

$\_\_\_ - 8 = 13$

$18 - \_\_\_ = 10$

$8 - \_\_\_ = 0$

$\_\_\_ - 8 = 4$

$\_\_\_ - 8 = 19$

$14 - 8 = \_\_\_$

$17 - 8 = \_\_\_$

$\_\_\_ - 8 = 22$

$\_\_\_ - 8 = 7$

$26 - \_\_\_ = 18$

$21 - 8 = \_\_\_$

$28 - 8 = \_\_\_$

Emily grew 27 pumpkins, but the rabbits ate 8 of them. How many pumpkins does Emily have left?

_____ pumpkins

Subtraction and adding by 7 and 8

Match.

20 - 7	18 - 8	16 - 7	15 - 7

9	8	13	9	10

7 - 1	8 + 2	8 + 5	7 + 2

Solve.

19 + 7 = 16	26 – 7 = 19
14 + 8 = ___	___ – 8 = ___
15 + 7 = ___	___ – 7 = ___
19 + 8 = ___	___ – 8 = ___
13 + 7 = ___	___ – 7 = ___
20 + 8 = ___	___ – 8 = ___
16 + 7 = ___	___ – 7 = ___

Write the answers in the boxes.

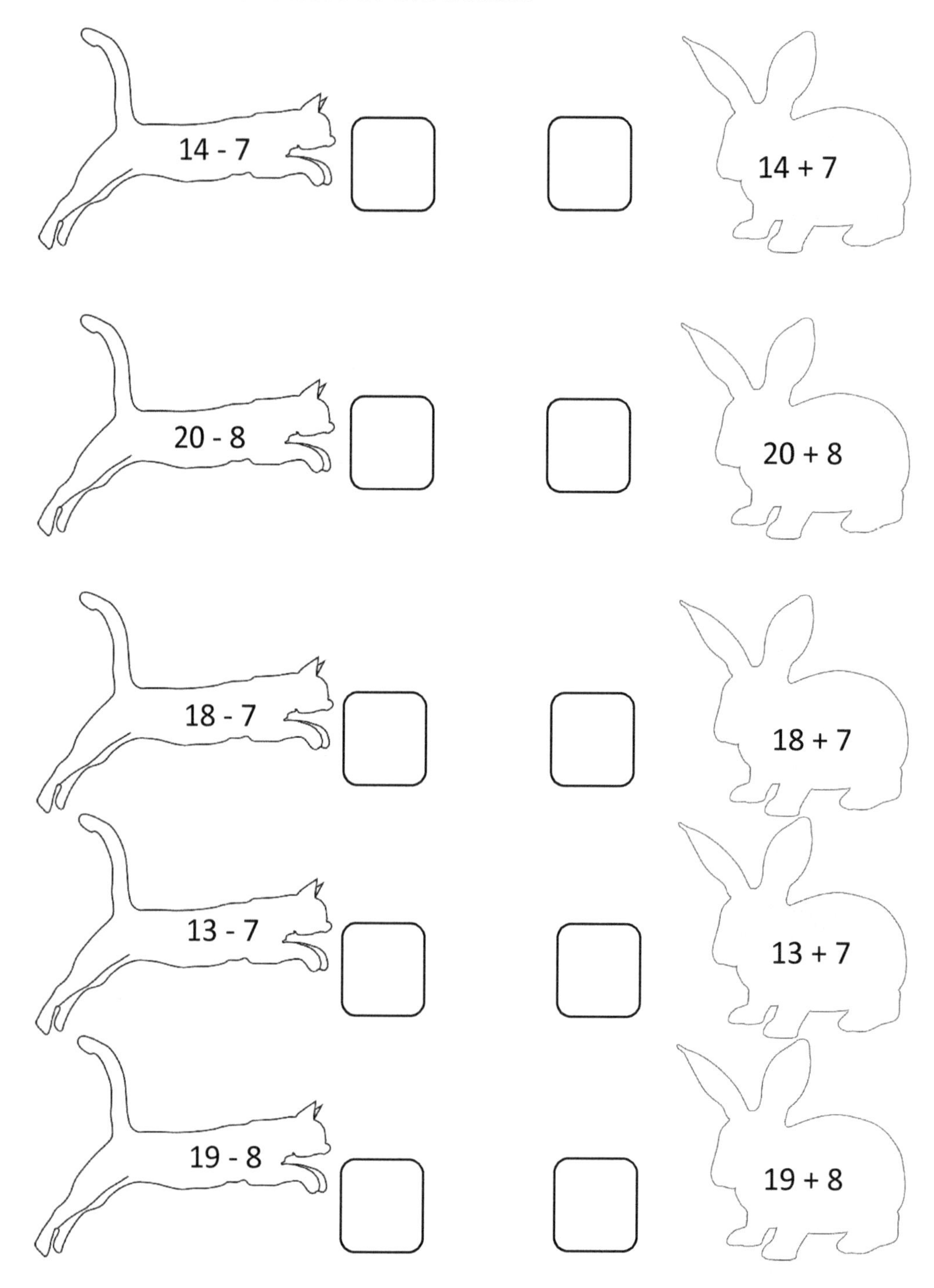

Find each difference.

$$\begin{array}{r} 20 \\ -\ \ 8 \\ \hline \end{array}$$
______

$$\begin{array}{r} 14 \\ -\ 7 \\ \hline \end{array}$$
______

$$\begin{array}{r} 16 \\ +\ 8 \\ \hline \end{array}$$
______

$$\begin{array}{r} 17 \\ +\ \ 7 \\ \hline \end{array}$$
______

$$\begin{array}{r} 18 \\ -\ 8 \\ \hline \end{array}$$
______

$$\begin{array}{r} 14 \\ +\ \ 7 \\ \hline \end{array}$$
______

$$\begin{array}{r} 12 \\ -\ \ 8 \\ \hline \end{array}$$
______

$$\begin{array}{r} 14 \\ -\ \ 8 \\ \hline \end{array}$$
______

$$\begin{array}{r} 13 \\ +\ 8 \\ \hline \end{array}$$
______

If there are 21 apples in a box and Ryan puts 8 more apples inside, how many apples are in the box?

______ apples

Lily picked 21 apples from the orchard, and gave 8 apples to her friend Aria. How many apples does Lily have now?

______ apples

Adding by 11

Write a fact for the following pictures.

☺☺☺☺ ☺☺☺☺ ☺☺☺	+	☺☺	=	☺☺☺☺☺ ☺☺☺☺☺ ☺☺☺	__ + __ = __
☺☺☺☺ ☺☺☺☺ ☺☺☺	+	☺☺☺ ☺☺	=	☺☺☺☺ ☺☺☺☺ ☺☺☺☺ ☺☺☺☺	__ + __ = __
☺☺☺☺ ☺☺☺☺ ☺☺☺	+	☺☺☺ ☺☺☺☺	=	☺☺☺☺☺ ☺☺☺☺☺ ☺☺☺☺☺ ☺☺☺	__ + __ = __
☺☺☺☺ ☺☺☺☺ ☺☺☺	+	☺☺☺ ☺☺☺ ☺☺☺	=	☺☺☺☺☺ ☺☺☺☺☺ ☺☺☺☺☺ ☺☺☺☺☺	__ + __ = __

Add each number in the top row by 11.

+	0	1	2	3	4	5	6	7	8	9	10	11	12
11													

Match.

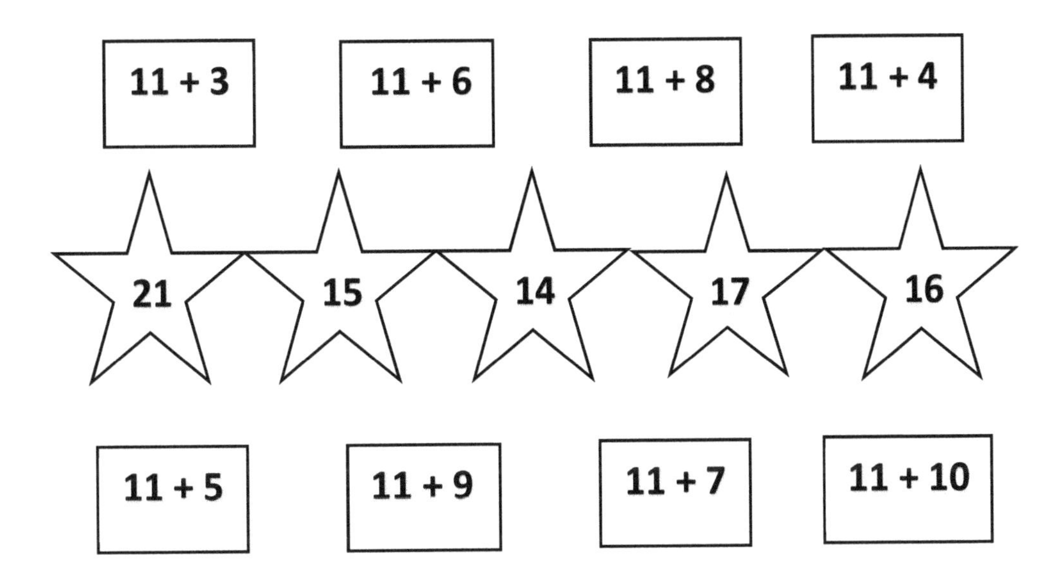

Write the answers in the boxes.

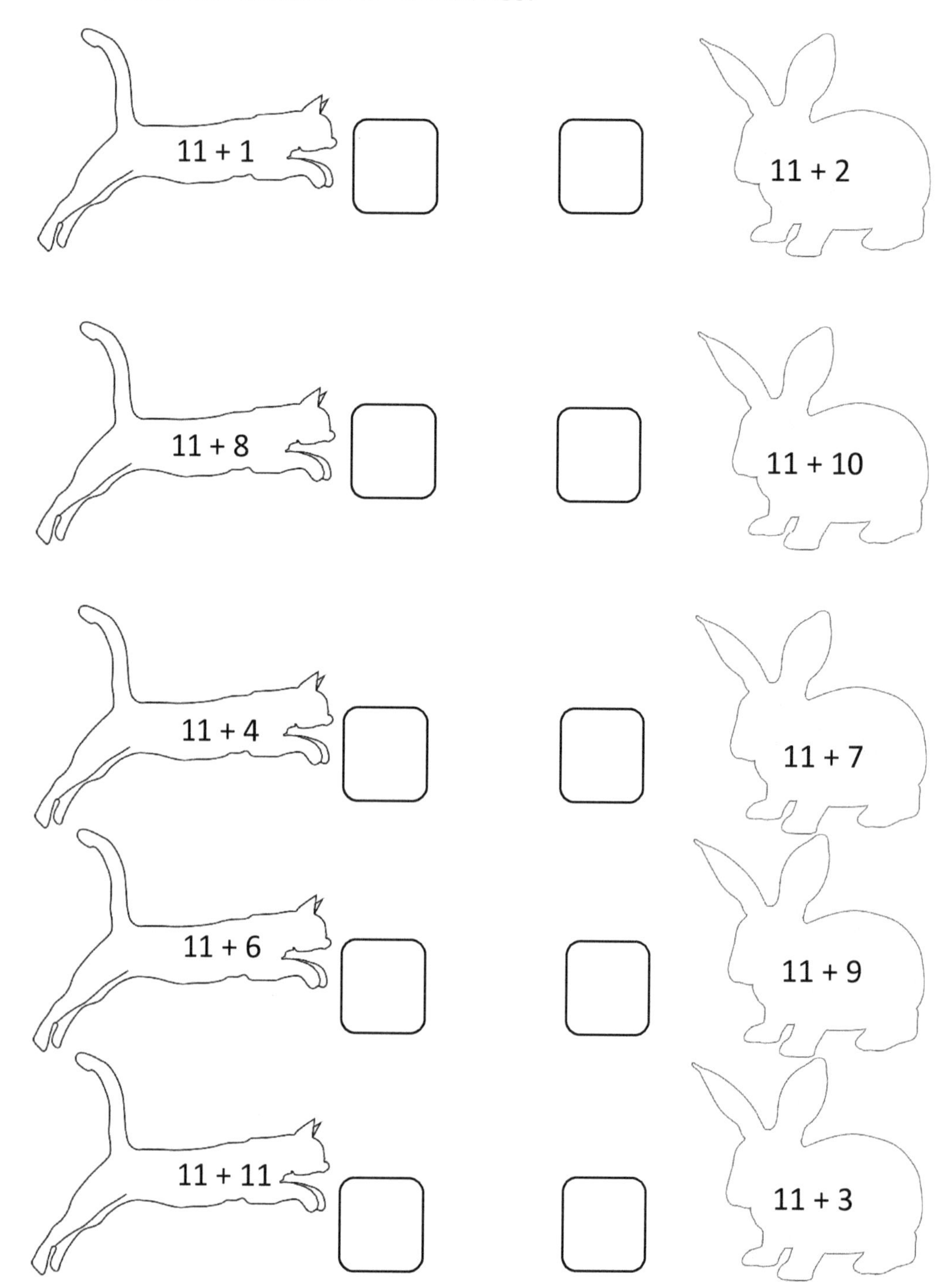

Find each sum.

$$\begin{array}{r} 11 \\ +\ 5 \\ \hline \_\_\_\_ \end{array} \quad \begin{array}{r} 11 \\ +\ 7 \\ \hline \_\_\_\_ \end{array} \quad \begin{array}{r} 11 \\ +\ 3 \\ \hline \_\_\_\_ \end{array}$$

$$\begin{array}{r} 11 \\ +\ 8 \\ \hline \_\_\_\_ \end{array} \quad \begin{array}{r} 11 \\ +\ 10 \\ \hline \_\_\_\_ \end{array} \quad \begin{array}{r} 11 \\ +\ 6 \\ \hline \_\_\_\_ \end{array}$$

$$\begin{array}{r} 11 \\ +\ 2 \\ \hline \_\_\_\_ \end{array} \quad \begin{array}{r} 11 \\ +\ 4 \\ \hline \_\_\_\_ \end{array} \quad \begin{array}{r} 11 \\ +\ 1 \\ \hline \_\_\_\_ \end{array}$$

Nora collects 11 candies. Nora's friend gives her 9 more. How many candies does Nora have?

_____ candies

Find each missing number.

11 + ___ = 13

___ + 4 = 15

11 + ___ = 17

___ + 8 = 19

11 + 9 = ___

___ + 5 = 15

11 + 3 = ___

11 + 11 = ___

11 + ___ = 23

___ + 13 = 24

11 + 10 = ___

___ + 1 = 6

11 + ___ = 11

11 + 7 = ___

Leah had 11 oranges. She gets 13 more from her friend Grace. How many oranges does Leah have now?

_____ oranges

Adding by 12

Write a fact for the following pictures.

☺☺☺☺
☺☺☺☺
☺☺☺☺ + ☺☺ = ☺☺☺☺☺
☺☺☺☺☺
☺☺☺☺ ___ + ___ = ___

☺☺☺☺
☺☺☺☺
☺☺☺☺ + ☺☺☺
☺☺ = ☺☺☺☺☺
☺☺☺☺☺☺
☺☺☺☺☺☺ ___ + ___ = ___

☺☺☺☺
☺☺☺☺
☺☺☺☺ + ☺☺☺
☺☺☺☺ = ☺☺☺☺☺
☺☺☺☺☺
☺☺☺☺☺
☺☺☺☺ ___ + ___ = ___

☺☺☺☺
☺☺☺☺
☺☺☺☺ + ☺☺☺
☺☺☺
☺☺☺ = ☺☺☺☺☺☺☺
☺☺☺☺☺☺☺
☺☺☺☺☺☺☺ ___ + ___ = ___

Add each number in the top row by 12.

+	0	1	2	3	4	5	6	7	8	9	10	11	12
12													

Match.

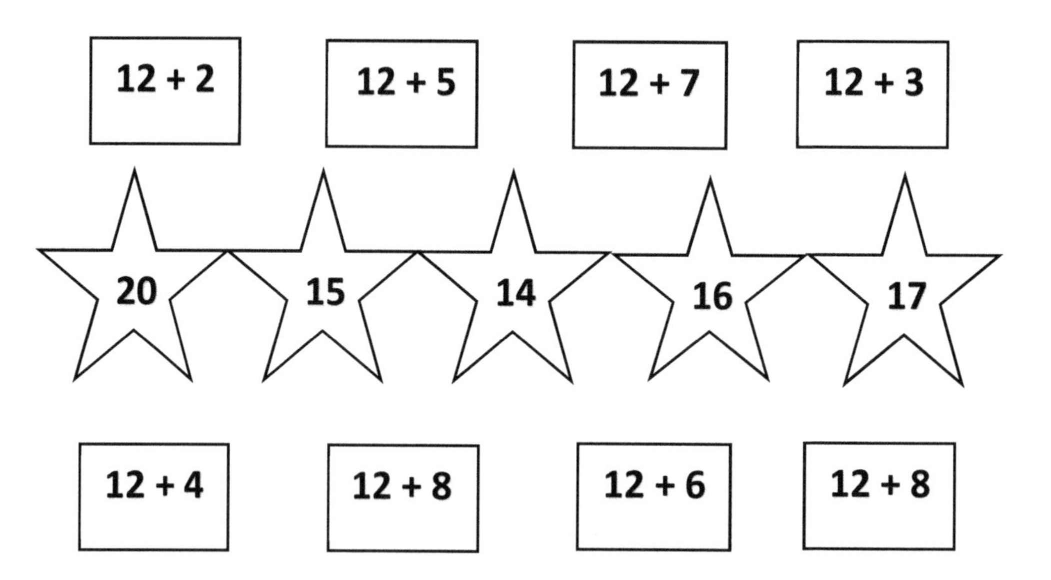

Write the answers in the boxes.

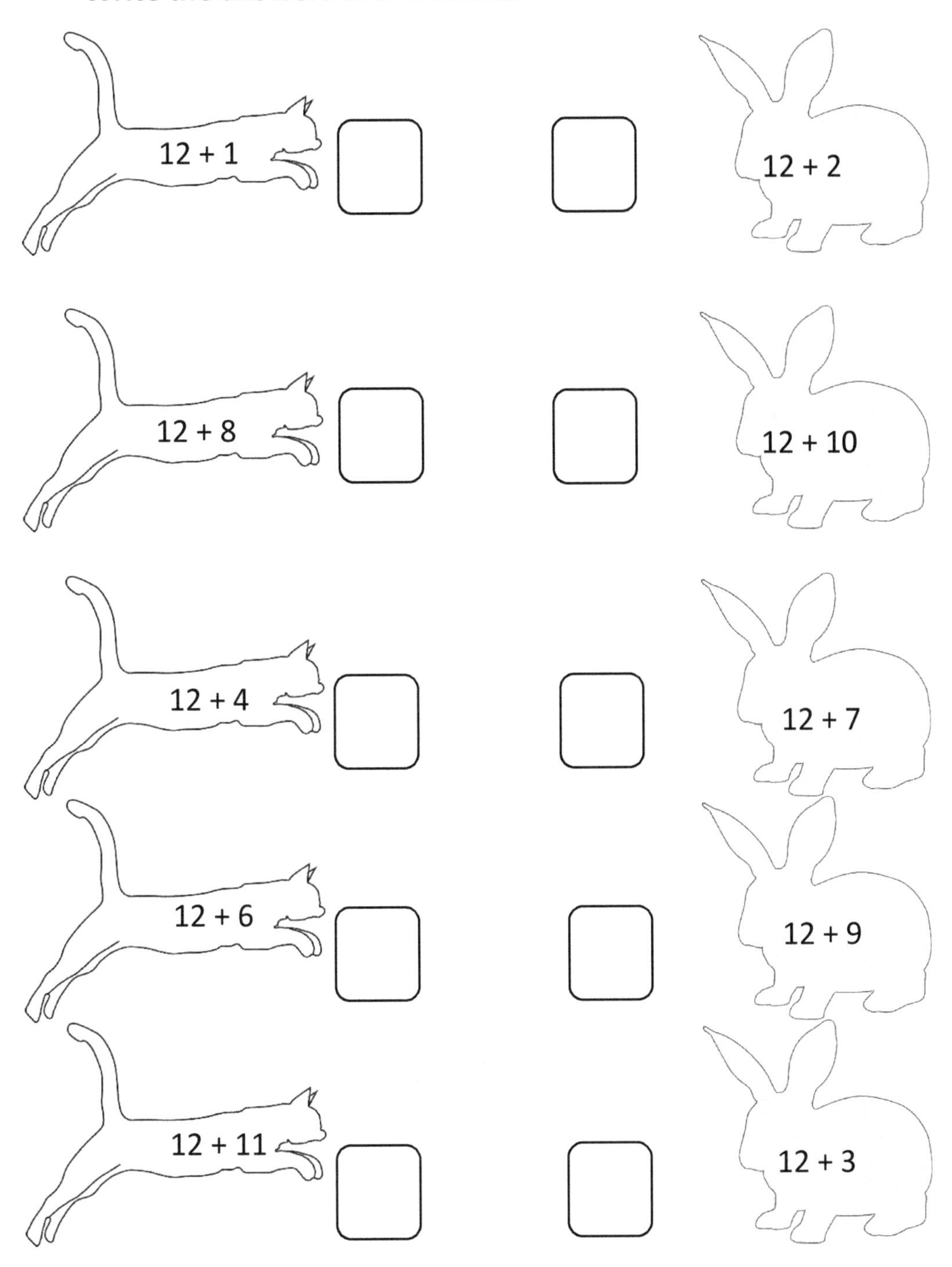

Find each sum.

$$\begin{array}{r} 12 \\ +\ 9 \\ \hline \end{array}$$

$$\begin{array}{r} 12 \\ +\ 7 \\ \hline \end{array}$$

$$\begin{array}{r} 12 \\ +\ 3 \\ \hline \end{array}$$

$$\begin{array}{r} 12 \\ +\ 8 \\ \hline \end{array}$$

$$\begin{array}{r} 12 \\ +\ 10 \\ \hline \end{array}$$

$$\begin{array}{r} 12 \\ +\ 6 \\ \hline \end{array}$$

$$\begin{array}{r} 12 \\ +\ 2 \\ \hline \end{array}$$

$$\begin{array}{r} 12 \\ +\ 4 \\ \hline \end{array}$$

$$\begin{array}{r} 12 \\ +\ 11 \\ \hline \end{array}$$

Anna has 12 candies. She was given 12 more candies. How many candies does Anna have now?

_____ candies

Find each missing number.

12 + ___ = 13

12 + 0 = ___

___ + 5 = 17

12 + ___ = 14

12 + ___ = 15

___ + 13 = 25

___ + 2 = 14

12 + 10 = ___

12 + 9 = ___

___ + 4 = 16

___ + 7 = 19

12 + ___ = 18

12 + 8 = ___

12 + 12 = ___

If there are 12 balls in a box and Lincoln puts 14 more balls inside, how many balls are in the box?

_____ balls

Complete the following addition table.

+	0	1	2	3	4	5	6	7	8	9	10	11	12
0													
1			3										
2													
3									11				
4													
5													
6												17	
7													
8													
9													
10													
11													
12													

Subtraction by 9

Write a subtraction fact for the following pictures.

☺☺☺☺☺
☺☺☺☺☺ – ☺☺☺☺
☺☺☺☺ ☺☺☺☺☺ = ___ - ___ = ___

☺☺☺☺☺ – ☺☺☺☺
☺☺☺☺☺ ☺☺☺☺☺ = ___ - ___ = ___

☺☺☺☺
☺☺☺☺ – ☺☺☺☺
☺☺☺☺ ☺☺☺☺☺ = ___ - ___ = ___

☺☺☺☺☺
☺☺☺☺☺ – ☺☺☺☺
☺☺☺☺☺ ☺☺☺☺☺ = ___ - ___ = ___

☺☺☺☺☺☺☺ ☺☺☺
☺☺☺☺☺☺☺ – ☺☺☺
☺☺☺☺☺☺☺ ☺☺☺ = ___ - ___ = ___

Subtract each number in the top row by 9.

—	9	10	11	12	13	14	15	16	17	18	19	20
9												

Match.

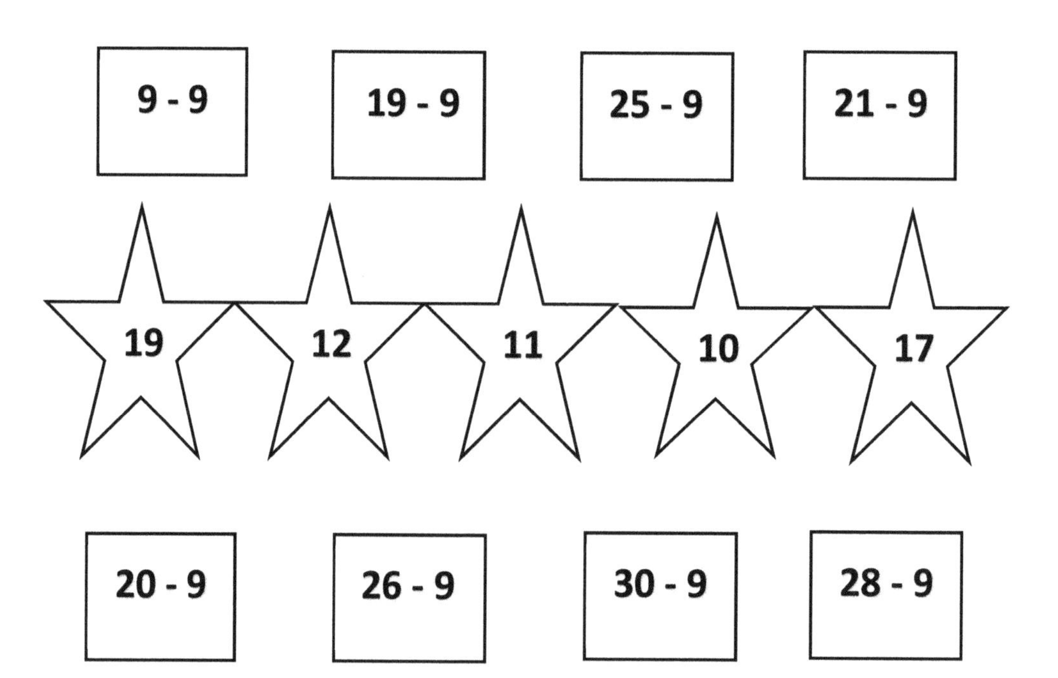

Write the answers in the boxes.

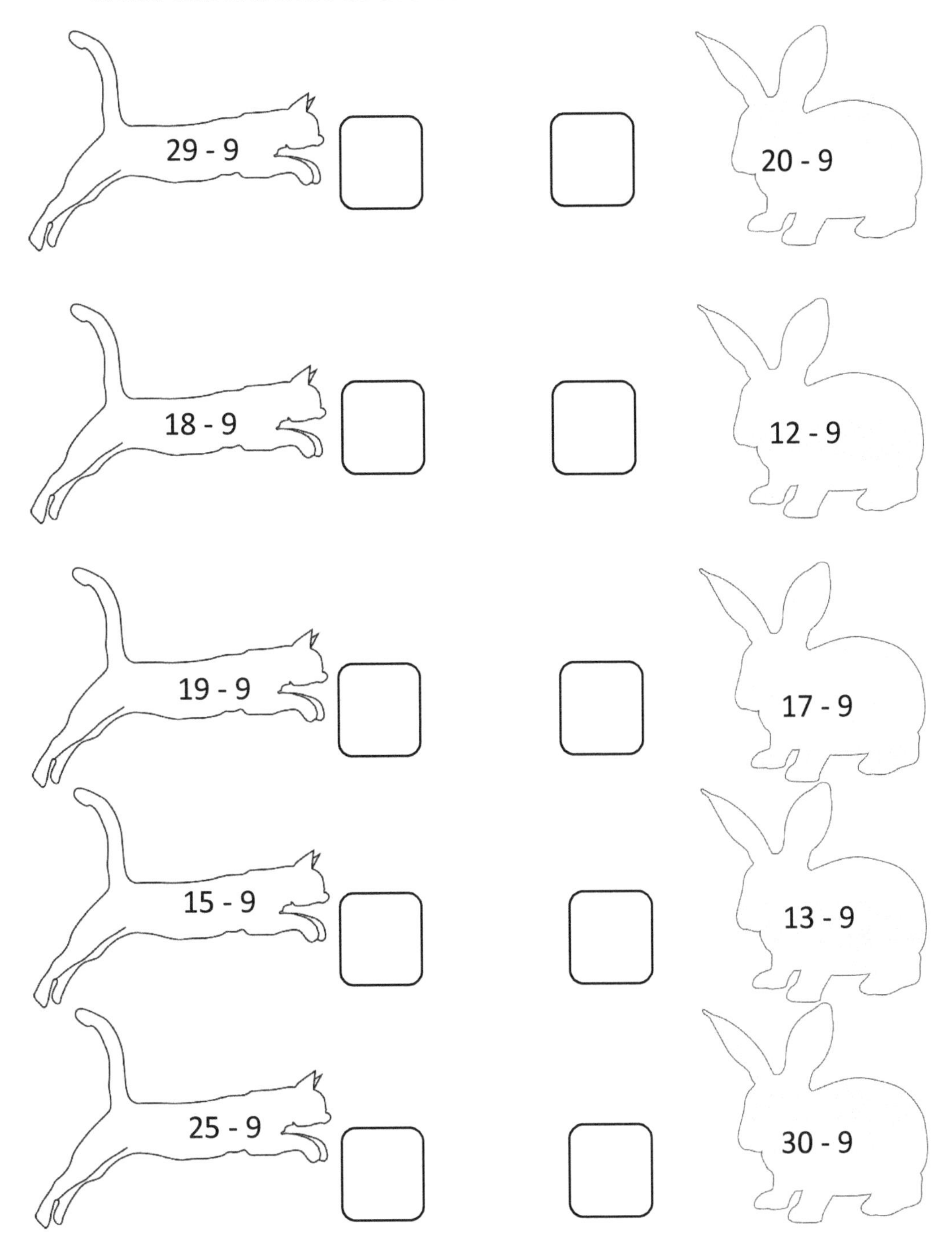

Find each difference.

32 − 9 _____	28 − 9 _____	39 − 9 _____
35 − 9 _____	31 − 9 _____	25 − 9 _____
29 − 9 _____	30 − 9 _____	35 − 9 _____

Ella's high school played 33 basketball games last year. She attended 9 games. How many basketball games did Ella miss?

______ basketball games

Find each missing number.

29 – ___ = 20

20 – 9 = ___

___ – 9 = 10

23 – ___ = 14

9 – ___ = 0

___ – 9 = 7

___ – 9 = 19

34 – 9 = ___

21 – 9 = ___

___ – 9 = 3

___ – 9 = 21

18 – ___ = 9

14 – 9 = ___

36 – 9 = ___

There are 26 trees currently in the park. Park workers cut down 9 trees that were damaged. How many trees will be in the park?

_____ trees

Subtraction by 10

Write a subtraction fact for the following pictures.

☺☺☺☺
☺☺☺☺ – ☺☺☺☺☺
☺☺☺☺ ☺☺☺☺☺ =

___ - ___ = ___

☺☺☺☺☺
☺☺☺☺☺ – ☺☺☺☺☺
☺☺☺☺☺ ☺☺☺☺☺ =

___ - ___ = ___

☺☺☺☺☺
☺☺☺☺☺ – ☺☺☺☺☺
☺☺☺☺☺ ☺☺☺☺☺ =
☺☺

___ - ___ = ___

☺☺☺☺☺
☺☺☺☺☺ – ☺☺☺☺☺
☺☺☺☺☺ ☺☺☺☺☺ =
☺☺☺

___ - ___ = ___

Subtract each number in the top row by 10.

—	10	11	12	13	14	15	16	17	18	19	20	21
10												

Match.

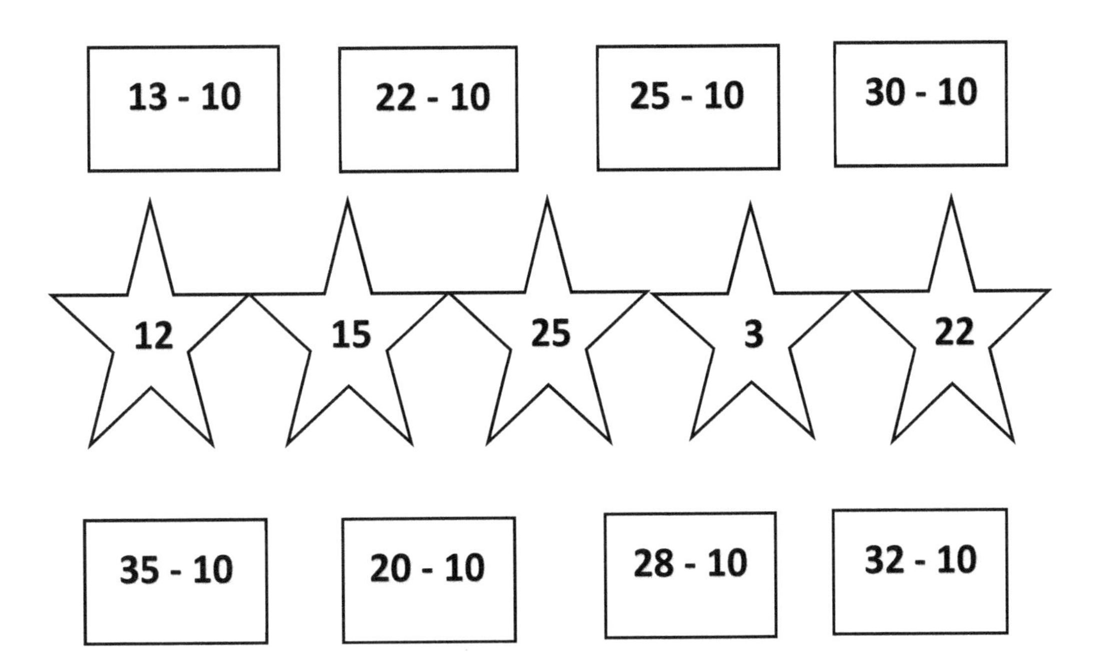

Write the answers in the boxes.

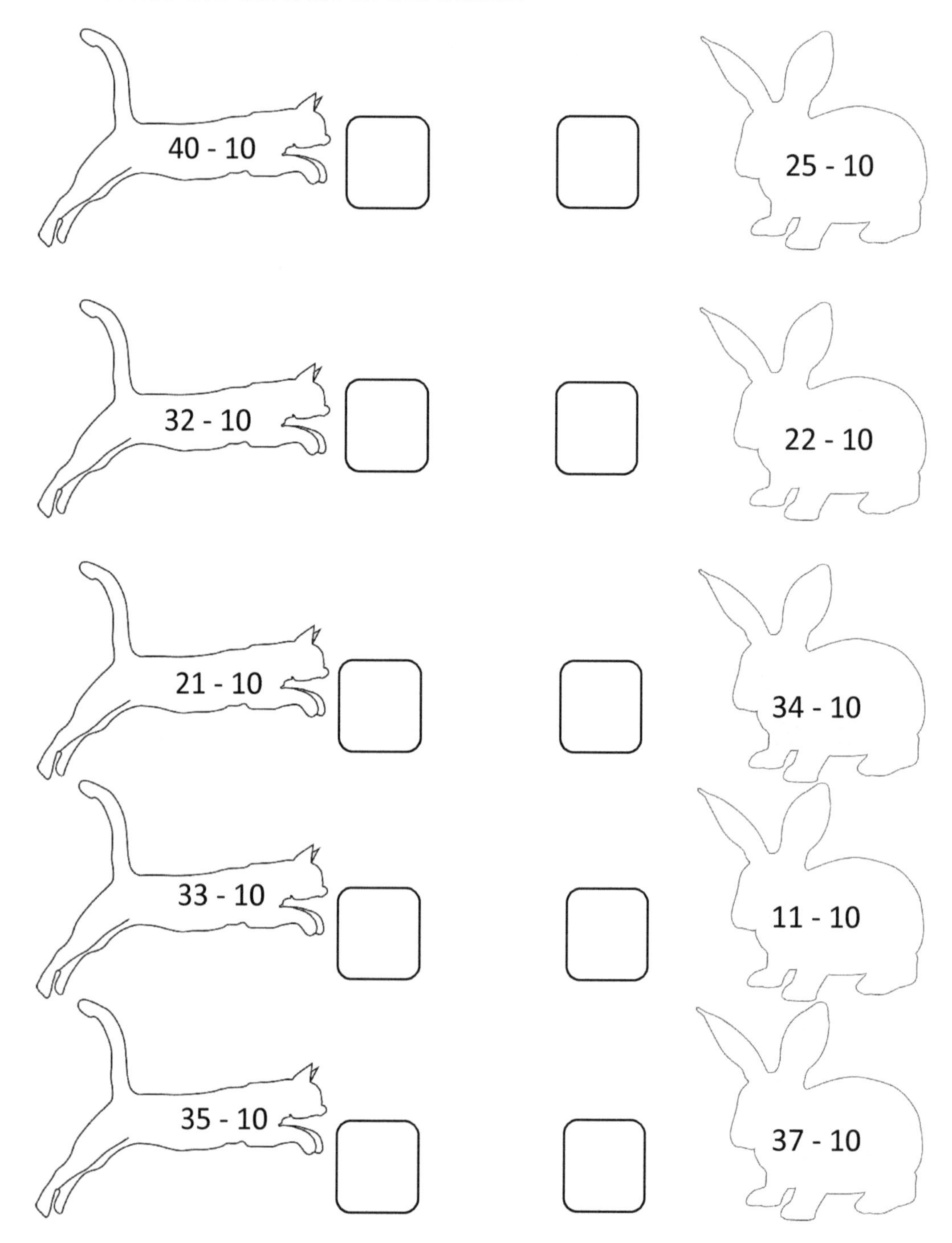

Find each difference.

$\begin{array}{r} 41 \\ -\ 10 \\ \hline \end{array}$ ______	$\begin{array}{r} 25 \\ -\ 10 \\ \hline \end{array}$ ______	$\begin{array}{r} 27 \\ -\ 10 \\ \hline \end{array}$ ______
$\begin{array}{r} 23 \\ -\ 10 \\ \hline \end{array}$ ______	$\begin{array}{r} 29 \\ -\ 10 \\ \hline \end{array}$ ______	$\begin{array}{r} 24 \\ -\ 10 \\ \hline \end{array}$ ______
$\begin{array}{r} 39 \\ -\ 10 \\ \hline \end{array}$ ______	$\begin{array}{r} 33 \\ -\ 10 \\ \hline \end{array}$ ______	$\begin{array}{r} 21 \\ -\ 10 \\ \hline \end{array}$ ______

Eliana had 34 old books. She sold 10 books. How many books does Eliana now have?

_____ books

Find each missing number.

25 – —— = 15 | 14 – 10 = ——

—— – 10 = 7 | 19 – —— = 9

20 – —— = 10 | —— – 10 = 23

—— – 10 = 13 | 28 – 10 = ——

27 – 10 = —— | —— – 10 = 21

—— – 10 = 15 | 34 – —— = 14

13 – 10 = —— | 40 – 10 = ——

Camilla has 24 basketball cards. John bought 10 of Camilla's cards. How many cards does Camilla have now?

_____ cards

Subtraction by 11

Write a subtraction fact for the following pictures.

☺☺☺☺☺ ☺☺☺☺
☺☺☺☺☺ – ☺☺☺☺ = ___ - ___ = ___
☺☺☺ ☺☺☺

☺☺☺☺ ☺☺☺☺
☺☺☺☺ – ☺☺☺☺ = ___ - ___ = ___
☺☺☺☺ ☺☺☺
☺☺☺☺

☺☺☺☺☺ ☺☺☺☺
☺☺☺☺☺ – ☺☺☺☺ = ___ - ___ = ___
☺☺☺☺☺ ☺☺☺
☺☺☺

☺☺☺☺☺ ☺☺☺☺
☺☺☺☺☺ – ☺☺☺☺ = ___ - ___ = ___
☺☺☺☺☺ ☺☺☺
☺☺☺☺☺

Subtract each number in the top row by 11.

—	11	12	13	14	15	16	17	18	19	20	21	22
11												

Match.

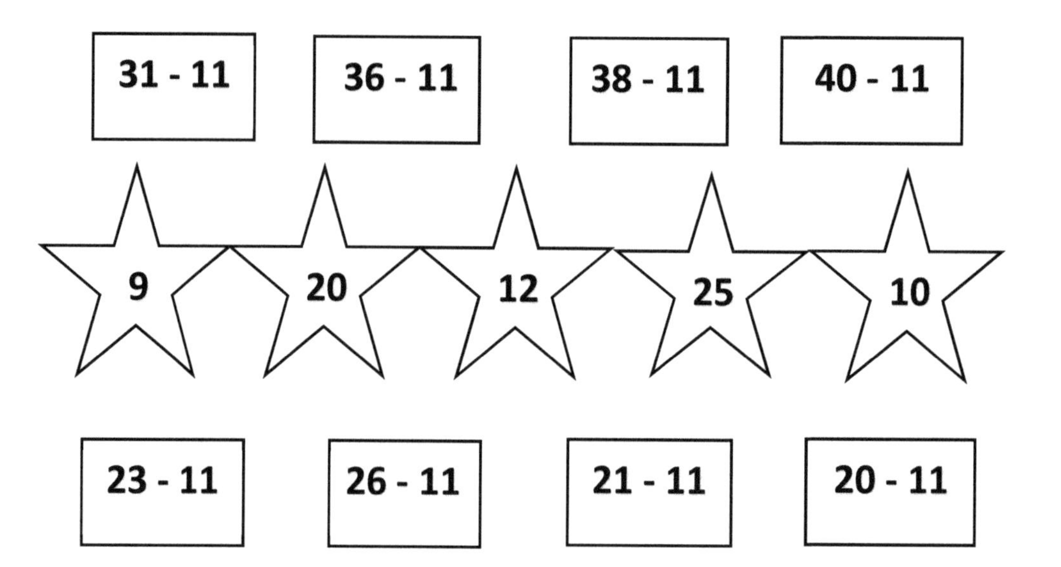

Write the answers in the boxes.

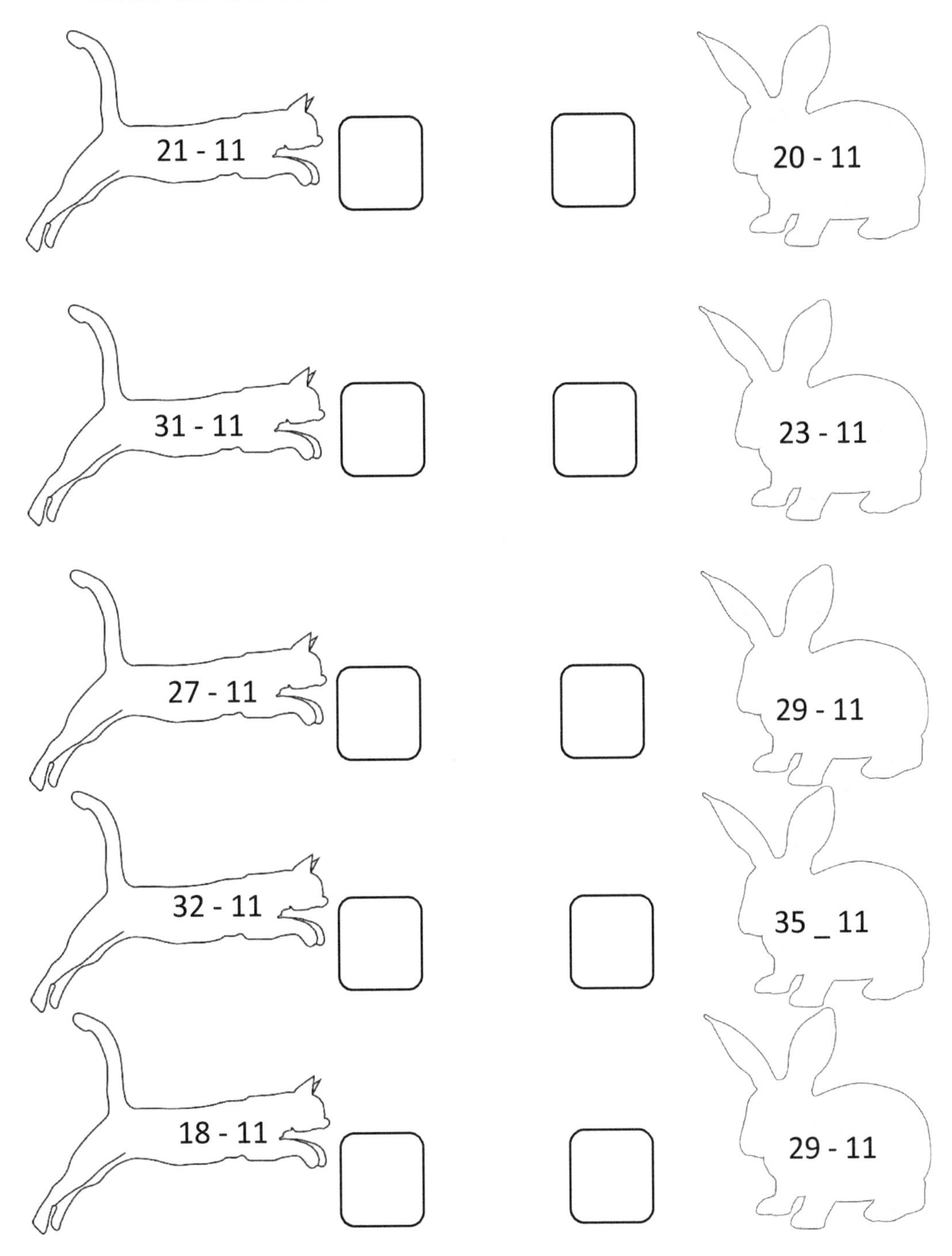

Find each difference.

$$\begin{array}{r} 41 \\ -\ 11 \\ \hline \end{array}$$

$$\begin{array}{r} 34 \\ -\ 11 \\ \hline \end{array}$$

$$\begin{array}{r} 21 \\ -\ 11 \\ \hline \end{array}$$

$$\begin{array}{r} 25 \\ -\ 11 \\ \hline \end{array}$$

$$\begin{array}{r} 27 \\ -\ 11 \\ \hline \end{array}$$

$$\begin{array}{r} 29 \\ -\ 11 \\ \hline \end{array}$$

$$\begin{array}{r} 15 \\ -\ 11 \\ \hline \end{array}$$

$$\begin{array}{r} 17 \\ -\ 11 \\ \hline \end{array}$$

$$\begin{array}{r} 19 \\ -\ 11 \\ \hline \end{array}$$

Lily picked 19 apples from the orchard, and gave 11 apples to her friend Aria. How many apples does Lily have now ?

______ apples

Find each missing number.

24 – ____ = 13

12 – 11 = ____

____ – 11 = 15

14 – ____ = 3

23 – ____ = 12

____ – 11 = 24

____ – 11 = 9

27 – 11 = ____

21 – 11 = ____

____ – 11 = 5

____ – 11 = 19

19 – ____ = 8

15 – 11 = ____

27 – 11 = ____

There are 20 cards in the drawer. Mia took 11 cards from the drawer. How many cards are now in the drawer?

_____ cards

Subtraction by 12

Write a subtraction fact for the following pictures.

☺☺☺☺☺ ☺☺☺☺
☺☺☺☺☺ – ☺☺☺☺ =
☺☺☺☺ ☺☺☺☺

___ - ___ = ___

☺☺☺☺☺ ☺☺☺☺
☺☺☺☺☺☺ – ☺☺☺☺ =
☺☺☺☺☺☺ ☺☺☺☺

___ - ___ = ___

☺☺☺☺☺ ☺☺☺☺
☺☺☺☺☺ – ☺☺☺☺ =
☺☺☺☺☺ ☺☺☺☺
☺☺☺☺

___ - ___ = ___

☺☺☺ ☺☺☺☺
☺☺☺☺ – ☺☺☺☺ =
☺☺☺ ☺☺☺☺
☺☺☺☺
☺☺☺
☺☺☺☺

___ - ___ = ___

Subtract each number in the top row by 12.

—	12	13	14	15	16	17	18	19	20	21	22	23
12												

Match.

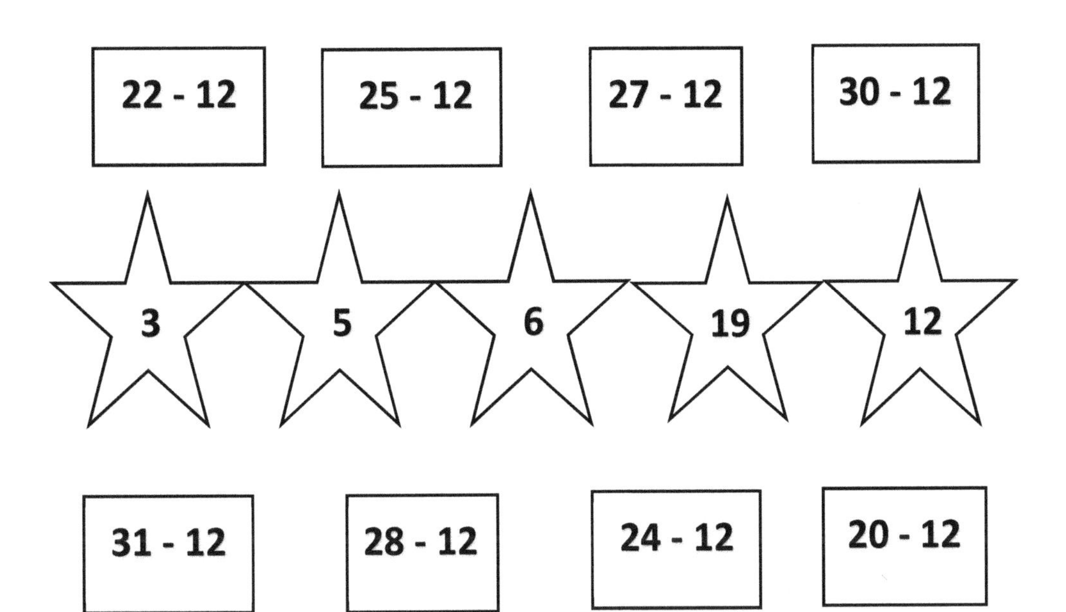

Write the answers in the boxes.

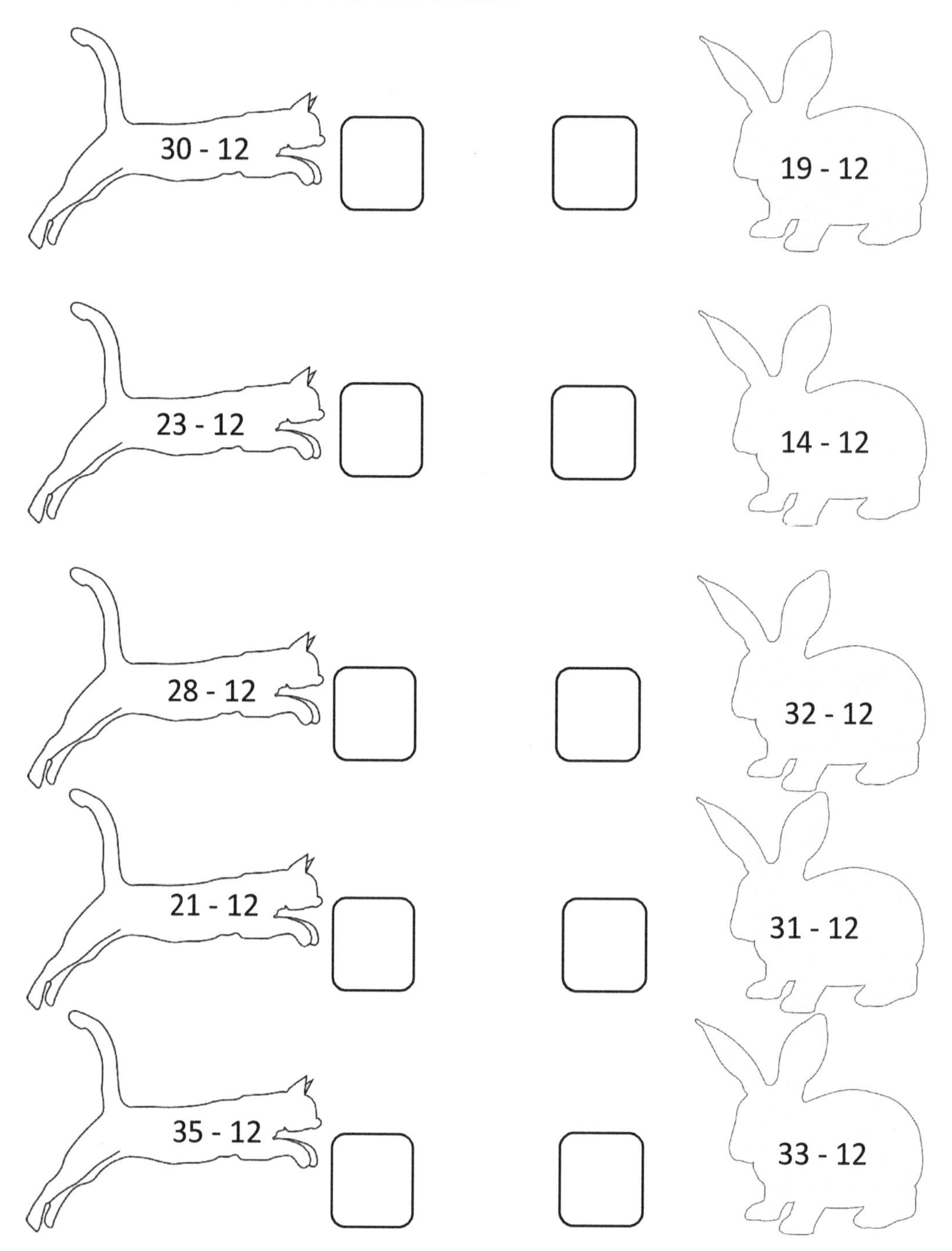

Find each difference.

$$\begin{array}{r} 23 \\ -\ 12 \\ \hline \end{array}$$ ______

$$\begin{array}{r} 28 \\ -\ 12 \\ \hline \end{array}$$ ______

$$\begin{array}{r} 32 \\ -\ 12 \\ \hline \end{array}$$ ______

$$\begin{array}{r} 40 \\ -\ 12 \\ \hline \end{array}$$ ______

$$\begin{array}{r} 17 \\ -\ 12 \\ \hline \end{array}$$ ______

$$\begin{array}{r} 35 \\ -\ 12 \\ \hline \end{array}$$ ______

$$\begin{array}{r} 34 \\ -\ 12 \\ \hline \end{array}$$ ______

$$\begin{array}{r} 39 \\ -\ 12 \\ \hline \end{array}$$ ______

$$\begin{array}{r} 37 \\ -\ 12 \\ \hline \end{array}$$ ______

Williams has 41 marbles, he gave Olivia 12 of the marbles. How many marbles does he now have?

_____ marbles

Find each missing number.

23 – ___ = 11

25 – 12 = ___

___ – 12 = 5

22 – ___ = 10

14 – ___ = 2

___ – 12 = 8

___ – 12 = 4

13 – 12 = ___

18 – 12 = ___

___ – 12= 16

___ – 12 = 19

32 – ___ = 20

29 – 12 = ___

30 – 12 = ___

Richard found 31 seashells on the beach, he gave Aria 12 of the seashells. How many seashells does he now have?

_____ seashells

—	10	11	12	13	14	15	16	17	18	19	20	21	22
0													
1													
2													
3													
4													
5													
6													
7													
8													
9													
10													
11													
12													

Subtraction and adding by 9, 10, 11 and 12

Match.

22 - 9	19 - 11	21 - 10	22 - 12

10 11 13 8 14

12 + 1	11 + 0	12 + 8	9 + 2

Solve.

20 + 9 = 29	29 – 9 = 20
19 + 10 = ___	___ – 10 = ___
21 + 12 = ___	___ – 12 = ___
18 + 11 = ___	___ – 11 = ___
15 + 12 = ___	___ – 12 = ___
16 + 11 = ___	___ – 11 = ___
12 + 10 = ___	___ – 10 = ___

Write the answers in the boxes.

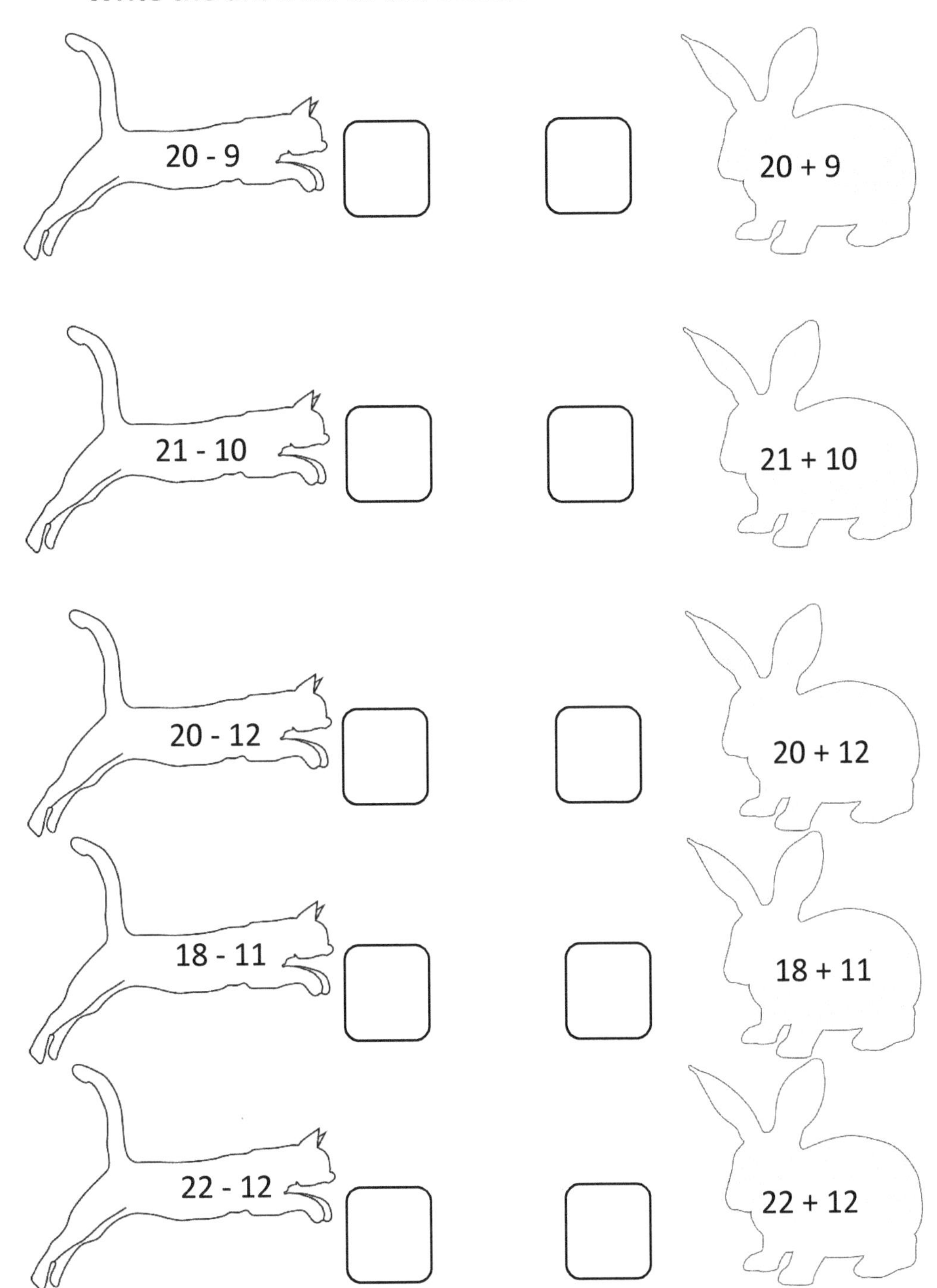

Find each difference.

$\begin{array}{r} 16 \\ -\ 12 \\ \hline \end{array}$	$\begin{array}{r} 18 \\ -\ 10 \\ \hline \end{array}$	$\begin{array}{r} 21 \\ +\ 12 \\ \hline \end{array}$
$\begin{array}{r} 19 \\ +\ 9 \\ \hline \end{array}$	$\begin{array}{r} 18 \\ -\ 12 \\ \hline \end{array}$	$\begin{array}{r} 14 \\ +\ 10 \\ \hline \end{array}$
$\begin{array}{r} 19 \\ -\ 10 \\ \hline \end{array}$	$\begin{array}{r} 13 \\ -\ 9 \\ \hline \end{array}$	$\begin{array}{r} 13 \\ +\ 12 \\ \hline \end{array}$

Hannah collects 24 oranges. Hannah's mother gives him 9 more. How many oranges does Hannah have?

_____ oranges

There are 24 cards in the drawer. Mia took 9 cards from the drawer. How many cards are now in the drawer?

_____ cards

Extra adding practices

Find each sum.

$$\begin{array}{r} 26 \\ +\,10 \\ \hline \end{array}$$

$$\begin{array}{r} 29 \\ +\,9 \\ \hline \end{array}$$

$$\begin{array}{r} 27 \\ +\,8 \\ \hline \end{array}$$

$$\begin{array}{r} 28 \\ +\,4 \\ \hline \end{array}$$

$$\begin{array}{r} 25 \\ +\,11 \\ \hline \end{array}$$

$$\begin{array}{r} 26 \\ +\,2 \\ \hline \end{array}$$

$$\begin{array}{r} 27 \\ +\,1 \\ \hline \end{array}$$

$$\begin{array}{r} 28 \\ +\,3 \\ \hline \end{array}$$

$$\begin{array}{r} 29 \\ +\,10 \\ \hline \end{array}$$

$$\begin{array}{r} 26 \\ +\,9 \\ \hline \end{array}$$

$$\begin{array}{r} 29 \\ +\,7 \\ \hline \end{array}$$

$$\begin{array}{r} 28 \\ +\,5 \\ \hline \end{array}$$

Solve.

30 + 8 = ___

38 + 4 = ___

32 + 4 = ___

39 + 9 = ___

33 + 10 = ___

39 + 7 = ___

32 + 3 = ___

38 + 5 = ___

31 + 2 = ___

37 + 3 = ___

35 + 7 = ___

36 + 10 = ___

Abigail has 38 pens. She buys 8 more. How many pens does Abigail have in all?

______ pens

Find each sum.

37 + 11 = ____	39 + 19 = ____	38 + 18 = ____
37 + 14 = ____	38 + 11 = ____	39 + 12 = ____
38 + 13 = ____	40 + 12 = ____	37 + 10 = ____
36 + 17 = ____	38 + 15 = ____	35 + 13 = ____

Solve.

46 + 20 = ___

48 + 15 = ___

45 + 16 = ___

49 + 9 = ___

49 + 15 = ___

46 + 7 = ___

43 + 3 = ___

48 + 5 = ___

41 + 9 = ___

44 + 13 = ___

40 + 6 = ___

45 + 9 = ___

There are 49 stamps. 12 stamps more are added. How many stamps are there in total?

_____ stamps

Find each sum.

$65 + 11 = \_\_\_$	$60 + 19 = \_\_\_$	$75 + 18 = \_\_\_$
$53 + 14 = \_\_\_$	$77 + 11 = \_\_\_$	$82 + 12 = \_\_\_$
$64 + 11 = \_\_\_$	$83 + 13 = \_\_\_$	$92 + 11 = \_\_\_$
$59 + 20 = \_\_\_$	$86 + 18 = \_\_\_$	$99 + 15 = \_\_\_$

Solve.

100 + 3 = ___

104 + 3 = ___

100 + 6 = ___

109 + 9 = ___

100 + 5 = ___

105 + 7 = ___

102 + 3 = ___

101 + 5 = ___

108 + 9 = ___

107 + 3 = ___

109 + 6 = ___

103 + 9 = ___

Isaac has 106 stickers. Owen has 7 stickers. How many stickers do they have in all?

_____ stickers

Find each sum.

$$\begin{array}{r} 111 \\ +\ 10 \\ \hline \end{array}$$

$$\begin{array}{r} 121 \\ +\ 9 \\ \hline \end{array}$$

$$\begin{array}{r} 125 \\ +\ 18 \\ \hline \end{array}$$

$$\begin{array}{r} 120 \\ +\ 14 \\ \hline \end{array}$$

$$\begin{array}{r} 125 \\ +\ 11 \\ \hline \end{array}$$

$$\begin{array}{r} 129 \\ +\ 22 \\ \hline \end{array}$$

$$\begin{array}{r} 145 \\ +\ 31 \\ \hline \end{array}$$

$$\begin{array}{r} 224 \\ +\ 33 \\ \hline \end{array}$$

$$\begin{array}{r} 229 \\ +\ 60 \\ \hline \end{array}$$

$$\begin{array}{r} 274 \\ +\ 39 \\ \hline \end{array}$$

$$\begin{array}{r} 226 \\ +\ 47 \\ \hline \end{array}$$

$$\begin{array}{r} 445 \\ +\ 95 \\ \hline \end{array}$$

Extra subtraction practices

Solve.

46 – 20 = ___

48 – 15 = ___

45 – 16 = ___

49 – 9 = ___

49 – 15 = ___

46 – 7 = ___

43 – 3 = ___

48 – 5 = ___

41 – 9 = ___

44 – 13 = ___

40 – 6 = ___

45 – 9 = ___

There are 49 cards in the drawer. Mia took 12 cards from the drawer. How many cards are now in the drawer?

_____ cards

Find each difference.

$$\begin{array}{r} 55 \\ -\ 11 \\ \hline \end{array}$$

$$\begin{array}{r} 50 \\ -\ 19 \\ \hline \end{array}$$

$$\begin{array}{r} 55 \\ -\ 18 \\ \hline \end{array}$$

$$\begin{array}{r} 53 \\ -\ 14 \\ \hline \end{array}$$

$$\begin{array}{r} 55 \\ -\ 11 \\ \hline \end{array}$$

$$\begin{array}{r} 52 \\ -\ 12 \\ \hline \end{array}$$

$$\begin{array}{r} 54 \\ -\ 11 \\ \hline \end{array}$$

$$\begin{array}{r} 54 \\ -\ 13 \\ \hline \end{array}$$

$$\begin{array}{r} 52 \\ -\ 11 \\ \hline \end{array}$$

$$\begin{array}{r} 59 \\ -\ 20 \\ \hline \end{array}$$

$$\begin{array}{r} 57 \\ -\ 18 \\ \hline \end{array}$$

$$\begin{array}{r} 59 \\ -\ 15 \\ \hline \end{array}$$

Solve.

63 – 5 = ___

61 – 15 = ___

67 – 9 = ___

69 – 19 = ___

70 – 15 = ___

64 – 9 = ___

68 – 3 = ___

65 – 10 = ___

66 – 19 = ___

70 – 3 = ___

63 – 6 = ___

71 – 9 = ___

Ella's high school played 76 basketball games last year. She attended 16 games. How many basketball games did Ella miss?

_____ basketball games

Find each difference.

$$\begin{array}{r} 70 \\ -\ 10 \\ \hline \end{array}$$

$$\begin{array}{r} 67 \\ -\ 19 \\ \hline \end{array}$$

$$\begin{array}{r} 65 \\ -\ 18 \\ \hline \end{array}$$

$$\begin{array}{r} 69 \\ -\ 14 \\ \hline \end{array}$$

$$\begin{array}{r} 66 \\ -\ 18 \\ \hline \end{array}$$

$$\begin{array}{r} 65 \\ -\ 12 \\ \hline \end{array}$$

$$\begin{array}{r} 61 \\ -\ 11 \\ \hline \end{array}$$

$$\begin{array}{r} 64 \\ -\ 13 \\ \hline \end{array}$$

$$\begin{array}{r} 63 \\ -\ 10 \\ \hline \end{array}$$

$$\begin{array}{r} 69 \\ -\ 17 \\ \hline \end{array}$$

$$\begin{array}{r} 68 \\ -\ 16 \\ \hline \end{array}$$

$$\begin{array}{r} 63 \\ -\ 13 \\ \hline \end{array}$$

Solve.

77 – 4 = ___

78 – 5 = ___

80 – 6 = ___

85 – 3 = ___

84 – 5 = ___

87 – 5 = ___

75 – 2 = ___

88 – 8 = ___

79 – 8 = ___

86 – 2 = ___

74 – 6 = ___

89 – 9 = ___

Wilson had 76 old books. he sold 9 books. How many books does Wilson now have?

_____ books

Find each difference.

$$\begin{array}{r} 90 \\ -\ 11 \\ \hline \end{array}$$

$$\begin{array}{r} 95 \\ -\ 30 \\ \hline \end{array}$$

$$\begin{array}{r} 90 \\ -\ 28 \\ \hline \end{array}$$

$$\begin{array}{r} 96 \\ -\ 24 \\ \hline \end{array}$$

$$\begin{array}{r} 95 \\ -\ 31 \\ \hline \end{array}$$

$$\begin{array}{r} 98 \\ -\ 42 \\ \hline \end{array}$$

$$\begin{array}{r} 99 \\ -\ 30 \\ \hline \end{array}$$

$$\begin{array}{r} 94 \\ -\ 63 \\ \hline \end{array}$$

$$\begin{array}{r} 92 \\ -\ 90 \\ \hline \end{array}$$

$$\begin{array}{r} 86 \\ -\ 89 \\ \hline \end{array}$$

$$\begin{array}{r} 91 \\ -\ 77 \\ \hline \end{array}$$

$$\begin{array}{r} 96 \\ -\ 35 \\ \hline \end{array}$$

Solve.

100 – 3 = ___

104 – 3 = ___

100 – 6 = ___

109 – 9 = ___

100 – 5 = ___

105 – 7 = ___

102 – 3 = ___

101 – 5 = ___

108 – 9 = ___

107 – 3 = ___

109 – 6 = ___

103 – 9 = ___

There are 110 cards in the drawer. Mia took 18 cards from the drawer. How many cards are now in the drawer?

_____ cards

Find each difference.

$$\begin{array}{r} 111 \\ -\ 10 \\ \hline \end{array}$$

$$\begin{array}{r} 121 \\ -\ 9 \\ \hline \end{array}$$

$$\begin{array}{r} 125 \\ -\ 18 \\ \hline \end{array}$$

$$\begin{array}{r} 120 \\ -\ 14 \\ \hline \end{array}$$

$$\begin{array}{r} 125 \\ -\ 11 \\ \hline \end{array}$$

$$\begin{array}{r} 129 \\ -\ 22 \\ \hline \end{array}$$

$$\begin{array}{r} 145 \\ -\ 31 \\ \hline \end{array}$$

$$\begin{array}{r} 224 \\ -\ 33 \\ \hline \end{array}$$

$$\begin{array}{r} 229 \\ -\ 60 \\ \hline \end{array}$$

$$\begin{array}{r} 274 \\ -\ 39 \\ \hline \end{array}$$

$$\begin{array}{r} 226 \\ -\ 47 \\ \hline \end{array}$$

$$\begin{array}{r} 445 \\ -\ 95 \\ \hline \end{array}$$

Solve.

600 – 30 = ___

847 – 43 = ___

450 – 65 = ___

930 – 40 = ___

367 – 45 = ___

680 – 70 = ___

489 – 63 = ___

793 – 45 = ___

320 – 39 = ___

834 – 44 = ___

890 – 60 = ___

934 – 90 = ___

Taylor grew 845 pumpkins, but the rabbits ate 57 of them. How many pumpkins does Taylor have left?

_____ pumpkins

Solve.

1000 – 90 = ___

1678 – 243 = ___

1000 – 88 = ___

3450 – 246 = ___

1234 – 66 = ___

5678 – 470 = ___

1643 – 88 = ___

3467 – 678 = ___

1799 – 90 = ___

4567 – 890 = ___

1654 – 60 = ___

2000 – 978 = ___

There are 2345 cards in the drawer. Mia took 180 cards from the drawer. How many cards are now in the drawer?

_____ cards

Find each difference.

$$\begin{array}{r} 2340 \\ -\ 370 \\ \hline \end{array}$$ ______

$$\begin{array}{r} 2910 \\ -\ 279 \\ \hline \end{array}$$ ______

$$\begin{array}{r} 3334 \\ -\ 290 \\ \hline \end{array}$$ ______

$$\begin{array}{r} 9100 \\ -\ 594 \\ \hline \end{array}$$ ______

$$\begin{array}{r} 6600 \\ -\ 800 \\ \hline \end{array}$$ ______

$$\begin{array}{r} 2334 \\ -\ 42 \\ \hline \end{array}$$ ______

$$\begin{array}{r} 3456 \\ -\ 201 \\ \hline \end{array}$$ ______

$$\begin{array}{r} 3442 \\ -\ 93 \\ \hline \end{array}$$ ______

$$\begin{array}{r} 5343 \\ -\ 440 \\ \hline \end{array}$$ ______

$$\begin{array}{r} 2630 \\ -\ 93 \\ \hline \end{array}$$ ______

$$\begin{array}{r} 9059 \\ -\ 197 \\ \hline \end{array}$$ ______

$$\begin{array}{r} 1722 \\ -\ 225 \\ \hline \end{array}$$ ______

Multiplication

Multiply by 0, 2 and 10

Write a multiplication fact for the following pictures.

☺☺ ☺☺

☺☺ ☺☺

☺☺ ☺☺

☺☺ ☺☺

8 x __ = __

☺☺☺☺☺☺☺☺☺☺

☺☺☺☺☺☺☺☺☺☺

☺☺☺☺☺☺☺☺☺☺

3 x __ = __

☺☺ ☺☺ ☺☺

☺☺ ☺☺ ☺☺

☺☺ ☺☺ ☺☺

☺☺

10 x __ = __

List the first ten multiples of each number.

2, ___, ___, ___, ___, ___, ___, ___, ___, ___

10, ___, ___, ___, ___, ___, ___, ___, ___, ___

Multiply each number in the top row by 0, 2 and then by 10.

×	1	2	3	4	5	6	7	8	9	10
0										
2										
10										

Match.

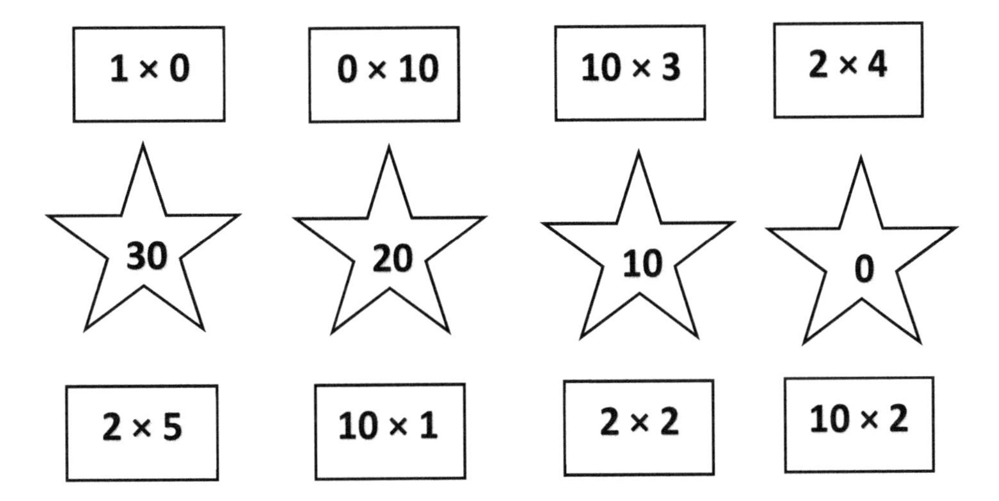

Complete.

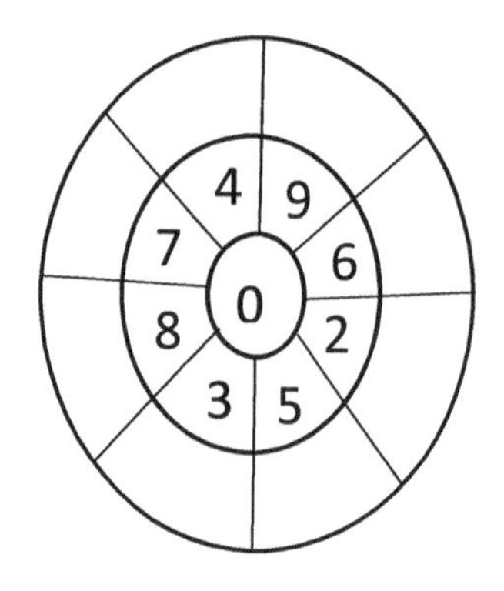

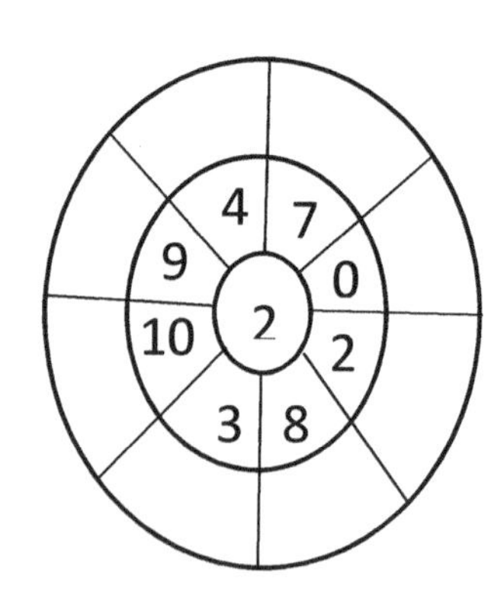

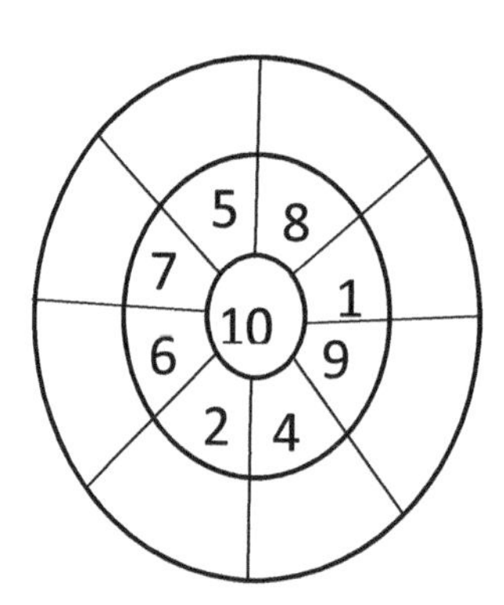

Find each missing number.

2 × ___ = 0

___ × 3 = 6

___ × 2 = 10

2 × ___ = 2

6 × ___ = 12

___ × 5 = 50

___ × 7 = 70

2 × ___ = 16

9 × ___ = 0

___ × 3 = 30

___ × 2 = 8

10 × ___ = 80

10 × ___ = 60

2 × ___ = 18

Write the answers in the boxes.

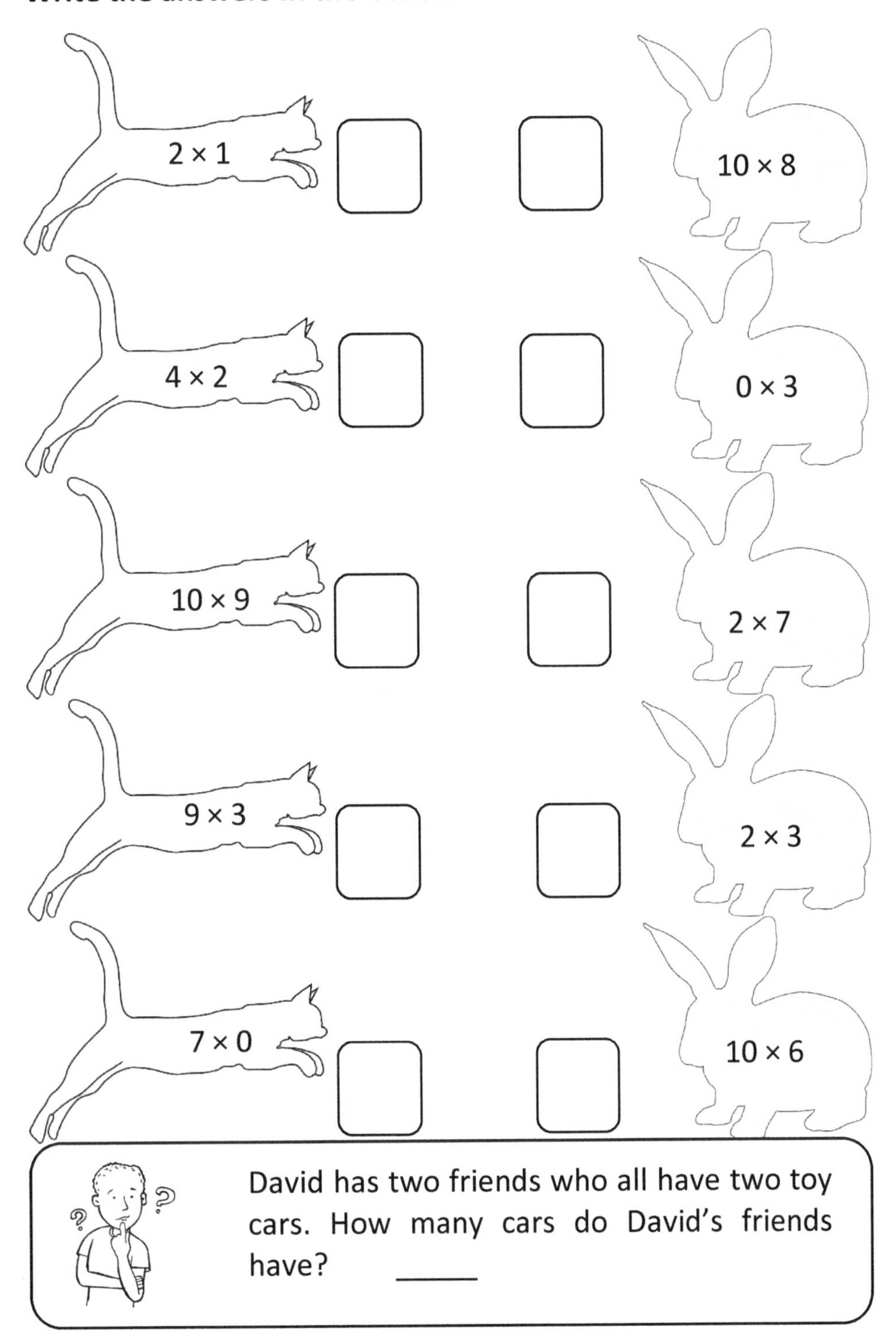

David has two friends who all have two toy cars. How many cars do David's friends have? ______

Multiply by 1

Write a multiplication fact for the following pictures.

☺ ☺ ☺

☺ ☺ ☺ 9 x __ = __

☺ ☺ ☺

☺ ☺ ☺ ☺ __ x __ = 8

☺ ☺ ☺ ☺

☺ ☺ ☺ ☺

☺ ☺ ☺ ☺ __ x 1 = __

List the first ten multiples of each number.

1, ___, 3, ___, ___, ___, ___, ___

Mr. smith usually eats 2 meals a day. How many meals does he eat in a week? _____

Multiply each number in the top row by 0, 2 and then by 10.

×	1	2	3	4	5	6	7	8	9	10
1										
2										
10										

Match.

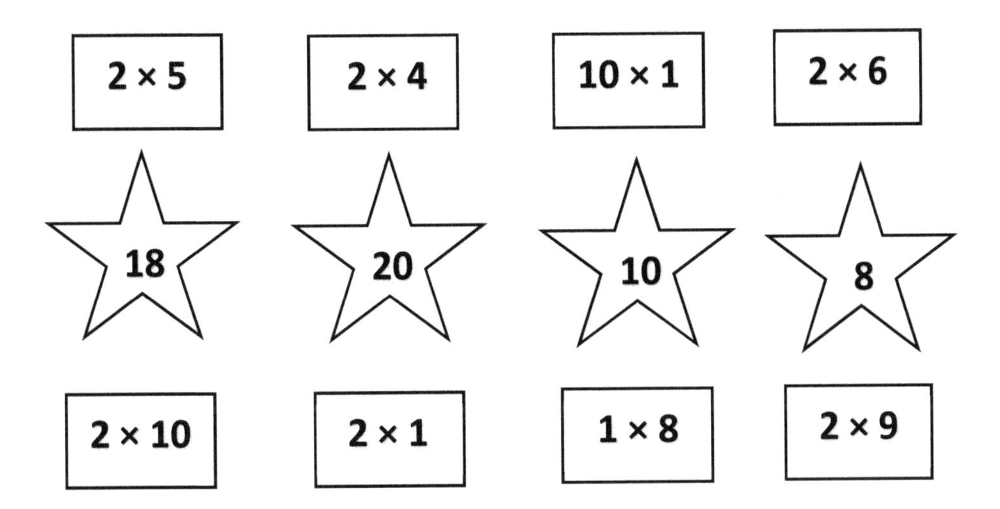

Complete.

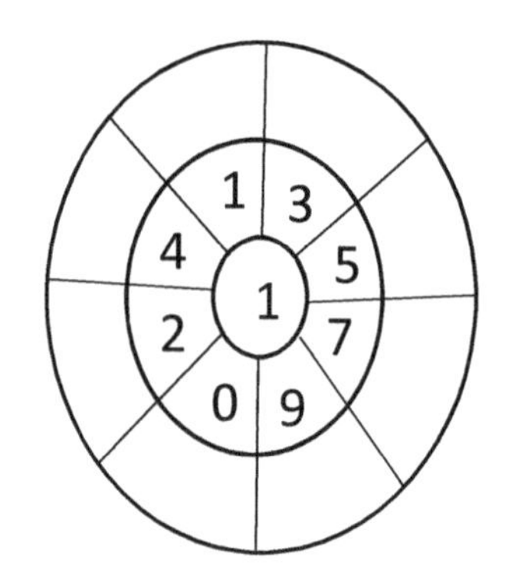

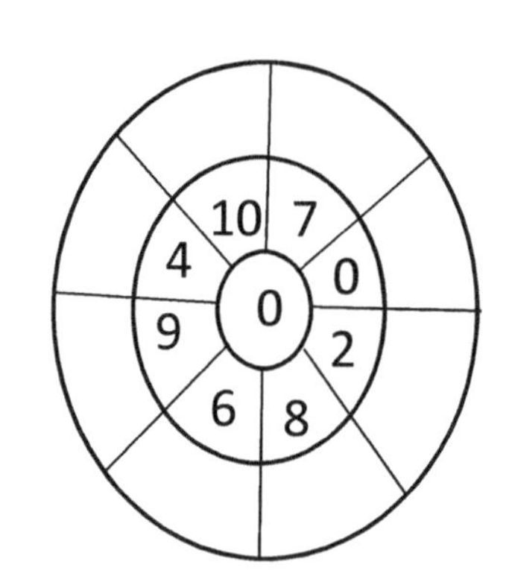

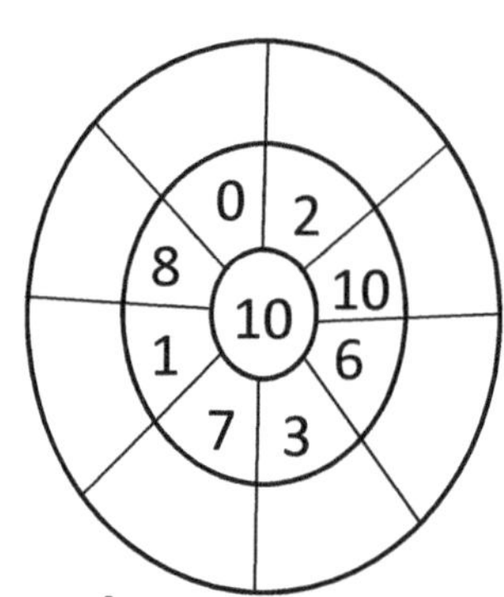

Find each missing number.

2 × ___ = 2	1 × 8 = ___
1 × 6 = ___	1 × ___ = 0
___ × 6 = 6	___ × 1 = 9
1 × ___ = 1	1 × 7 = ___
5 × 1 = ___	4 × ___ = 1
___ × 3 = 3	10 × ___ = 10
8 × 1 = ___	10 × 1 = ___

Write the answers in the boxes.

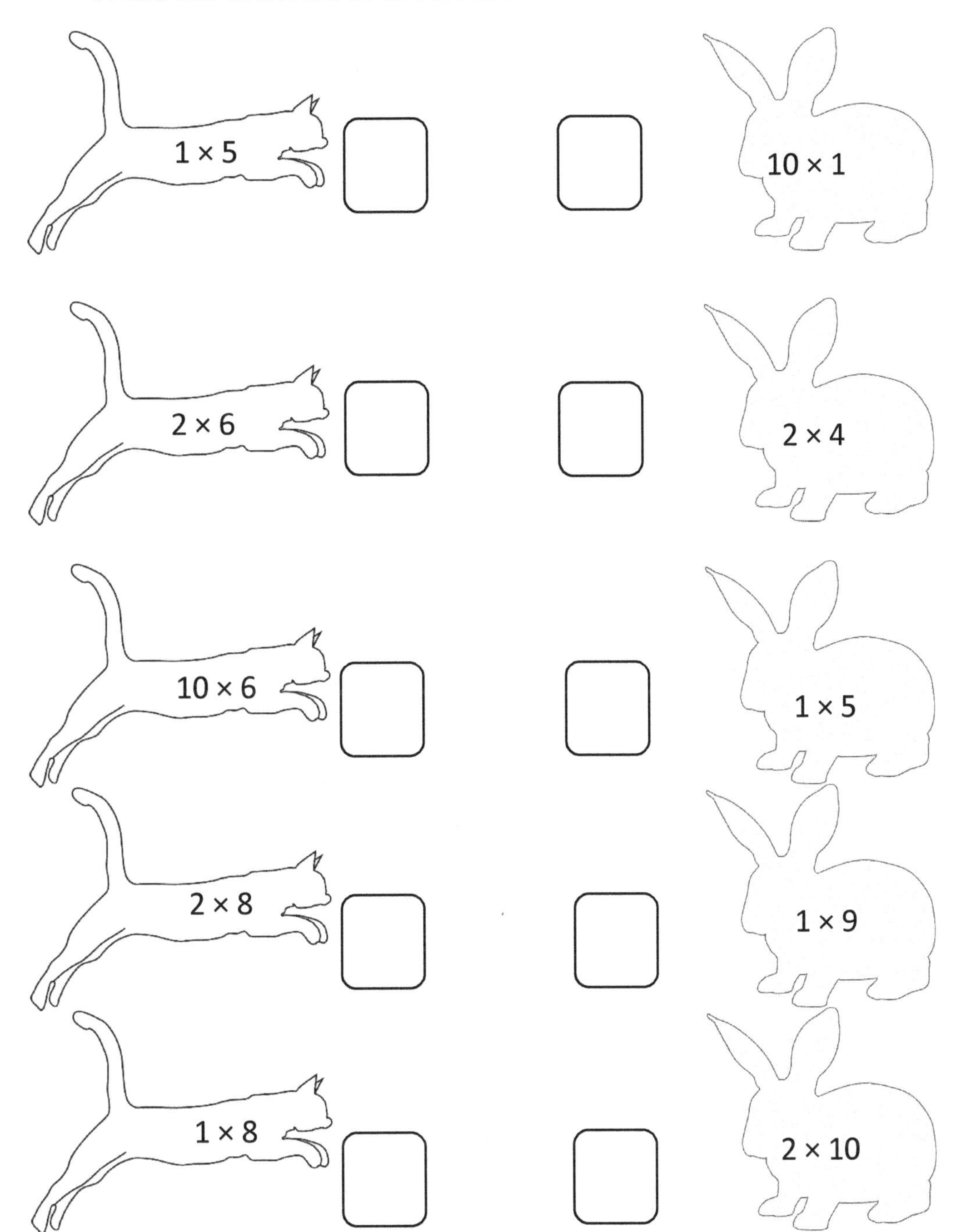

Multiply by 3

Write a multiplication fact for the following pictures.

☺☺☺ ☺☺☺

☺☺☺ ☺☺☺ 4 x __ = __

☺☺☺ ☺☺☺

☺☺☺ ☺☺☺ __ x __ = 18

☺☺☺ ☺☺☺

☺☺☺ ☺☺☺

☺☺☺ ☺☺☺ __ x 3 = __

List the first ten multiples of each number.

3, ___, ___, ___, ___, ___, ___

2, ___, ___, ___, ___, ___, ___

The multiplication symbol (×) simply mear "groups of". For example, 3 × 4 = 12 mean 3 groups of 4 objects!

Multiply each number in the top row by 1, 2 and then by 3.

×	1	2	3	4	5	6	7	8	9	10
1										
2										
3										

Match.

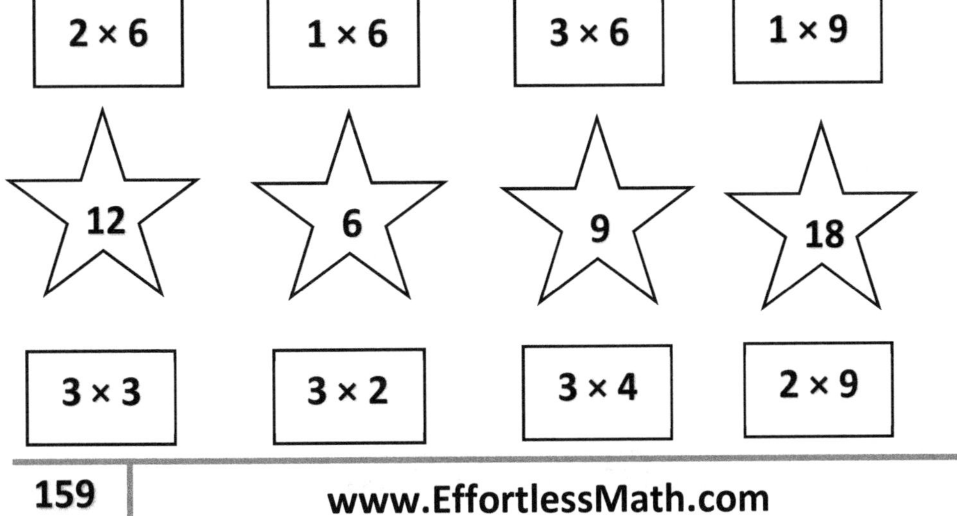

Complete.

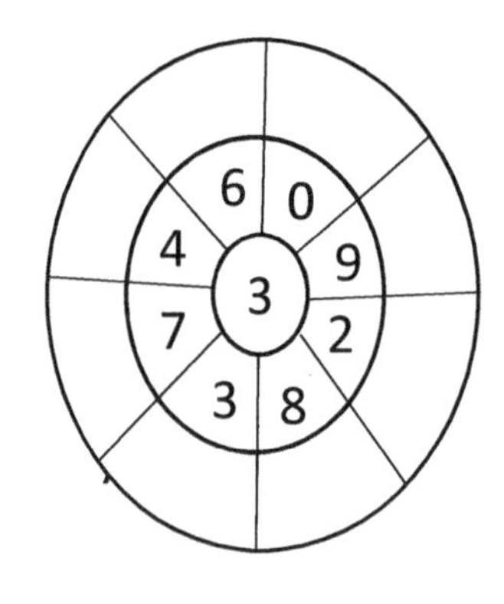

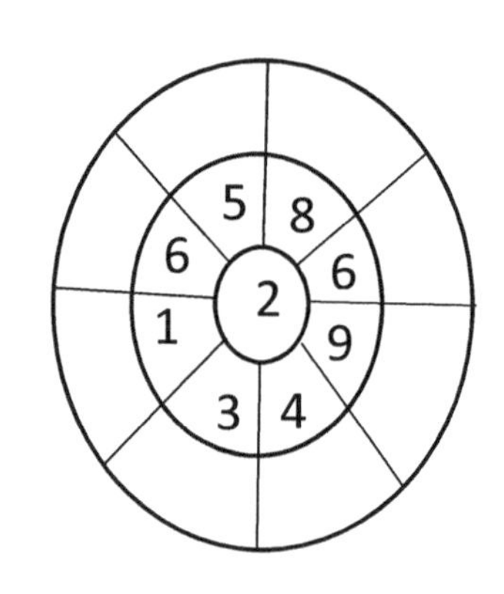

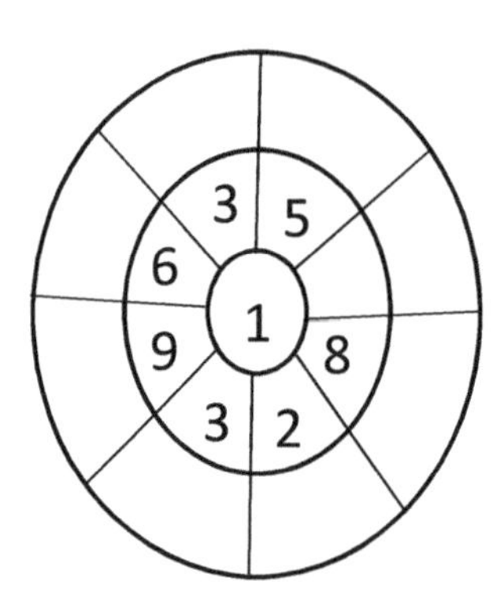

Find each missing number.

3 × ___ = 27

7 × 3 = ___

___ × 5 = 15

3 × ___ = 0

6 × ___ = 18

___ × 2 = 6

___ × 3 = 6

3 × 10 = ___

3 × 4 = ___

___ × 3 = 24

Write the answers in the boxes.

3 × 6 ☐ ☐ 3 × 3

3 × 4 ☐ ☐ 3 × 8

3 × 0 ☐ ☐ 2 × 3

1 × 3 ☐ ☐ 3 × 7

3 × 5 ☐ ☐ 3 × 9

There are 3 sets of tables in the backyard and each set has 5 chairs, how many chairs are in the backyard? ______

Multiply by 5

Write a multiplication fact for the following pictures.

☺☺☺☺☺
☺☺☺☺☺
☺☺☺☺☺

4 x __ = __

☺☺☺☺☺ ☺☺☺☺☺
☺☺☺☺☺ ☺☺☺☺☺

__ x __ = 20

☺☺☺☺☺ ☺☺☺☺☺
☺☺☺☺☺ ☺☺☺☺☺
☺☺☺☺☺ ☺☺☺☺☺
☺☺☺☺☺ ☺☺☺☺☺

__ x 5 = __

List the first ten multiples of each number.

5, ___, 15, ___, ___, ___, ___, ___

On a family dinner table, there are five plates for everybody. Eight people came to the dinner. How many plates were on the table? _____

Multiply each number in the top row by 2, 3 and then by 5.

×	1	2	3	4	5	6	7	8	9	10
2										
3										
5										

Match.

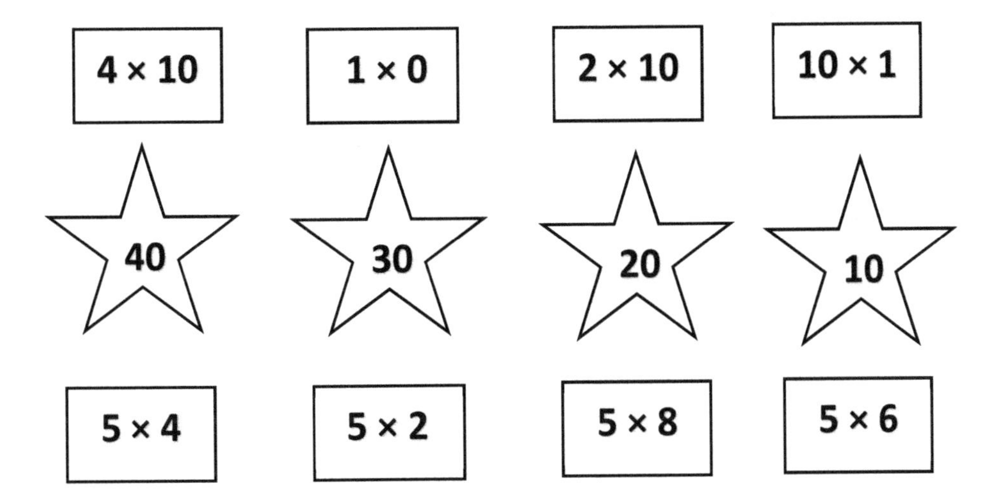

Complete.

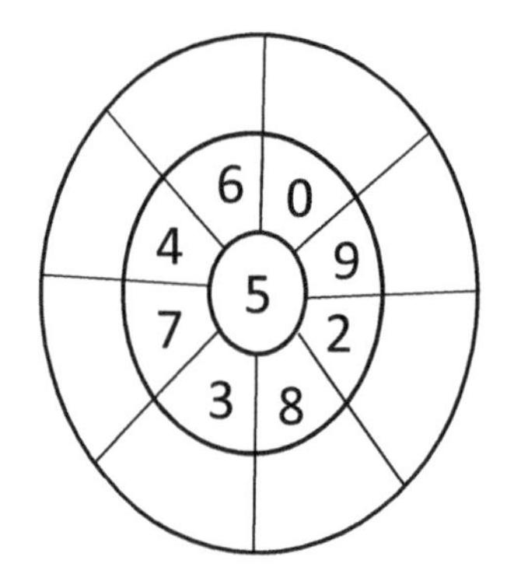

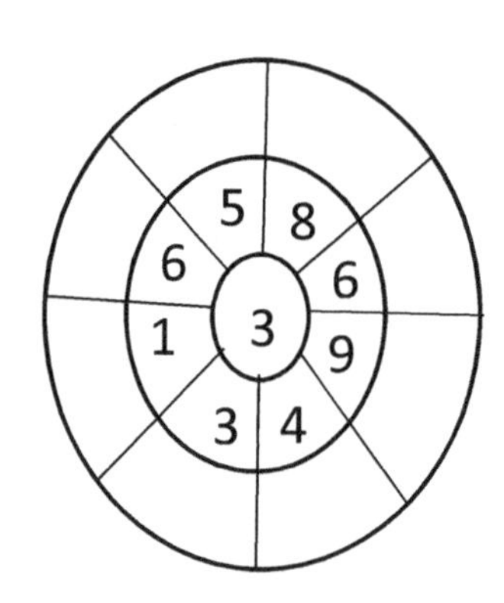

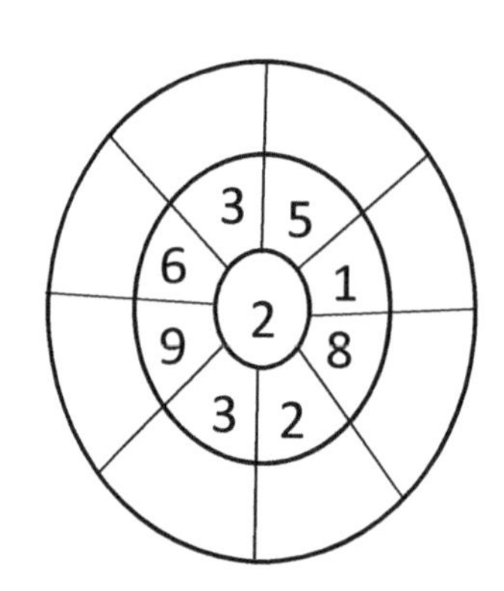

Find each missing number.

5 × ___ = 10

___ × 8 = 40

5 × ___ = 0

5 × 3 = ___

5 × ___ = 20

___ × 5 = 25

5 × 9 = ___

5 × 7 = ___

5 × ___ = 5

___ × 5 = 30

5 × 11 = ___

___ × 5 = 45

5 × ___ = 50

5 × 5 = ___

Write the answers in the boxes.

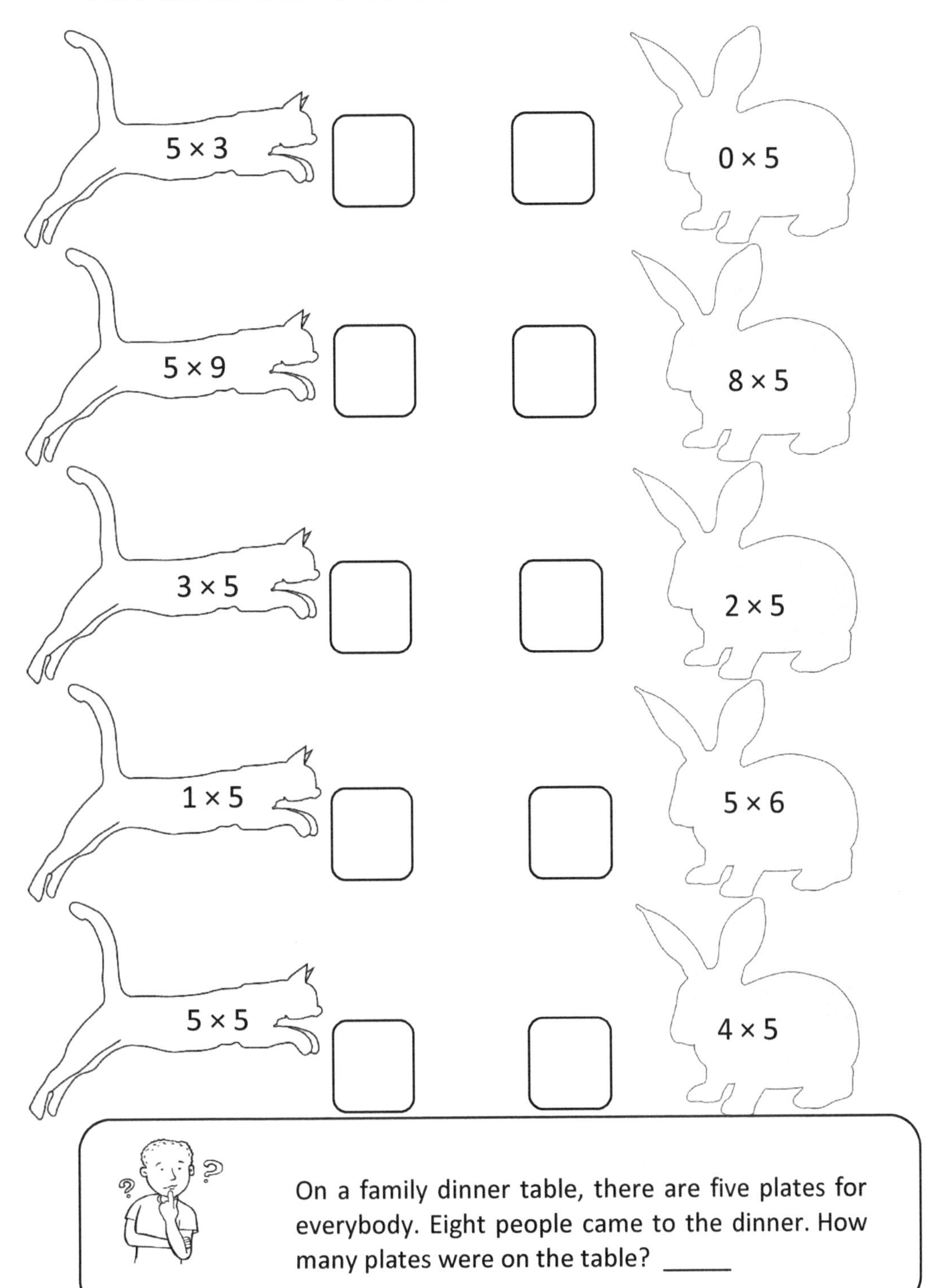

On a family dinner table, there are five plates for everybody. Eight people came to the dinner. How many plates were on the table? _____

Multiply by 1, 3 and 5

Write a multiplication fact for the following pictures.

☺☺☺ ☺☺☺
☺☺☺ ☺☺☺
☺☺☺ ☺☺☺
☺☺☺ ☺☺☺

3 x __ = __

☺☺☺☺☺ ☺☺☺☺☺
☺☺☺☺☺ ☺☺☺☺☺
☺☺☺☺☺ ☺☺☺☺☺
☺☺☺☺☺ ☺☺☺☺☺
☺☺☺☺☺ ☺☺☺☺☺

5 x __ = __

☺☺☺ ☺☺☺ ☺☺☺
☺☺☺ ☺☺☺ ☺☺☺

__ x 3 = __

List the first ten multiples of each number.

3, ____, 9, ____, ____, ____, ____, ____

5, ____, 15, ____, ____, ____, ____, ____

Mrs. Torres bakes 3 dozen cookies every day and sales them for $2 per cookie. How much money would Mrs. Torres make every day? ______

Multiply each number in the top row by 1, 2, 3 and then by 5.

×	1	2	3	4	5	6	7	8	9	10
1										
2										
3										
5										

Match.

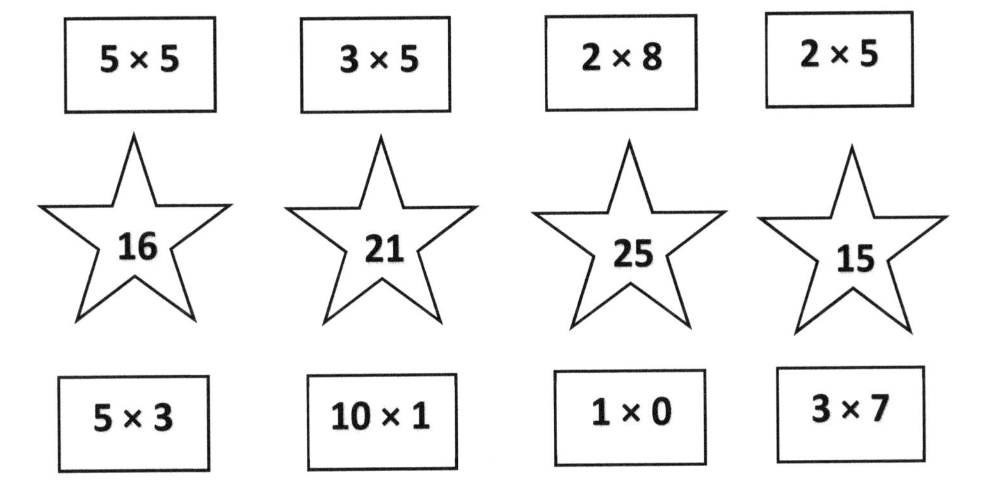

Complete.

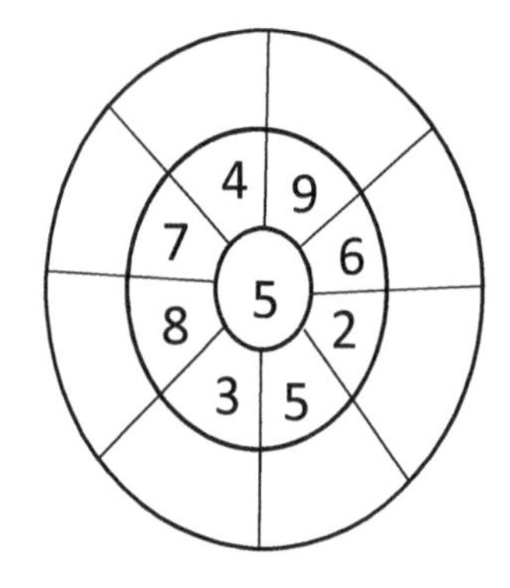

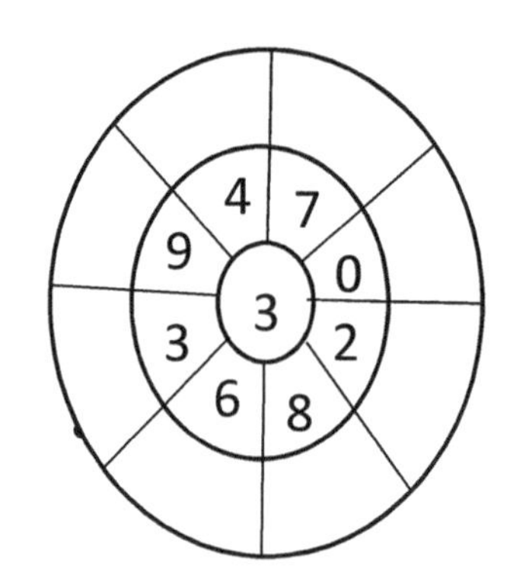

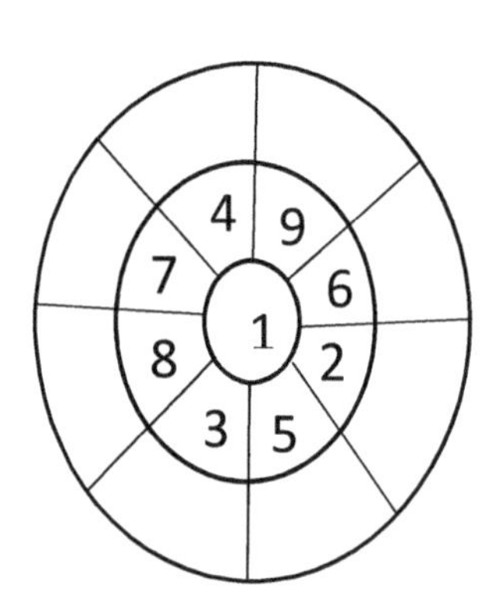

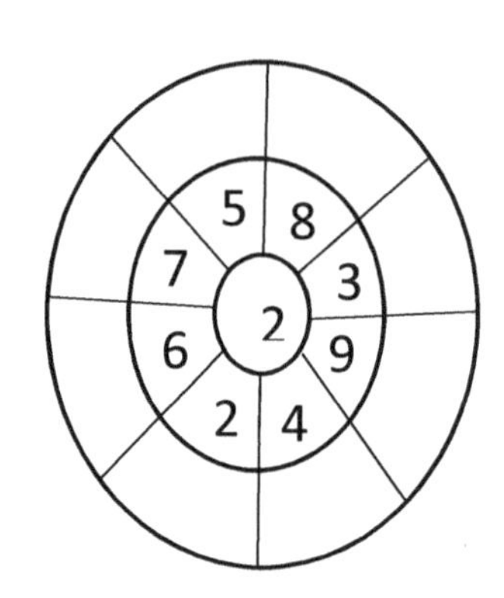

Find each missing number.

$5 \times$ ___ $= 40$

___ $\times 3 = 27$

$1 \times$ ___ $= 9$

___ $\times 3 = 9$

$5 \times 4 =$ ___

___ $\times 3 = 18$

$5 \times 7 =$ ___

$1 \times 10 =$ ___

$3 \times$ ___ $= 24$

___ $\times 5 = 35$

$5 \times 10 =$ ___

___ $\times 3 = 15$

$5 \times$ ___ $= 25$

$3 \times 10 =$ ___

Write the answers in the boxes.

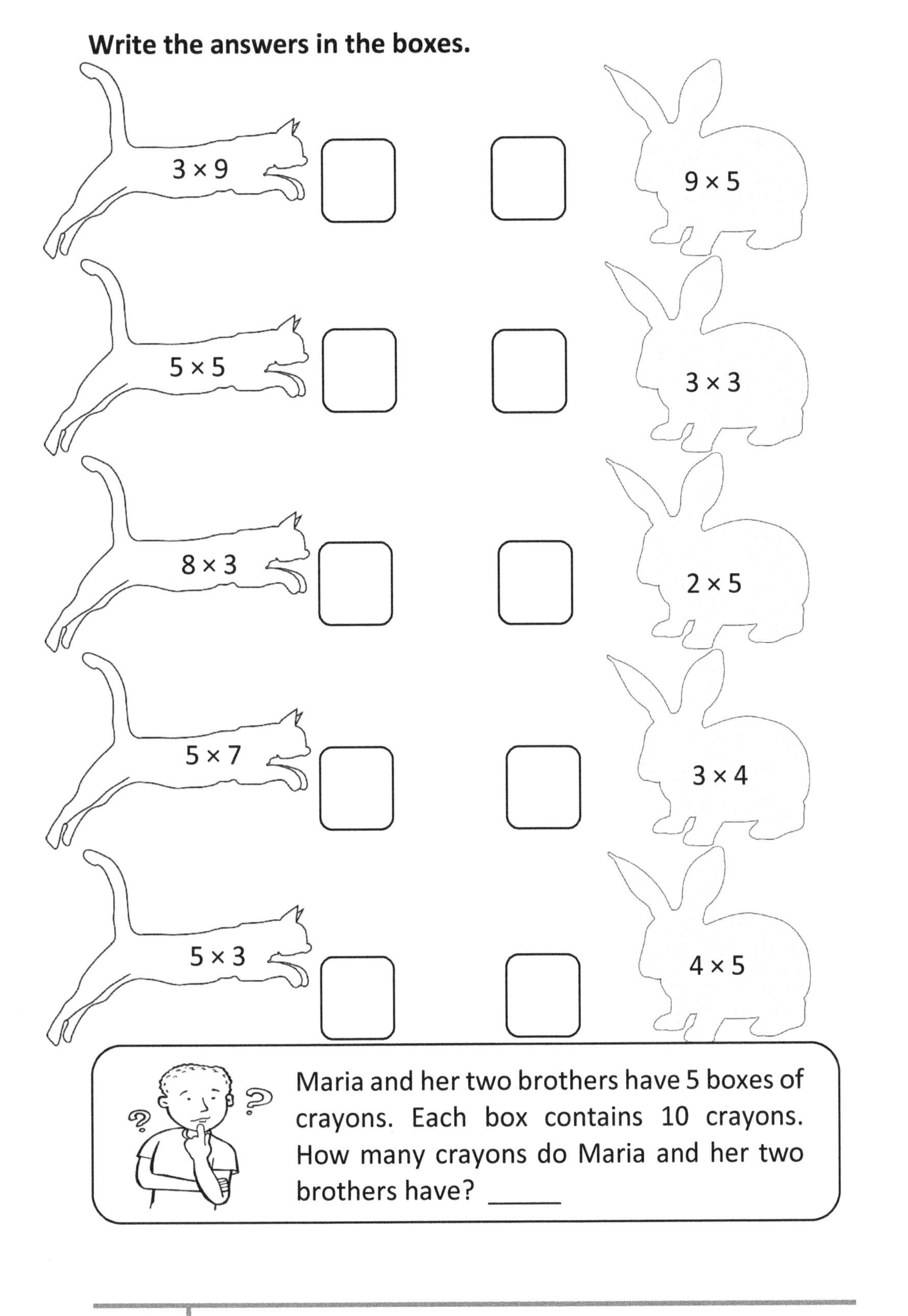

Maria and her two brothers have 5 boxes of crayons. Each box contains 10 crayons. How many crayons do Maria and her two brothers have? _____

Find each missing number.

$10 \times \_\_\_ = 30$	$\_\_\_ \times 5 = 25$	$\_\_\_ \times 3 = 12$
$2 \times \_\_\_ = 10$	$3 \times \_\_\_ = 9$	$5 \times \_\_\_ = 50$
$\_\_\_ \times 5 = 30$	$\_\_\_ \times 2 = 4$	$2 \times \_\_\_ = 16$
$10 \times \_\_\_ = 90$	$5 \times \_\_\_ = 20$	$\_\_\_ \times 4 = 40$
$\_\_\_ \times 3 = 27$	$2 \times \_\_\_ = 10$	$5 \times \_\_\_ = 30$
$2 \times \_\_\_ = 12$	$\_\_\_ \times 5 = 5$	$\_\_\_ \times 6 = 60$
$\_\_\_ \times 1 = 9$	$2 \times \_\_\_ = 6$	$3 \times \_\_\_ = 21$
$5 \times \_\_\_ = 45$	$\_\_\_ \times 1 = 10$	$10 \times 9 = \_\_\_$
$2 \times \_\_\_ = 14$	$5 \times \_\_\_ = 40$	$3 \times \_\_\_ = 24$
$5 \times 7 = \_\_\_$	$5 \times 3 = \_\_\_$	$\_\_\_ \times 9 = 27$
$2 \times 2 = \_\_\_$	$2 \times \_\_\_ = 18$	$10 \times \_\_\_ = 80$
$10 \times 4 = \_\_\_$	$\_\_\_ \times 5 = 35$	$\_\_\_ \times 7 = 70$
$5 \times 8 = \_\_\_$	$1 \times \_\_\_ = 7$	$10 \times \_\_\_ = 60$

$$\begin{array}{r} 10 \\ \times 5 \\ \hline \end{array}$$

$$\begin{array}{r} 9 \\ \times 3 \\ \hline \end{array}$$

$$\begin{array}{r} 8 \\ \times 2 \\ \hline \end{array}$$

$$\begin{array}{r} 6 \\ \times 5 \\ \hline \end{array}$$

$$\begin{array}{r} 3 \\ \times 2 \\ \hline \end{array}$$

$$\begin{array}{r} 7 \\ \times 5 \\ \hline \end{array}$$

$$\begin{array}{r} 9 \\ \times 3 \\ \hline \end{array}$$

$$\begin{array}{r} 8 \\ \times 5 \\ \hline \end{array}$$

$$\begin{array}{r} 10 \\ \times 2 \\ \hline \end{array}$$

$$\begin{array}{r} 10 \\ \times 3 \\ \hline \end{array}$$

$$\begin{array}{r} 4 \\ \times 5 \\ \hline \end{array}$$

$$\begin{array}{r} 7 \\ \times 3 \\ \hline \end{array}$$

$$\begin{array}{r} 9 \\ \times 2 \\ \hline \end{array}$$

$$\begin{array}{r} 6 \\ \times 3 \\ \hline \end{array}$$

$$\begin{array}{r} 3 \\ \times 5 \\ \hline \end{array}$$

Multiply by 4

Write a multiplication fact for the following pictures.

☺☺☺☺ ☺☺☺☺
☺☺☺☺ ☺☺☺☺
☺☺☺☺ ☺☺☺☺

6 x __ = __

☺☺☺☺ ☺☺☺☺
☺☺☺☺ ☺☺☺☺
☺☺☺☺ ☺☺☺☺
☺☺☺☺ ☺☺☺☺
☺☺☺☺ ☺☺☺☺

__ x 4 = __

☺☺☺☺ ☺☺☺☺
☺☺☺☺ ☺☺☺☺

__ x 4 = __

List the first ten multiples of each number.

4, ___, 12, ___, ___, ___, ___, ___, ___, ___

Mr. King went to the store 4 times last month. He buys 9 eggs each time he goes to the store. How many eggs did Mr. King buy last month? _____ eggs

Complete the table.

×	1	2	3	4	5	6	7	8	9	10
2										
3										
4										
5										

Match.

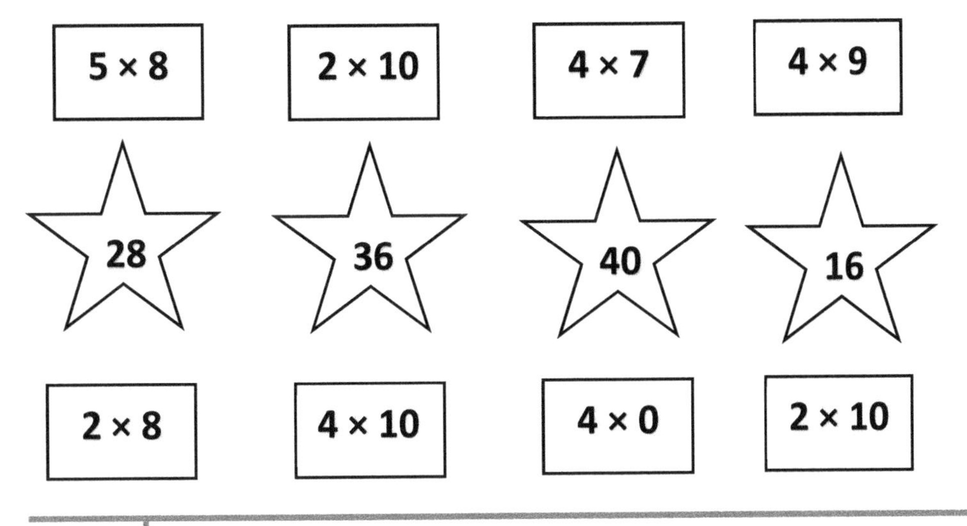

Complete.

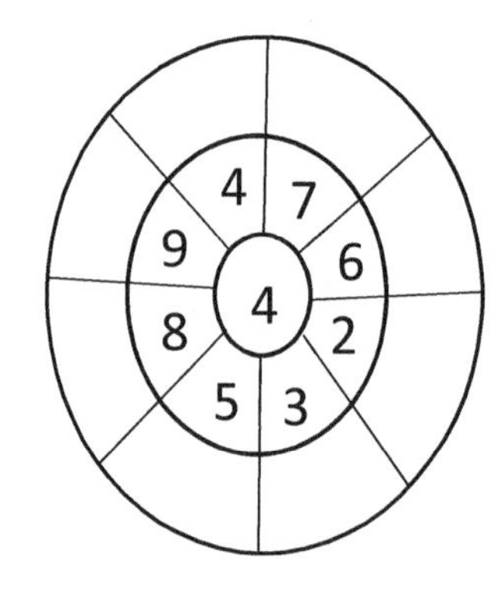

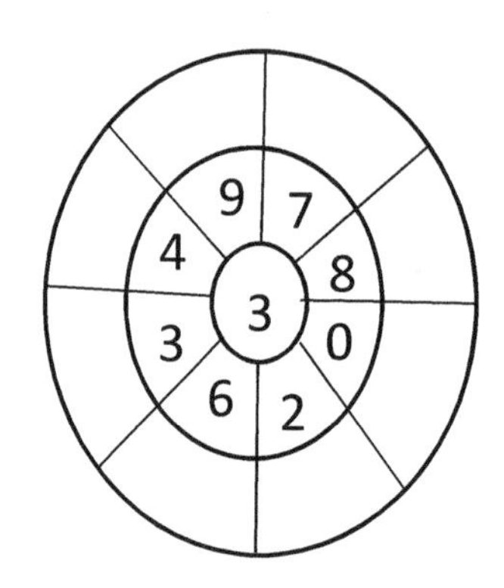

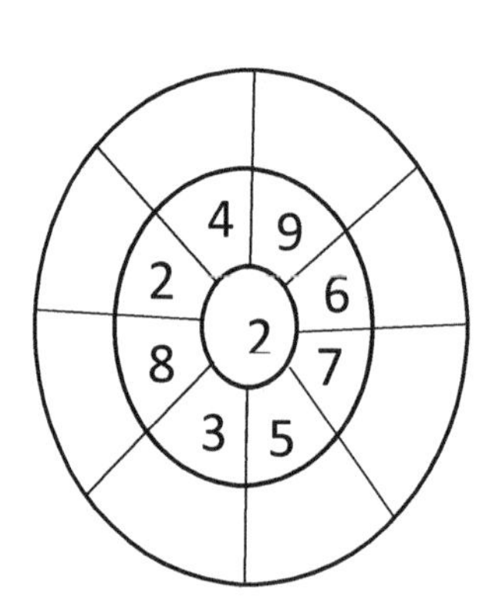

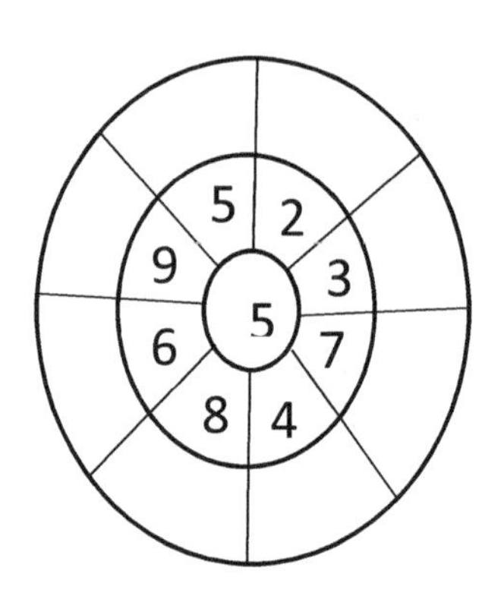

Find each missing number.

4 × ___ = 16	4 × 10 = ___
___ × 4 = 32	5 × ___ = 20
1 × ___ = 4	8 × 4 = ___
___ × 4 = 12	4 × 9 = ___
2 × 4 = ___	___ × 4 = 0
___ × 4 = 28	4 × 7 = ___
4 × 6 = ___	4 × ___ = 8

Write the answers in the boxes.

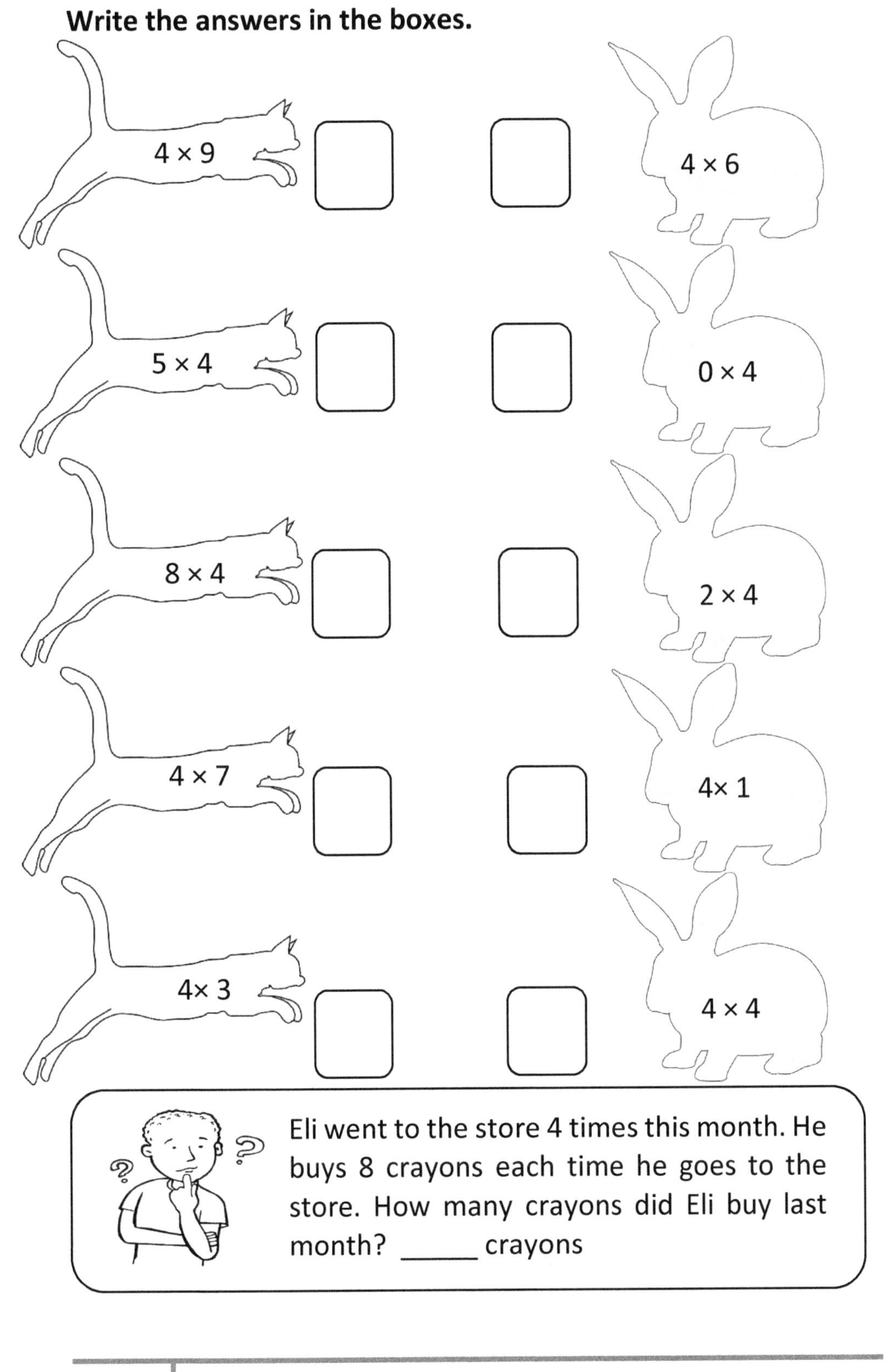

Eli went to the store 4 times this month. He buys 8 crayons each time he goes to the store. How many crayons did Eli buy last month? ______ crayons

Multiply by 6

Write a multiplication fact for the following pictures.

☺☺☺☺☺☺
☺☺☺☺☺☺
☺☺☺☺☺☺

3 x __ = __

☺ ☺ ☺ ☺
☺ ☺ ☺ ☺
☺ ☺ ☺ ☺
☺ ☺ ☺ ☺
☺ ☺ ☺ ☺
☺ ☺ ☺ ☺

4 x __ = __

☺☺☺☺☺☺
☺☺☺☺☺☺
☺☺☺☺☺☺
☺☺☺☺☺☺
☺☺☺☺☺☺

__ x 5 = __

List the first ten multiples of each number.

6, ___, 18, ___, ___, ___, ___, ___, ___

Anna has 6 boxes of eggs. Each box holds 9 eggs. How many eggs does Anna have?

_____ eggs

Multiply each number in the top row by 2, 3, 4, 5 and then by 6.

×	1	2	3	4	5	6	7	8	9	10
2										
3										
4										
5										
6										

Match.

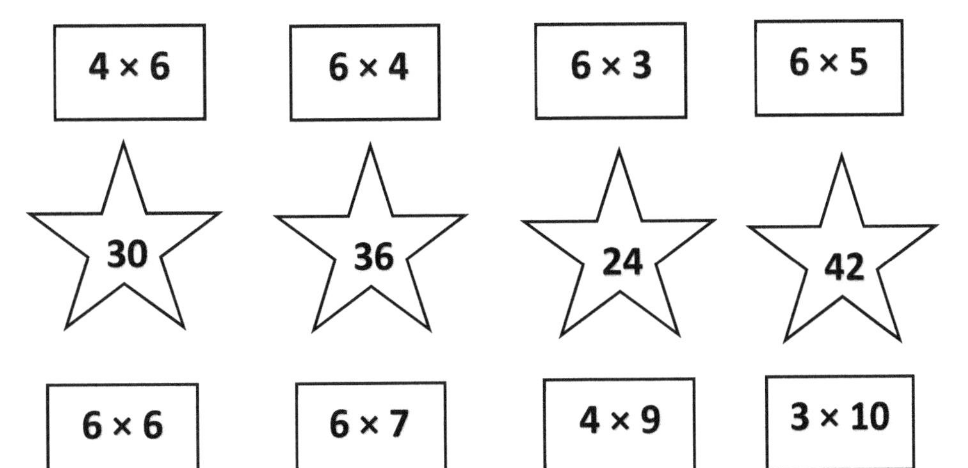

Complete.

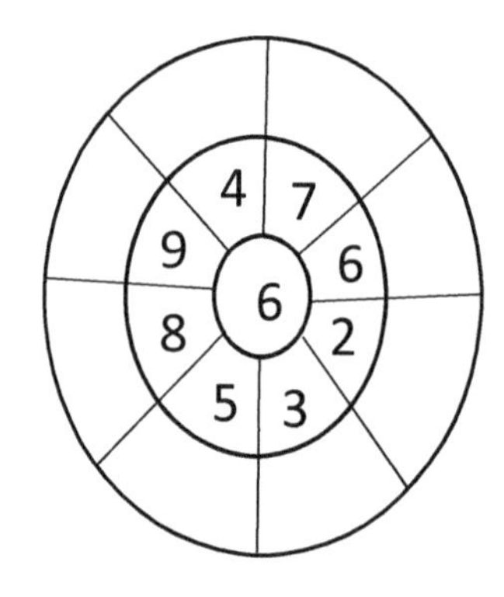

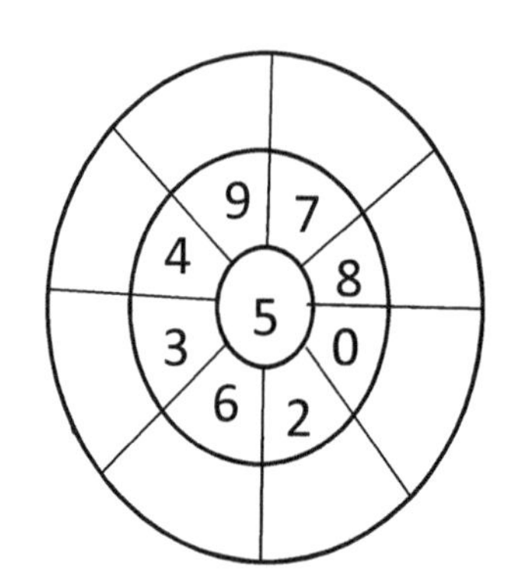

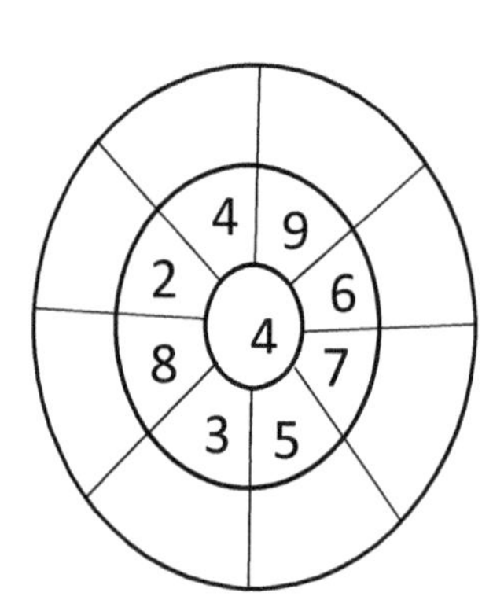

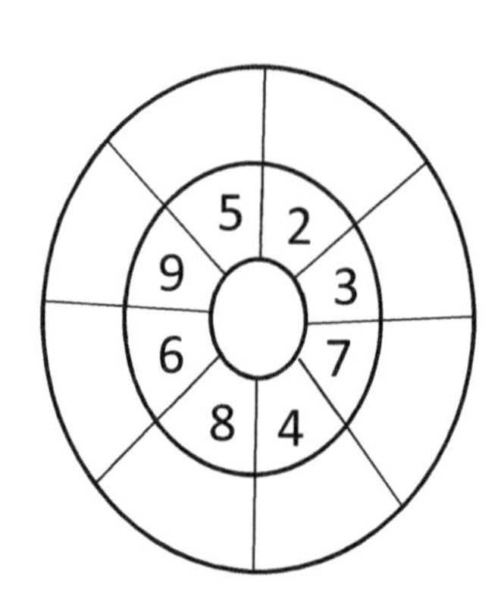

Find each missing number.

6 × ___ = 36

___ × 6 = 12

6 × ___ = 18

___ × 4 = 24

5 × 6 = ___

___ × 6 = 42

9 × 6 = ___

6 × 10 = ___

6 × ___ = 48

6 × 7 = ___

6 × 9 = ___

___ × 6 = 54

6 × 6 = ___

6 × ___ = 60

Write the answers in the boxes.

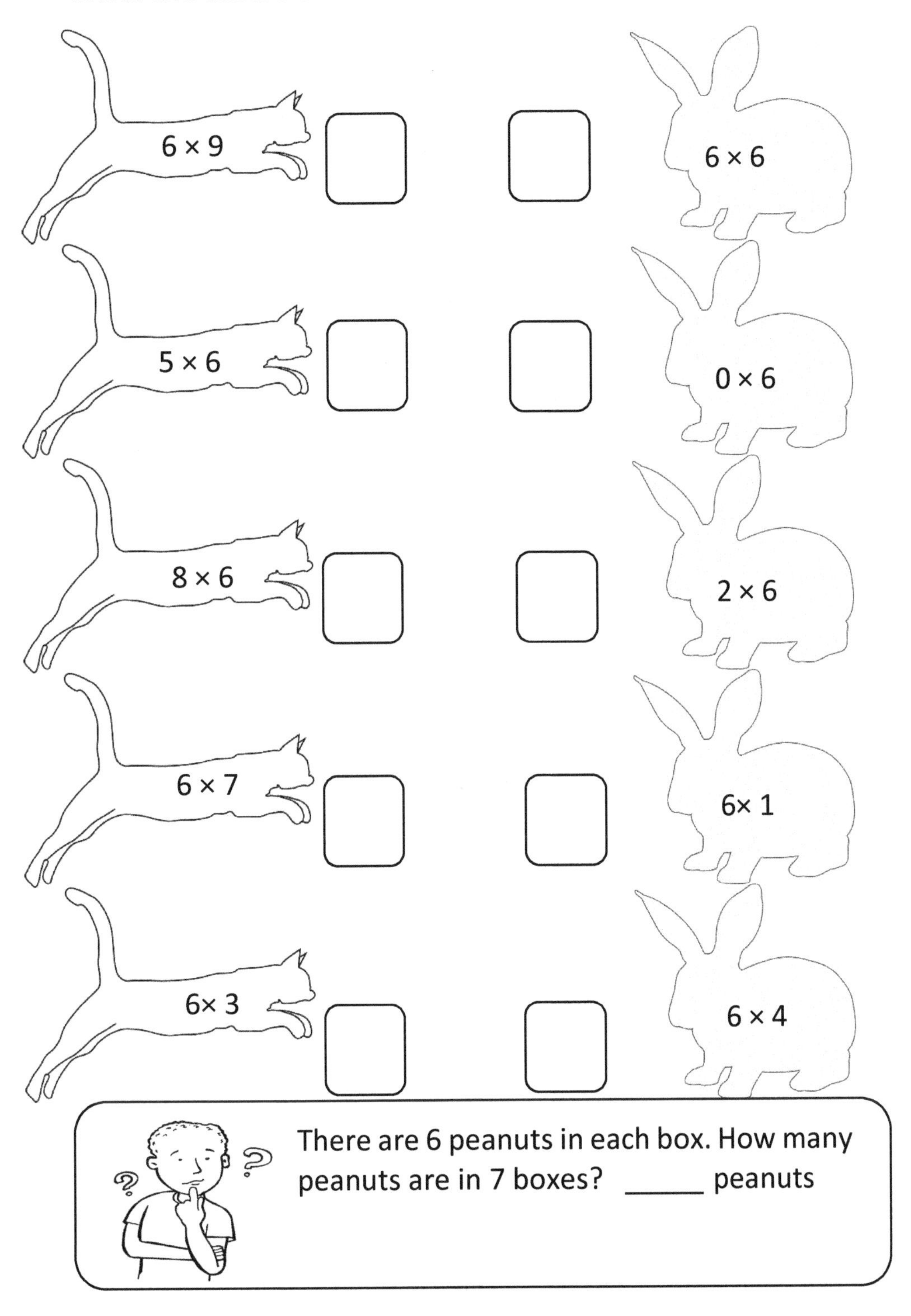

Find each missing number.

2 × ___ = 18	___ × 5 = 50	___ × 3 = 18
4 × ___ = 16	5 × ___ = 15	6 × ___ = 42
___ × 5 = 10	___ × 4 = 32	2 × ___ = 16
6 × ___ = 36	5 × ___ = 45	___ × 4 = 36
___ × 3 = 9	6 × ___ = 12	5 × ___ = 40
2 × ___ = 2	___ × 5 = 20	___ × 6 = 48
___ × 1 = 6	2 × ___ = 8	6 × ___ = 24
5 × ___ = 25	___ × 1 = 5	5 × 4 = ___
6 × ___ = 0	6 × ___ = 30	3 × ___ = 21
4 × 3 = ___	5 × 3 = ___	___ × 6 = 60
6 × 2 = ___	2 × ___ = 6	3 × ___ = 15
9 × 4 = ___	___ × 5 = 15	___ × 4 = 32
6 × 7 = ___	1 × ___ = 3	5 × ___ = 45

Multiply by 8

Write a multiplication fact for the following pictures.

☺☺☺☺☺☺☺☺
☺☺☺☺☺☺☺☺
☺☺☺☺☺☺☺☺

3 x __ = __

☺ ☺ ☺ ☺
☺ ☺ ☺ ☺
☺ ☺ ☺ ☺
☺ ☺ ☺ ☺
☺ ☺ ☺ ☺
☺ ☺ ☺ ☺
☺ ☺ ☺ ☺
☺ ☺ ☺ ☺

__ x 8 = __

☺☺☺☺☺☺☺☺
☺☺☺☺☺☺☺☺

__ x __ = 16

List the first ten multiples of each number.

8, ___, 27, ___, ___, ___, ___, ___

There are 8 Skittles in each box. How many Skittles are in 5 boxes? _____ skittles

Multiply each number in the top row by 0, 2, 4, 6 and then by 8.

×	1	2	3	4	5	6	7	8	9	10
0										
2										
4										
6										
8										

Match.

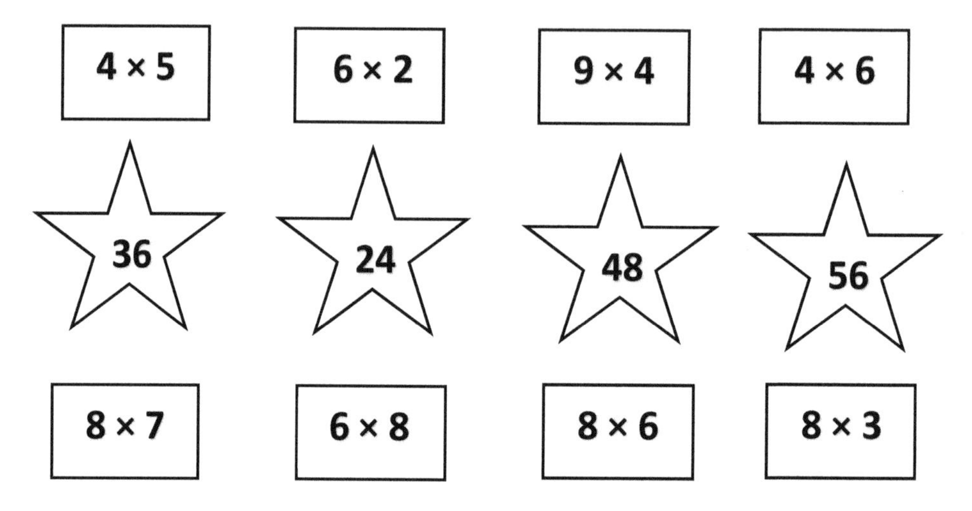

Complete.

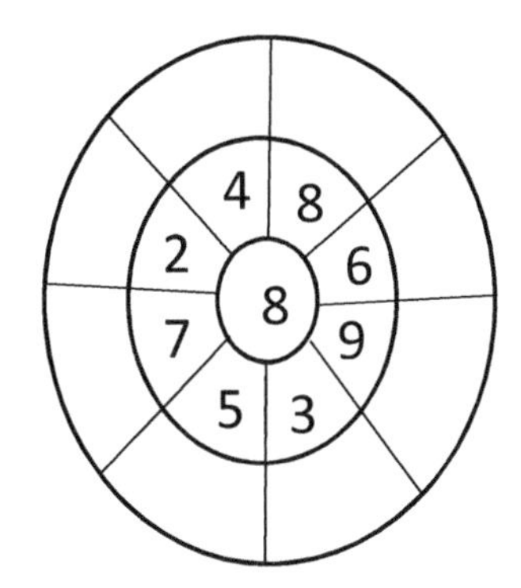

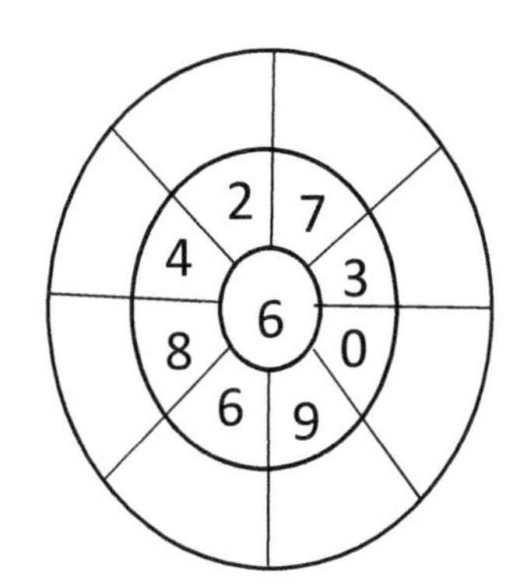

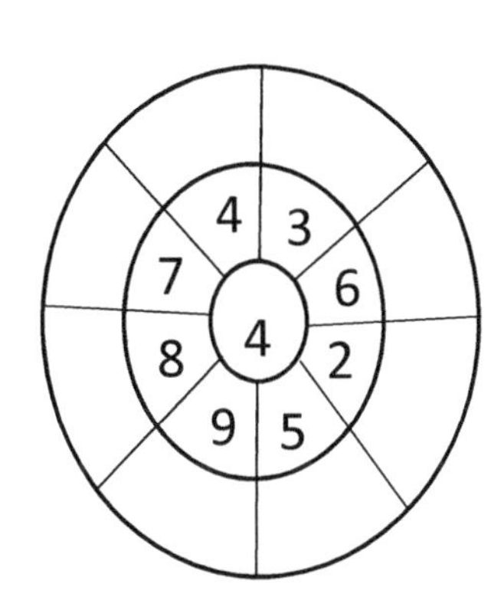

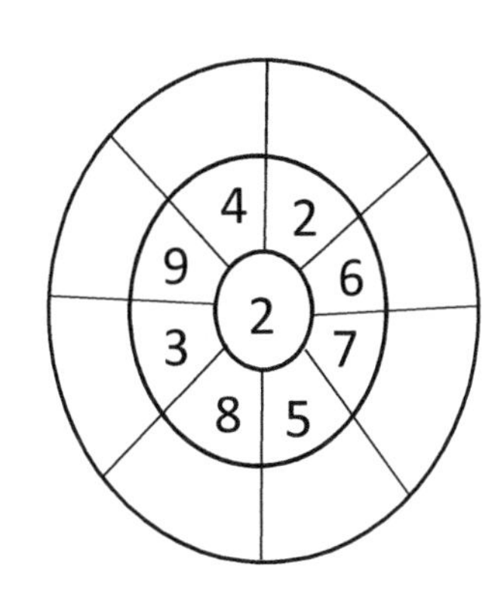

Find each missing number.

8 × ___ = 64

___ × 8 = 72

8 × 2 = ___

8 × ___ = 80

___ × 8 = 16

8 × 1 = ___

___ × 6 = 48

8 × ___ = 32

8 × 8 = ___

___ × 8 = 56

5 × 8 = ___

9 × 8 = ___

8 × 6 = ___

8 × ___ = 40

Write the answers in the boxes.

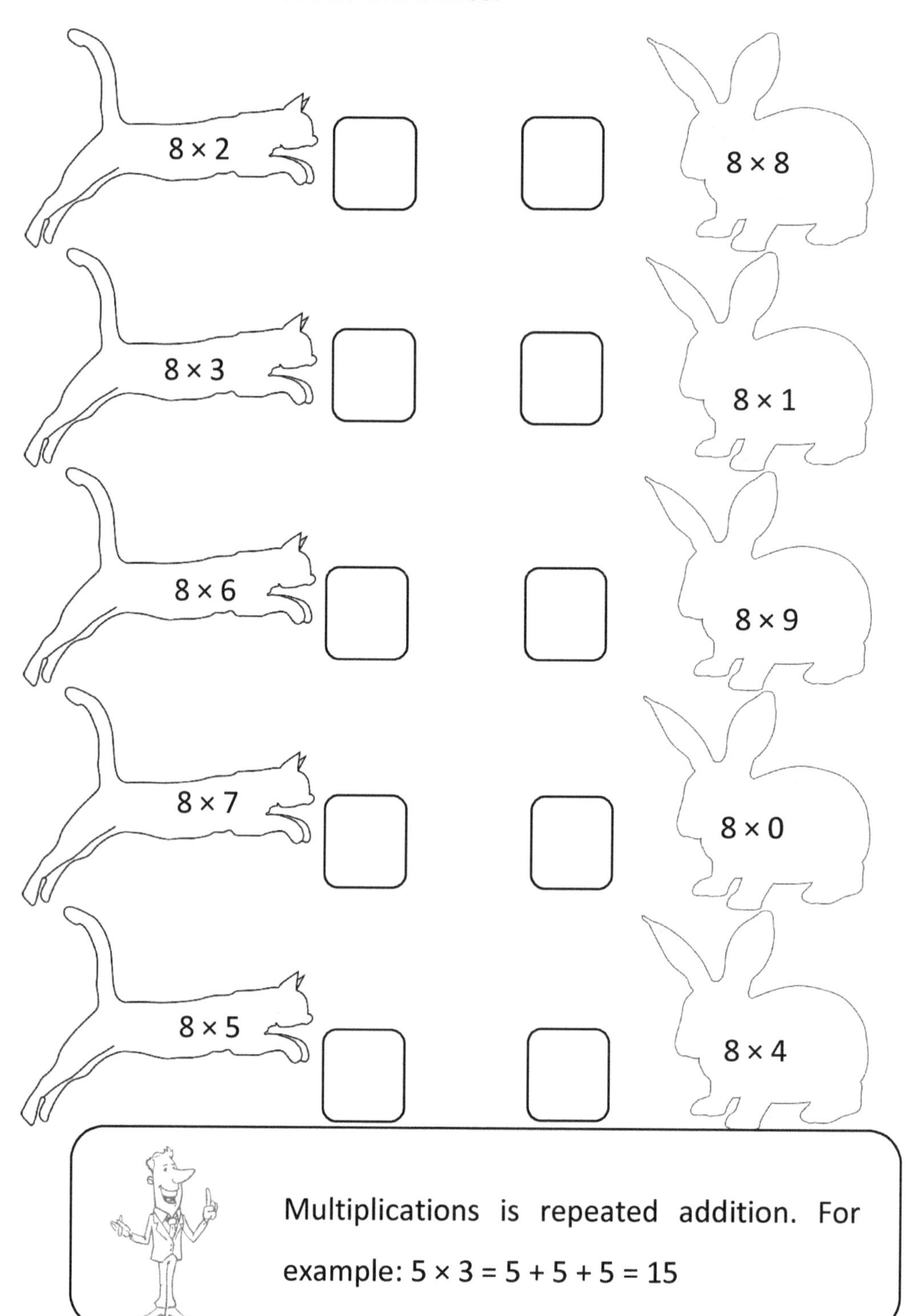

Multiplications is repeated addition. For example: 5 × 3 = 5 + 5 + 5 = 15

Multiply by 7

Write a multiplication fact for the following pictures.

☺☺☺☺☺☺☺
☺☺☺☺☺☺☺
☺☺☺☺☺☺☺
☺☺☺☺☺☺☺

4 x __ = __

☺ ☺ ☺ ☺ ☺
☺ ☺ ☺ ☺ ☺
☺ ☺ ☺ ☺ ☺
☺ ☺ ☺ ☺ ☺
☺ ☺ ☺ ☺ ☺
☺ ☺ ☺ ☺ ☺
☺ ☺ ☺ ☺ ☺

5 x __ = __

☺☺☺☺☺☺☺
☺☺☺☺☺☺☺

__ x 7 = __

List the first ten multiples of each number.

7, ____, 21, ____, ____, ____, ____, ____

Mr. King has 7 boxes of Skittles. Each box holds 9 Skittles. How many Skittles does Mr. King have?

______ Skittles

Multiply each number in the top row by 1, 3, 5 and then by 7.

×	1	2	3	4	5	6	7	8	9	10
1										
3										
5										
7										

Match.

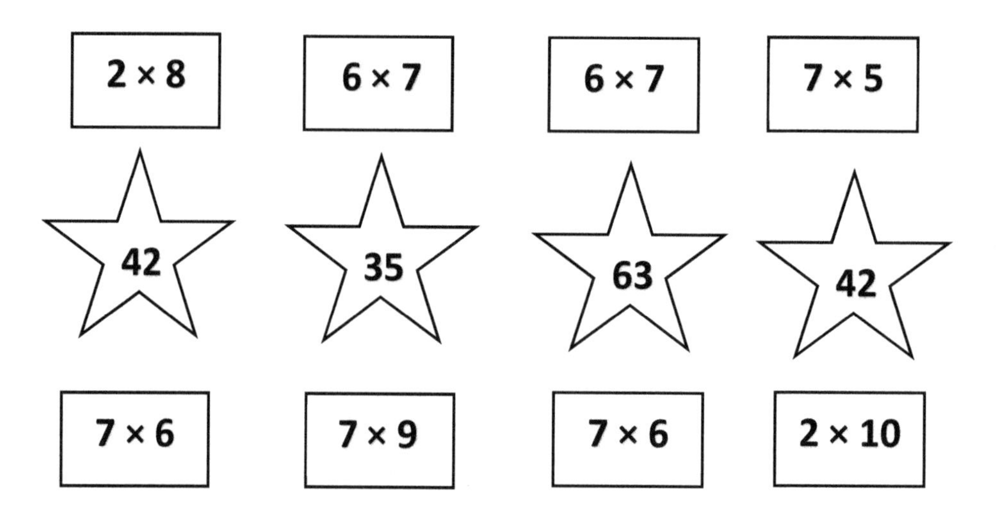

Complete.

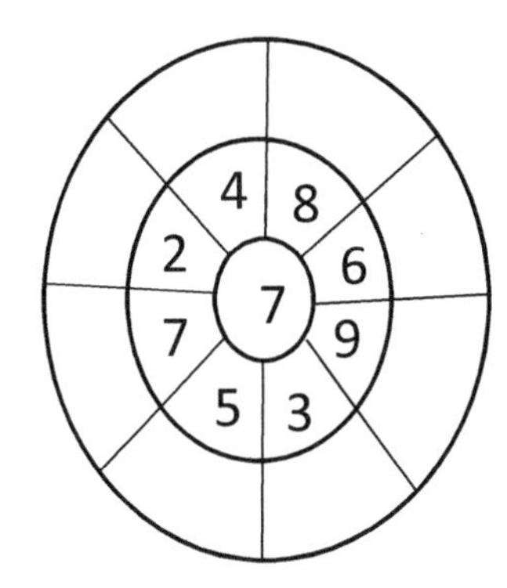

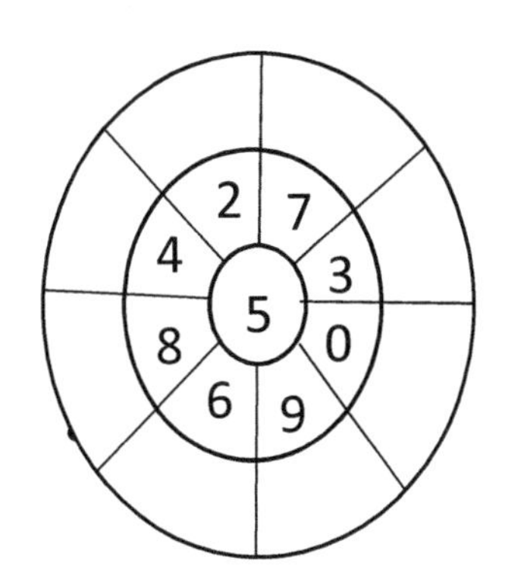

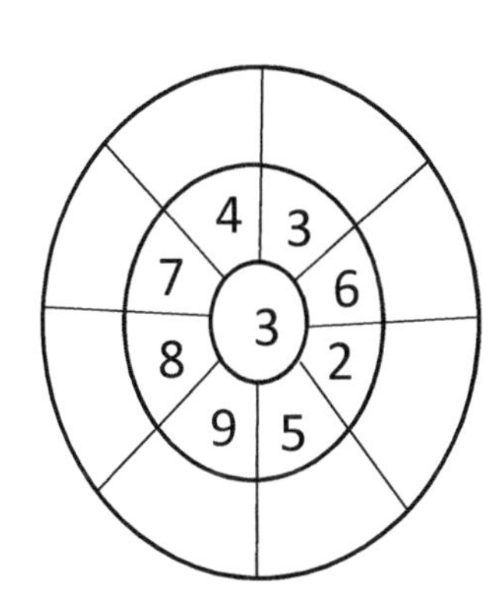

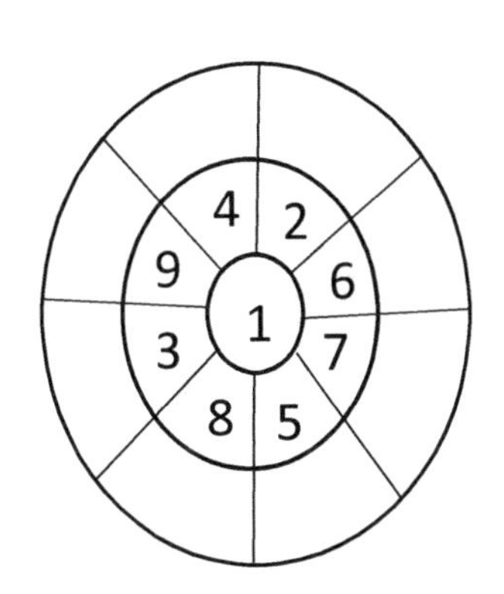

Find each missing number.

7 × ____ = 35

____ × 7 = 70

7 × ____ = 14

____ × 7 = 7

3 × 7 = ____

____ × 7 = 49

9 × 4 = ____

7 × 2 = ____

7 × ____ = 63

7 × 8 = ____

6 × 7 = ____

____ × 7 = 0

7 × 5 = ____

6 × ____ = 60

Write the answers in the boxes.

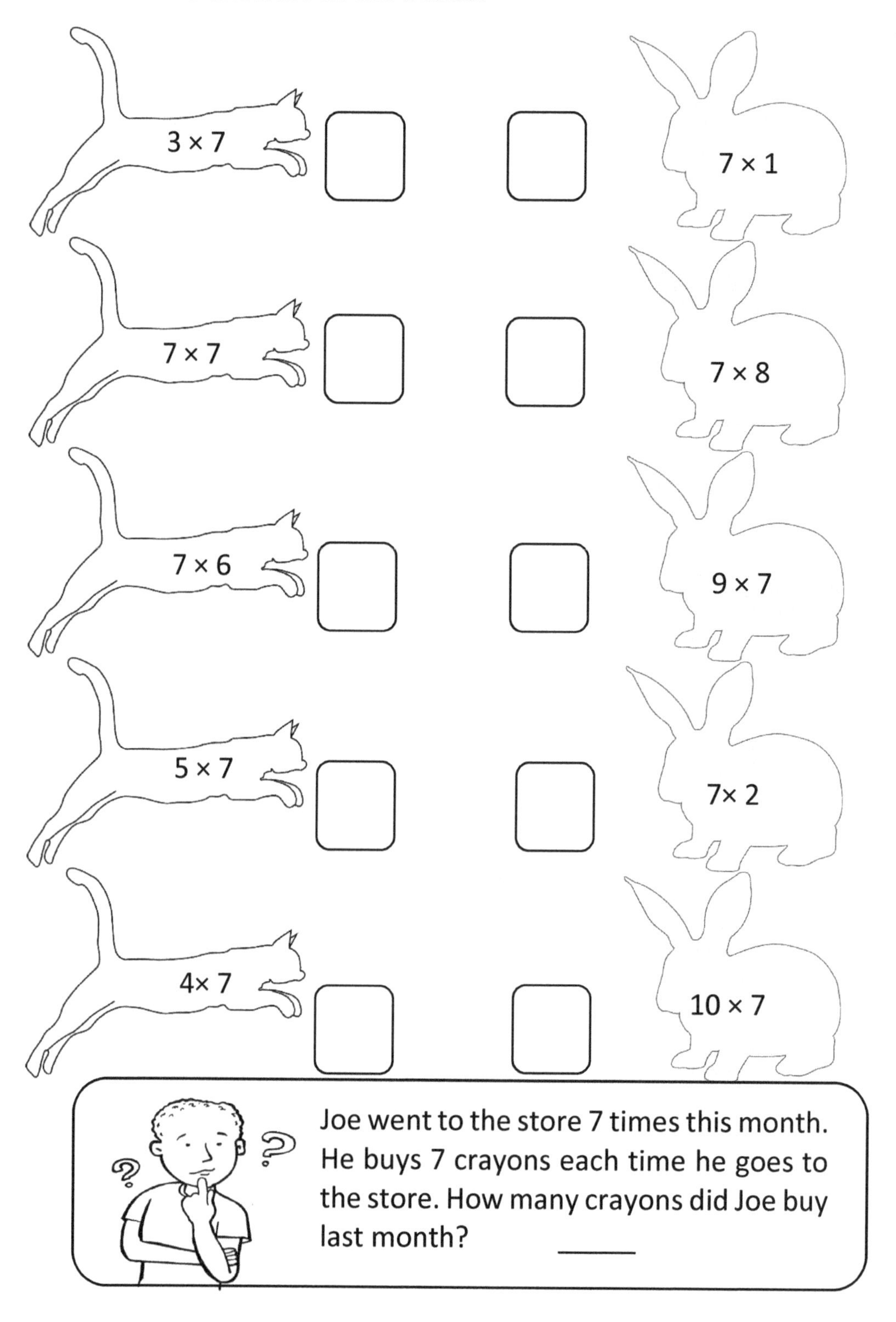

Multiply by 9

Write a multiplication fact for the following pictures.

☺☺☺☺☺☺☺☺☺
☺☺☺☺☺☺☺☺☺ __ x 9 = __

☺ ☺ ☺ ☺
☺ ☺ ☺ ☺ 4 x __ = __
☺ ☺ ☺ ☺
☺ ☺ ☺ ☺
☺ ☺ ☺ ☺
☺ ☺ ☺ ☺
☺ ☺ ☺ ☺
☺ ☺ ☺ ☺
☺ ☺ ☺ ☺

☺☺☺☺☺☺☺☺☺ __ x 9 = __

List the first ten multiples of each number.

9, ___, 27, ___, ___, ___, ___, ___

Each child has 9 pens. If there are 8 children, how many pens are there in total?

_____ pens

Multiply each number in the top row by 1, 3, 5 and then by 7.

×	1	2	3	4	5	6	7	8	9	10
1										
3										
5										
7										
9										

Match.

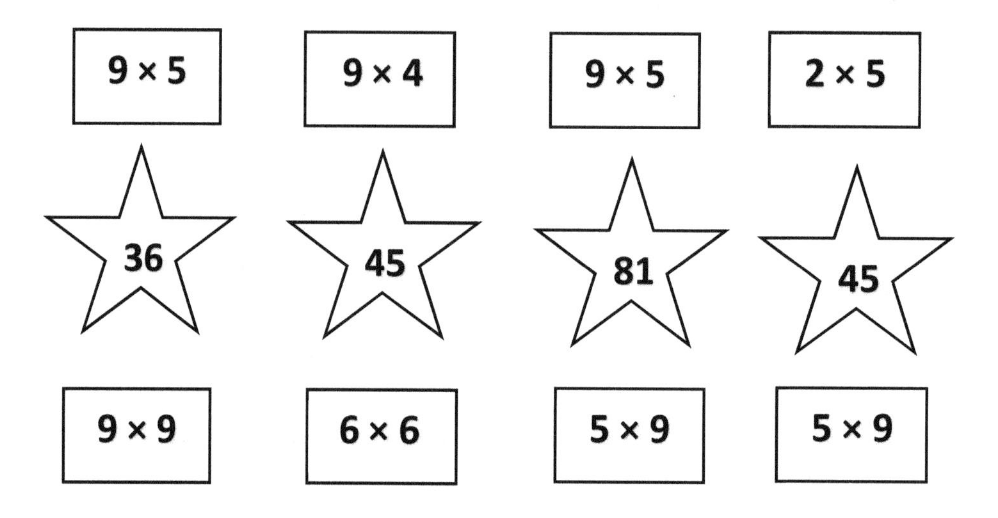

Complete.

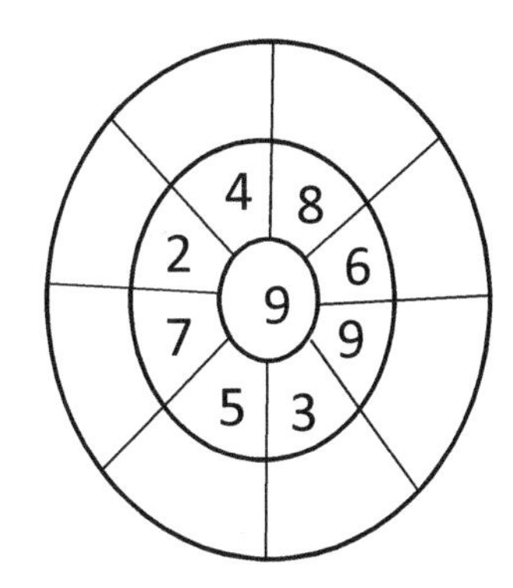

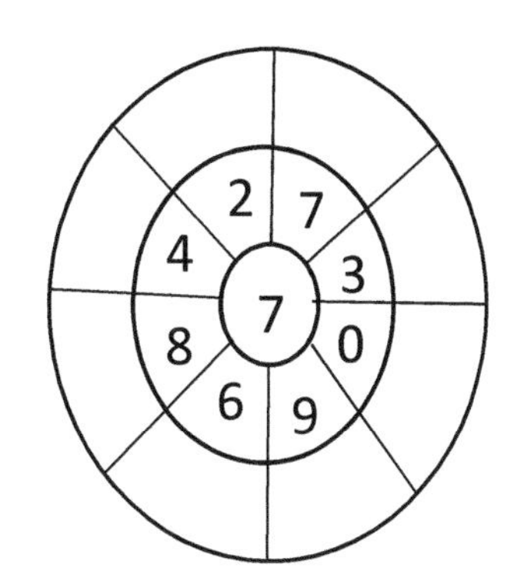

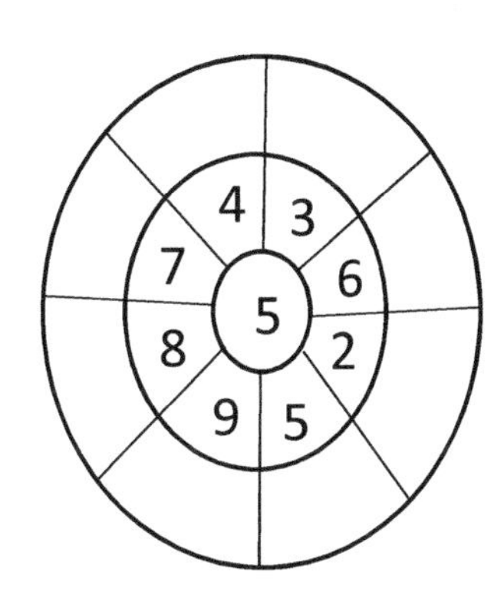

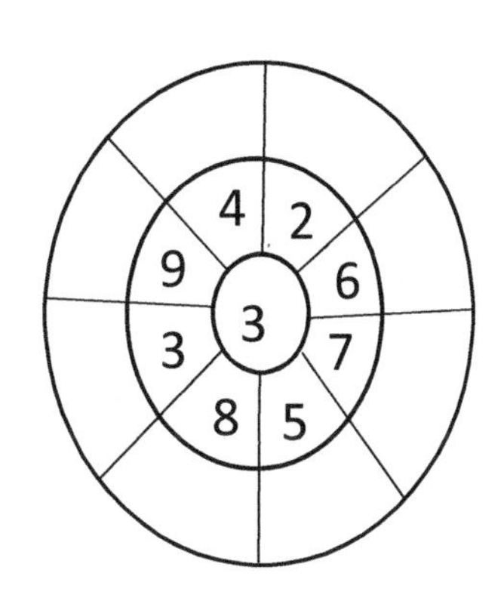

Find each missing number.

9 × ___ = 81

___ × 9 = 63

9 × ___ = 45

___ × 9 = 27

9 × 2 = ___

___ × 9 = 36

9 × 6 = ___

9 × 8 = ___

9 × ___ = 9

9 × 9 = ___

9× 5 = ___

___ × 9 = 0

7 × 4 = ___

9 × ___ = 90

Write the answers in the boxes.

3 × 7 ☐ ☐ 7 × 1

7 × 7 ☐ ☐ 7 × 8

7 × 6 ☐ ☐ 9 × 7

5 × 7 ☐ ☐ 7× 2

4× 7 ☐ ☐ 10 × 7

There are 9 bottle caps in each box. How many bottle caps are in 8 boxes?

_____ bottles caps

Find each missing number.

2 × ___ = 18	___ × 5 = 50	___ × 3 = 18
4 × ___ = 16	5 × ___ = 15	6 × ___ = 42
___ × 5 = 10	___ × 4 = 32	2 × ___ = 16
6 × ___ = 36	5 × ___ = 45	___ × 4 = 36
___ × 3 = 9	6 × ___ = 12	5 × ___ = 40
2 × ___ = 2	___ × 5 = 20	___ × 6 = 48
___ × 1 = 6	2 × ___ = 8	6 × ___ = 24
5 × ___ = 25	___ × 1 = 5	5 × 4 = ___
6 × ___ = 0	6 × ___ = 30	3 × ___ = 21
4 × 3 = ___	5 × 3 = ___	___ × 6 = 60
6 × 2 = ___	2 × ___ = 6	3 × ___ = 15
9 × 4 = ___	___ × 5 = 15	___ × 4 = 32
6 × 7 = ___	1 × ___ = 3	5 × ___ = 45

Multiply by 11

Write a multiplication fact for the following pictures.

☺☺☺☺☺☺☺☺☺☺☺
☺☺☺☺☺☺☺☺☺☺☺ 2 x __ = __

☺ ☺ ☺ ☺
☺ ☺ ☺ ☺ __ x 11 = __
☺ ☺ ☺ ☺
☺ ☺ ☺ ☺
☺ ☺ ☺ ☺
☺ ☺ ☺ ☺
☺ ☺ ☺ ☺
☺ ☺ ☺ ☺
☺ ☺ ☺ ☺
☺ ☺ ☺ ☺
☺ ☺ ☺ ☺

List the first ten multiples of each number.

11, ___, ___, ___, ___, ___, ___, ___

There are 8 marbles in each box. How many marbles are in 6 boxes?

_____ marbles

Multiply each number in the top row by 3, 5, 7, 9 and then by 11.

×	1	2	3	4	5	6	7	8	9	10
3										
5										
7										
9										
11										

Match.

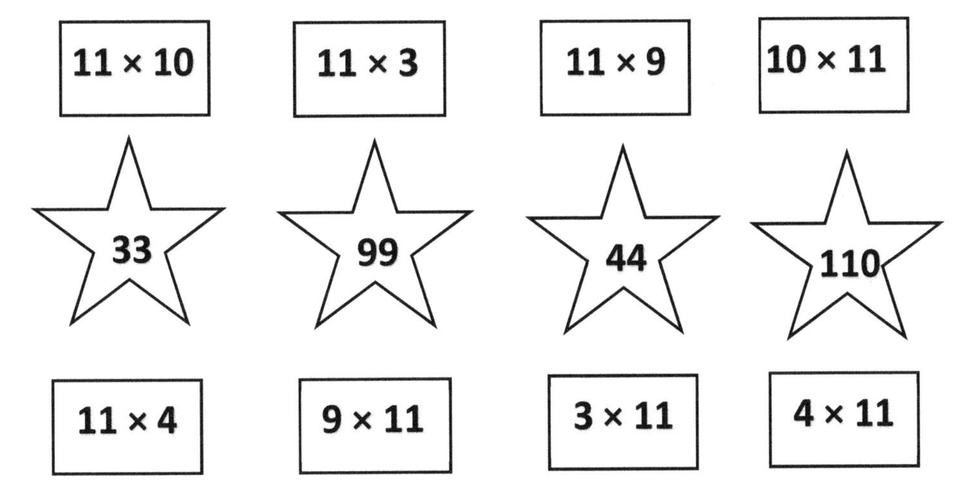

Complete.

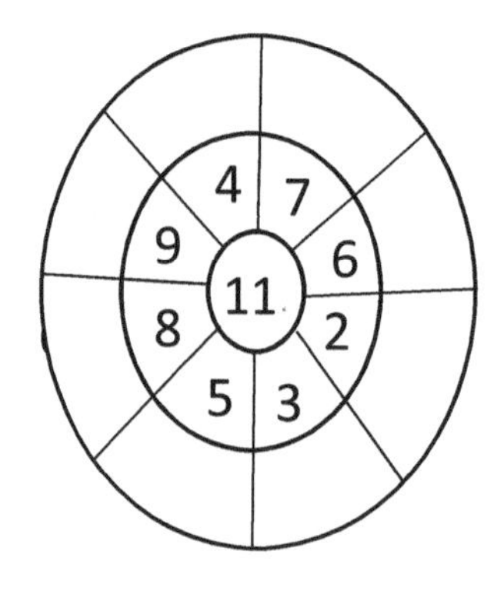

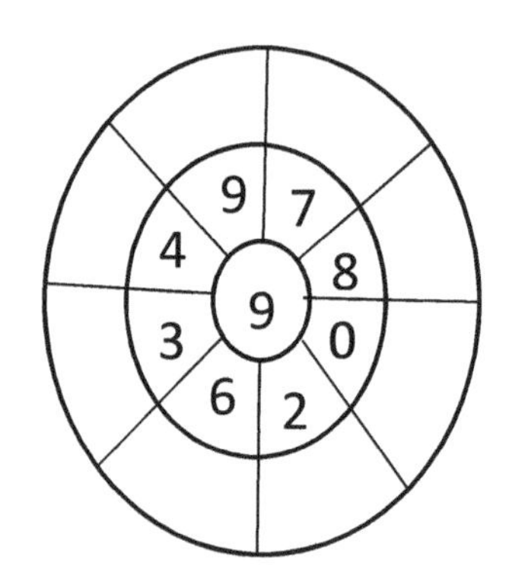

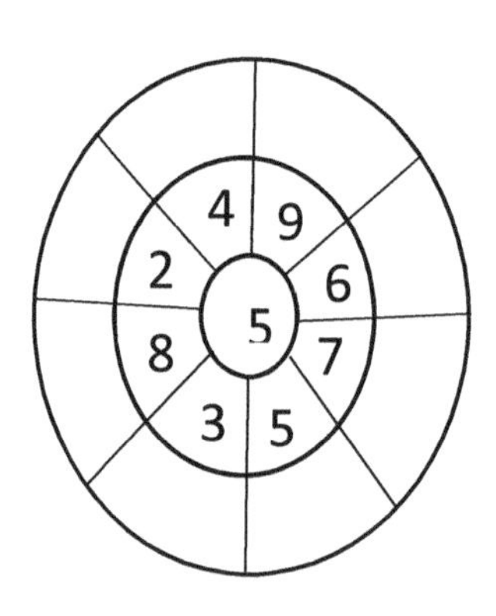

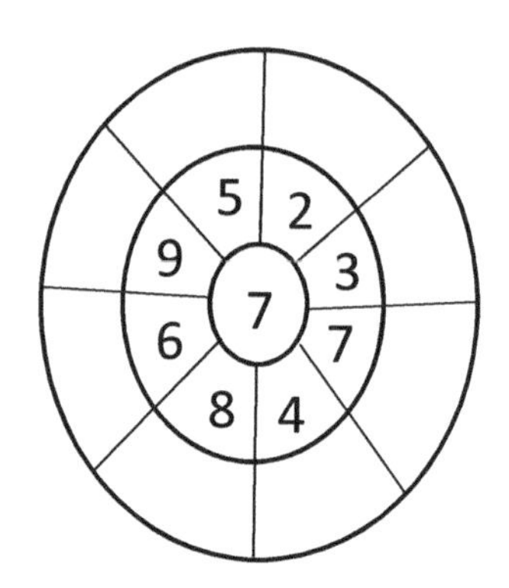

Find each missing number.

11 × ___ = 66

___ × 7 = 77

11 × ___ = 99

___ × 11 = 55

11 × 3 = ___

___ × 11 = 11

8 × 11 = ___

11 × 4 = ___

11 × ___ = 33

0 × 11 = ___

11 × 2 = ___

___ × 11 = 44

11 × 9 = ___

11 × ___ = 0

Write the answers in the boxes.

11×6 | 11×9

5×11 | 0×11

8×11 | 2×11

11×3 | 11×1

8×11 | 11×4

Mr. Jonson has 11 boxes of cards. Each box holds 9 cards. How many cards does Mr. Jonson have? _____ cards

Multiply by 12

Write a multiplication fact for the following pictures.

☺☺☺☺☺☺☺☺☺☺☺☺
☺☺☺☺☺☺☺☺☺☺☺☺
☺☺☺☺☺☺☺☺☺☺☺☺
☺☺☺☺☺☺☺☺☺☺☺☺

4 x __ = __

☺ ☺ ☺ ☺ ☺
☺ ☺ ☺ ☺ ☺
☺ ☺ ☺ ☺ ☺
☺ ☺ ☺ ☺ ☺
☺ ☺ ☺ ☺ ☺
☺ ☺ ☺ ☺ ☺
☺ ☺ ☺ ☺ ☺
☺ ☺ ☺ ☺ ☺
☺ ☺ ☺ ☺ ☺
☺ ☺ ☺ ☺ ☺
☺ ☺ ☺ ☺ ☺
☺ ☺ ☺ ☺ ☺

__ x 12 = __

List the first ten multiples of each number.

12, ___, ___, ___, ___, ___, ___, ___, ___, ___

Anna went to the store 11 times last month. She buys 7 eggs each time he goes to the store. How many eggs did Anna buy last month? _____

Multiply each number in the top row by 2, 4, 6, 8, 10 and then by 12.

×	1	2	3	4	5	6	7	8	9	10
2										
4										
6										
8										
10										
12										

Match.

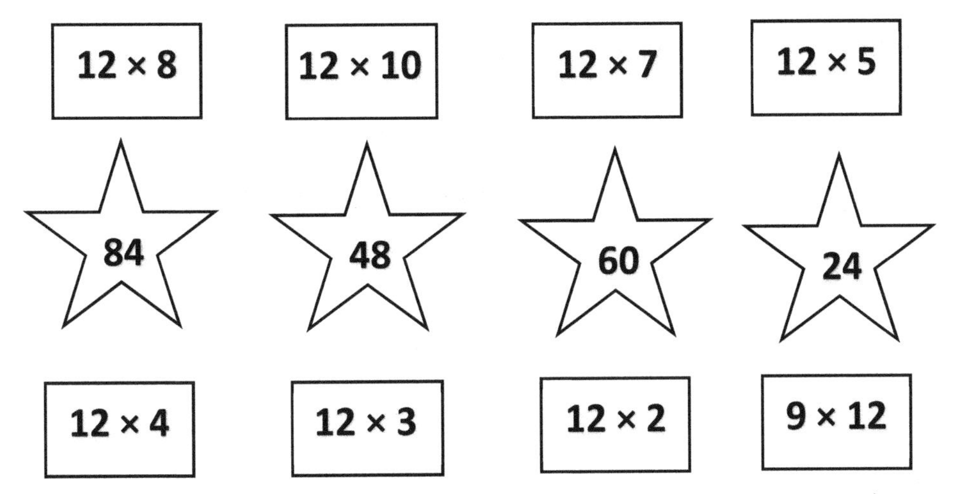

Complete.

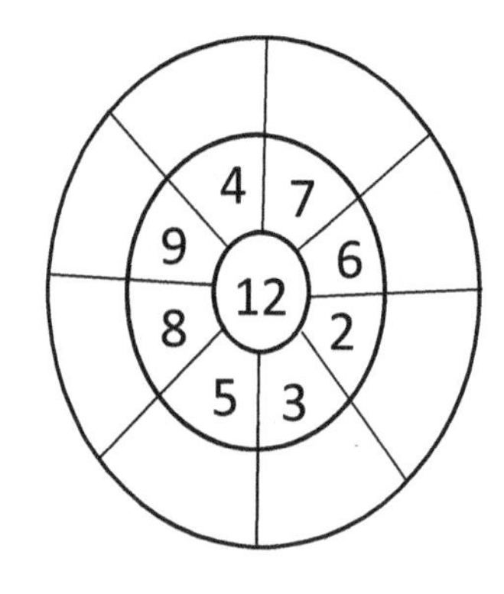

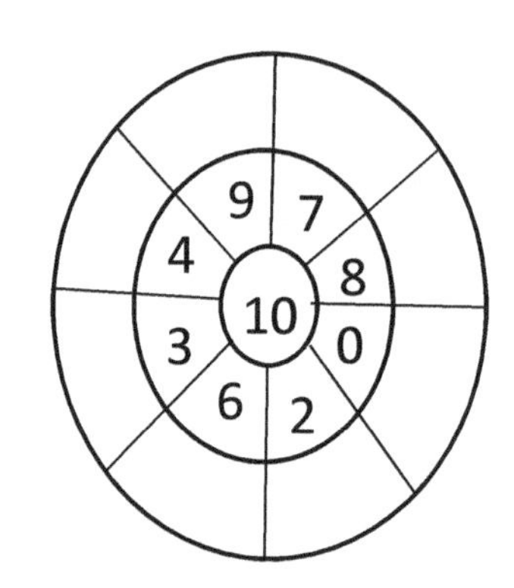

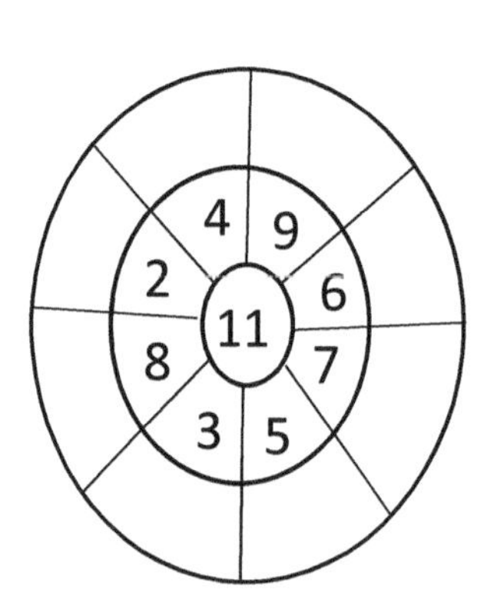

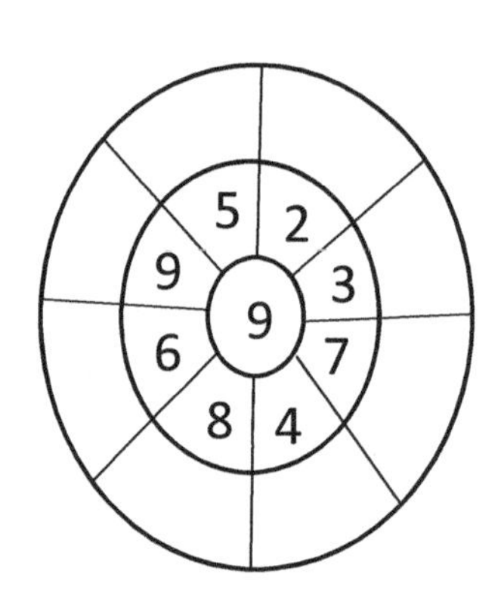

Find each missing number.

12 × ___ = 36

___ × 11 = 88

9 × ___ = 108

___ × 12 = 96

12 × 4 = ___

___ × 12 = 84

12 × 5 = ___

12 × 9 = ___

12 × ___ = 12

7 × 12 = ___

12 × 2 = ___

___ × 12 = 72

12 × 0 = ___

12 × ___ = 48

Write the answers in the boxes.

12 × 5

12 × 9

6 × 12

0 × 12

8 × 12

2 × 12

12 × 3

12× 1

8 × 12

12 × 4

There are 12 Skittles in each box. How many Skittles are in 11 boxes? _____

Find each missing number.

12 × ___ = 36 ___ × 5 = 60 ___ × 3 = 18

11 × ___ = 22 11 × ___ = 66 11 × ___ = 11

___ × 10 = 30 ___ × 4 = 44 12 × ___ = 72

12 × ___ = 24 10 × ___ = 60 ___ × 4 = 36

___ × 9 = 54 7 × ___ = 70 11 × ___ = 66

12 × ___ = 48 ___ × 11 = 88 ___ × 6 = 48

___ × 1 = 12 12 × ___ = 96 12 × ___ = 108

11 × ___ = 55 ___ × 11 = 99 11 × 0 = ___

10 × ___ = 50 11 × ___ = 99 12 × ___ = 84

11 × 3 = ___ 11 × 7 = ___ ___ × 6 = 60

10 × 2 = ___ 12 × ___ = 60 11 × ___ = 11

11 × 4 = ___ ___ × 11 = 44 ___ × 10 = 20

11 × 7 = ___ 12 × ___ = 12 12 × ___ = 0

Extra multiplication practice

Complete.

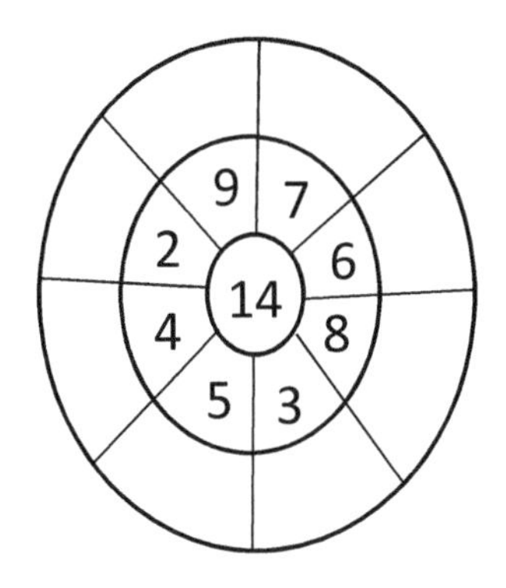

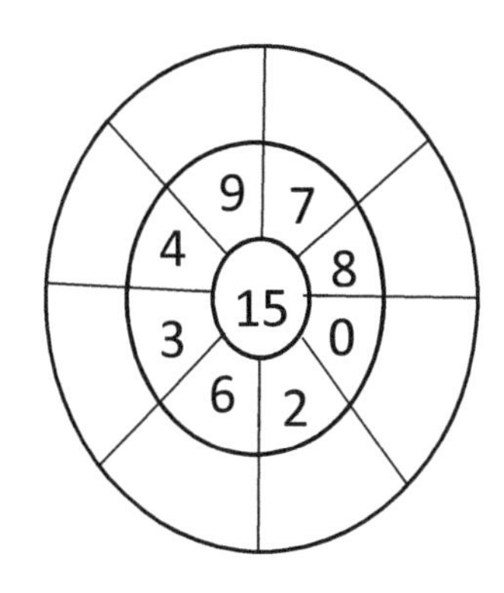

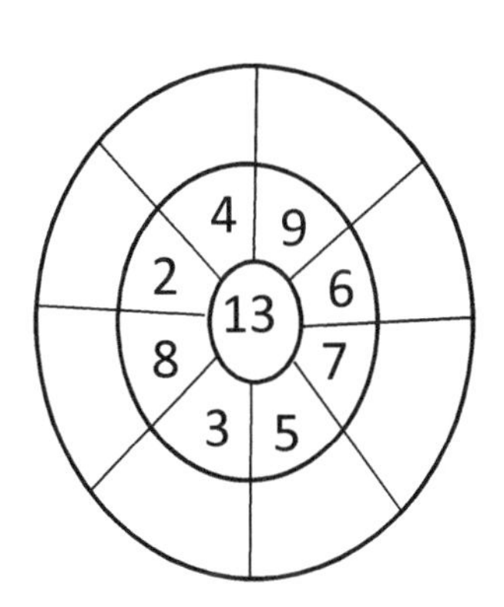

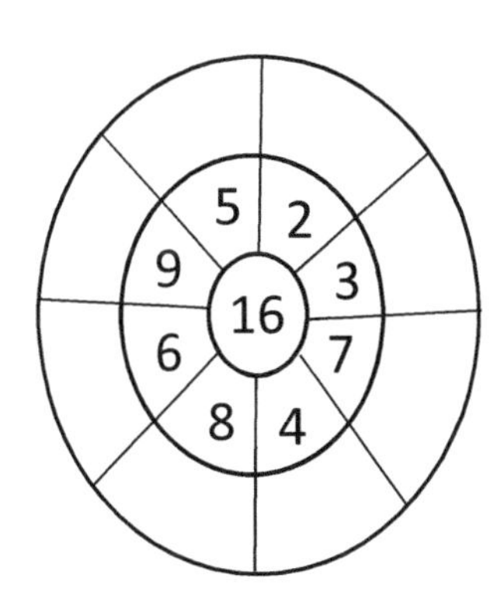

Mark went to the store 6 times this month. He buys 15 crayons each time he goes to the store. How many crayons did Mark buy last month?

_____ crayons

Write the answers in the boxes.

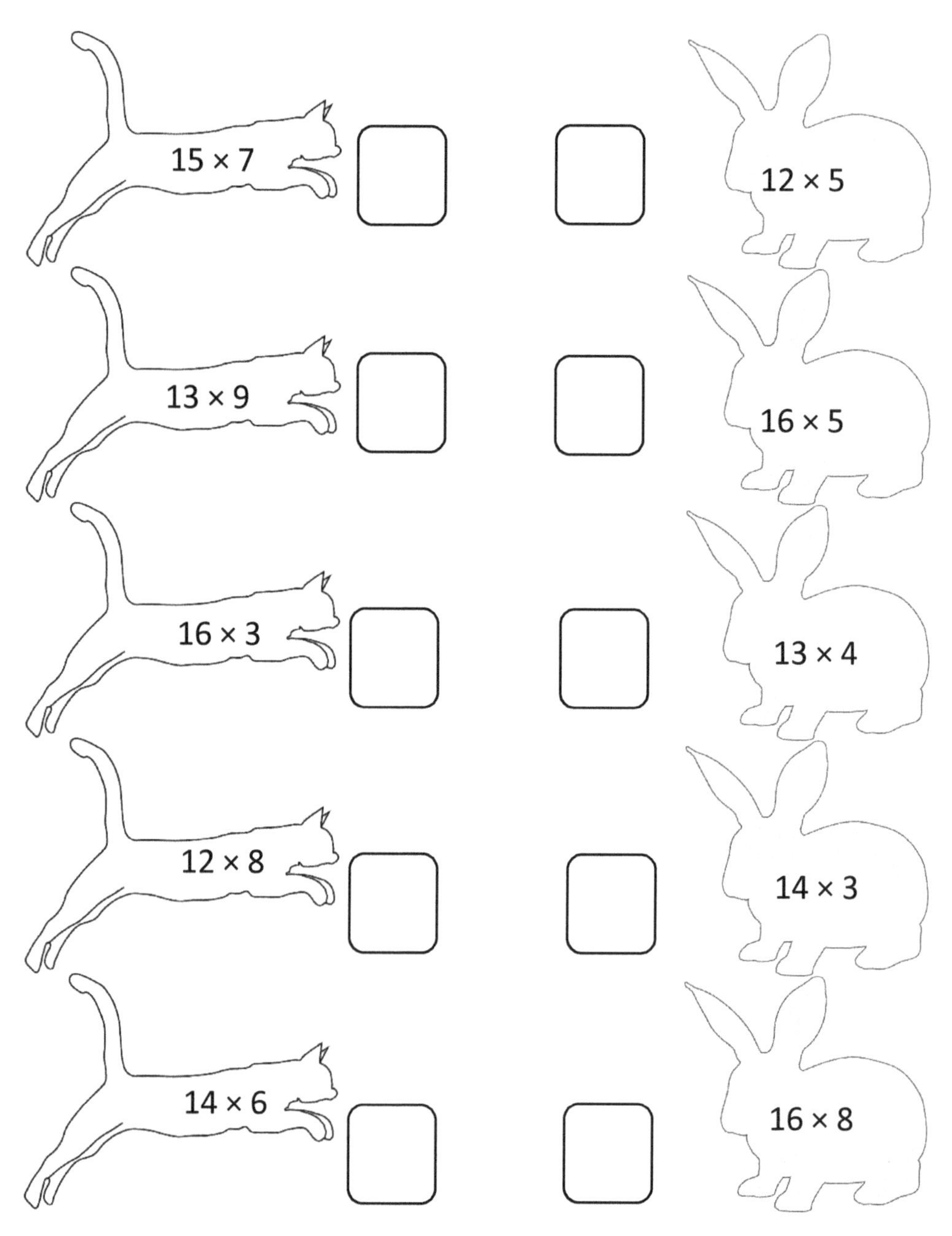

A square number is a number multiplied by itself. For example, 2 × 2 = 4
3 × 3 = 9

$$\begin{array}{r} 18 \\ \times 9 \\ \hline \end{array}$$ ______

$$\begin{array}{r} 11 \\ \times 6 \\ \hline \end{array}$$ ______

$$\begin{array}{r} 10 \\ \times 3 \\ \hline \end{array}$$ ______

$$\begin{array}{r} 13 \\ \times 7 \\ \hline \end{array}$$ ______

$$\begin{array}{r} 14 \\ \times 8 \\ \hline \end{array}$$ ______

$$\begin{array}{r} 19 \\ \times 4 \\ \hline \end{array}$$ ______

$$\begin{array}{r} 20 \\ \times 9 \\ \hline \end{array}$$ ______

$$\begin{array}{r} 11 \\ \times 8 \\ \hline \end{array}$$ ______

$$\begin{array}{r} 17 \\ \times 4 \\ \hline \end{array}$$ ______

$$\begin{array}{r} 16 \\ \times 3 \\ \hline \end{array}$$ ______

$$\begin{array}{r} 12 \\ \times 5 \\ \hline \end{array}$$ ______

$$\begin{array}{r} 10 \\ \times 7 \\ \hline \end{array}$$ ______

Kevin has 10 boxes of cards. Each box holds 6 cards. How many cards does Kevin have?

______ cards

Find each missing number.

20 × ___ = 60

___ × 25 = 75

___ × 23 = 46

16 × ___ = 32

24 × ___ = 120

25 × ___ = 225

___ × 14 = 84

22 × 4 = ___

22 × ___ = 88

16 × ___ = 80

20 × ___ = 140

___ ×14 = 28

___ × 19 = 38

17 × ___ = 153

26 × ___ = 104

17 × ___ = 34

___ × 15 = 120

___ × 26 = 78

___ × 1 = 18

21 × 6 = ___

25 × ___ = 125

21 × ___ = 42

___ × 22 = 154

26 × 0 = ___

20 × ___ = 80

19 × ___ = 76

26 × ___ = 182

15 × 7 = ___

23 × 9 = ___

___ × 26 = 52

18 × 9 = ___

25 × 6 = ___

26 × ___ = 26

21 × 4 = ___

___ × 18 = 36

___ × 27 = 54

23 × 7 = ___

24 × ___ = 48

27 × ___ = 216

Complete.

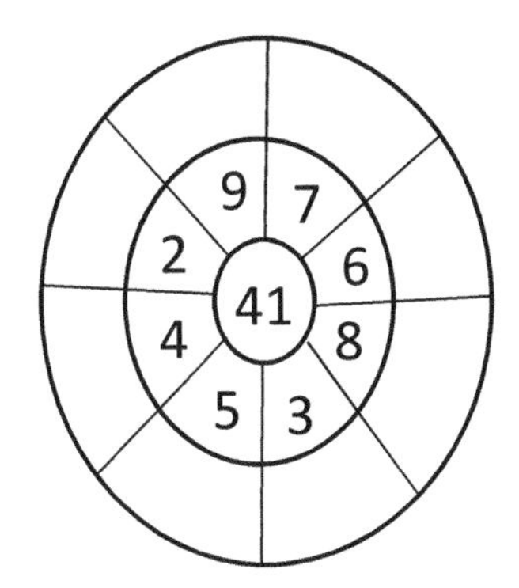

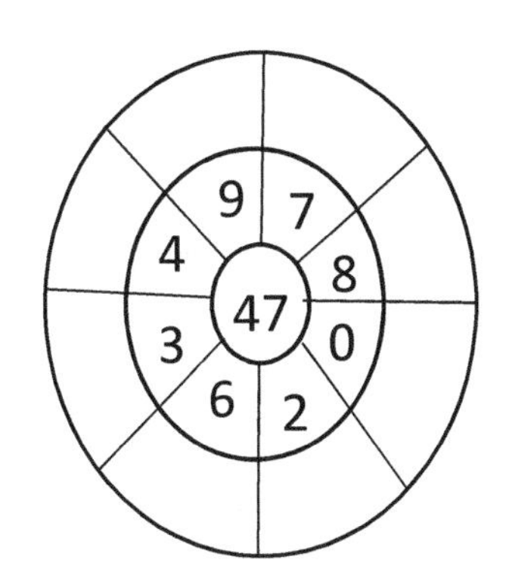

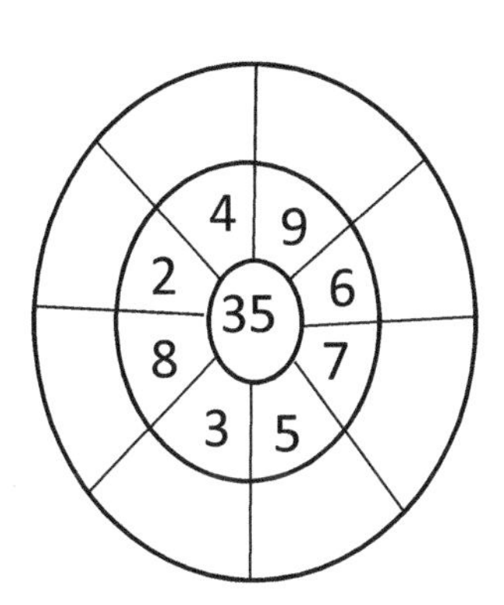

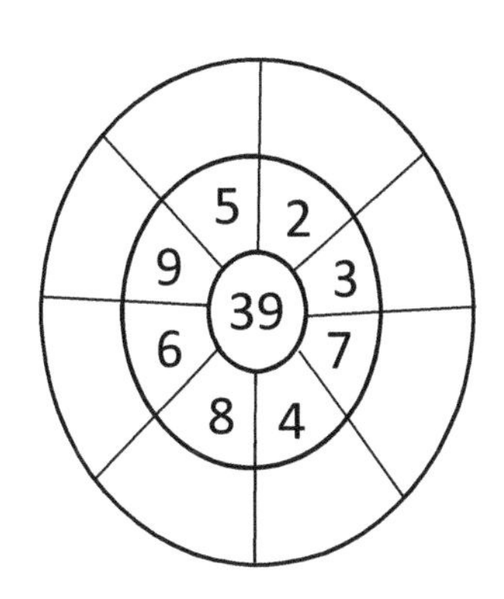

Each peanut costs \$3.00. How much do 47 peanuts cost?

\$ _____

Each Skittle costs \$6.00. How much do 35 Skittles cost?

\$ _____

Write the answers in the boxes.

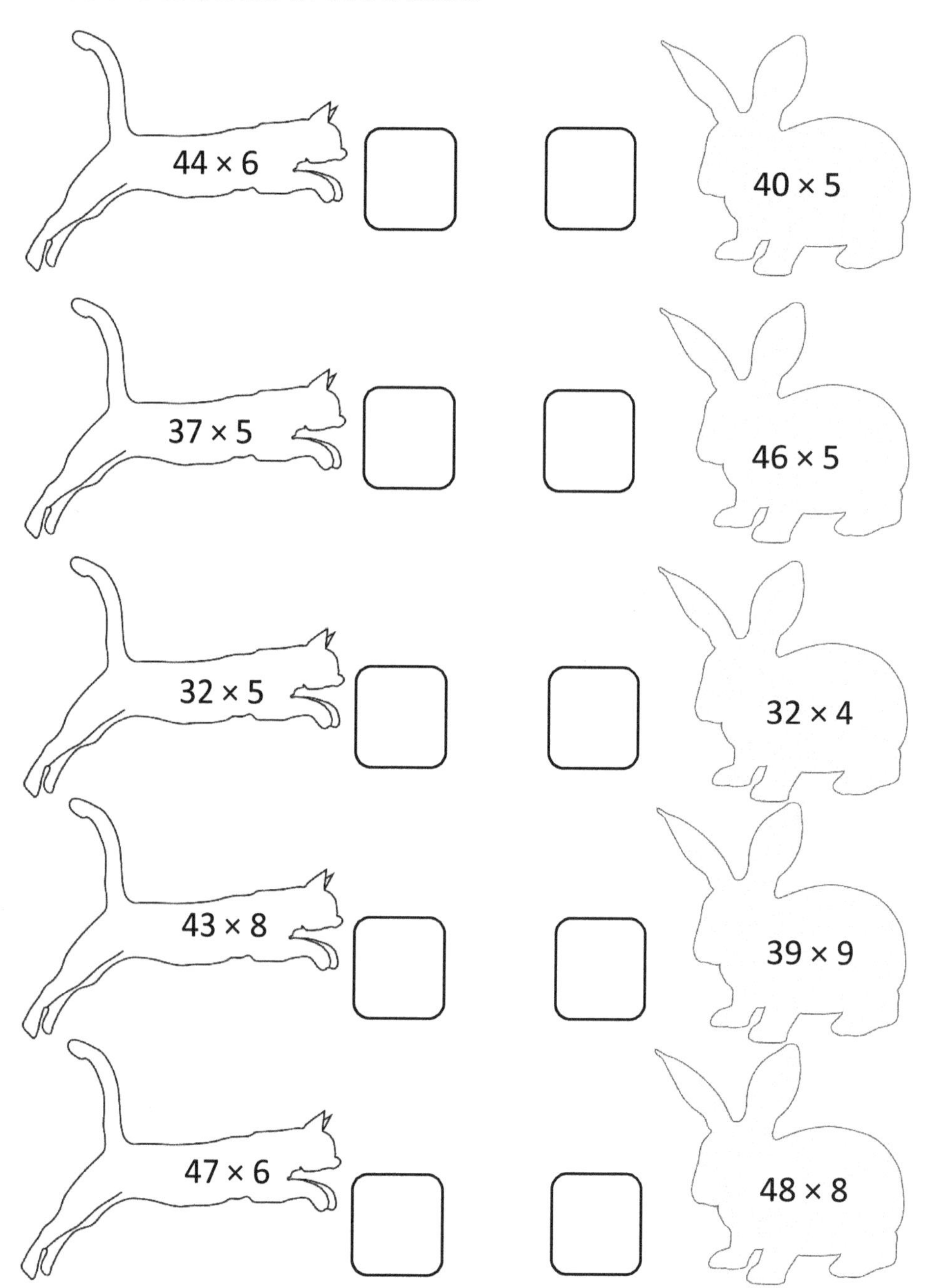

$$\begin{array}{r} 55 \\ \times 8 \\ \hline \end{array}$$
______

$$\begin{array}{r} 53 \\ \times 2 \\ \hline \end{array}$$
______

$$\begin{array}{r} 57 \\ \times 7 \\ \hline \end{array}$$
______

$$\begin{array}{r} 53 \\ \times 9 \\ \hline \end{array}$$
______

$$\begin{array}{r} 50 \\ \times 8 \\ \hline \end{array}$$
______

$$\begin{array}{r} 59 \\ \times 6 \\ \hline \end{array}$$
______

$$\begin{array}{r} 52 \\ \times 9 \\ \hline \end{array}$$
______

$$\begin{array}{r} 51 \\ \times 8 \\ \hline \end{array}$$
______

$$\begin{array}{r} 56 \\ \times 6 \\ \hline \end{array}$$
______

$$\begin{array}{r} 54 \\ \times 9 \\ \hline \end{array}$$
______

$$\begin{array}{r} 57 \\ \times 5 \\ \hline \end{array}$$
______

$$\begin{array}{r} 58 \\ \times 9 \\ \hline \end{array}$$
______

There are 55 peanuts in each box. How many peanuts are in 7 boxes?

______ peanuts

Find each missing number.

63 × ___ = 126	___ × 67 = 134	___ × 62 = 124
66 × ___ = 132	66 × ___ = 264	61 × ___ = 549
___ × 65 = 130	65 × 8 = ___	65 × ___ = 325
63 × ___ = 126	63 × ___ = 441	___ × 66 = 198
___ × 66 = 330	65 × ___ = 520	67 × ___ = 201
62 × ___ = 310	___ × 69 = 138	___ × 60 = 180
___ × 60 = 120	66 × 6 = ___	68 × ___ = 68
63 × ___ = 378	___ × 61 = 305	61 × 8 = ___
65 × ___ = 325	69 × ___ = 414	69 × 4 = ___
67 × 9 = ___	67 × 9 = ___	___ × 69 = 138
69 × 7 = ___	68 × 3 = ___	68 × ___ = 340
66 × 4 = ___	___ × 67 = 335	___ × 65 = 260
64 × 2 = ___	64 × ___ = 128	69 × 9 = ___

Complete.

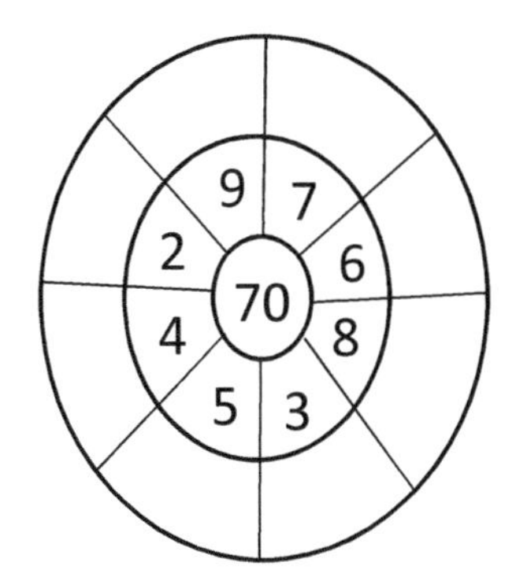

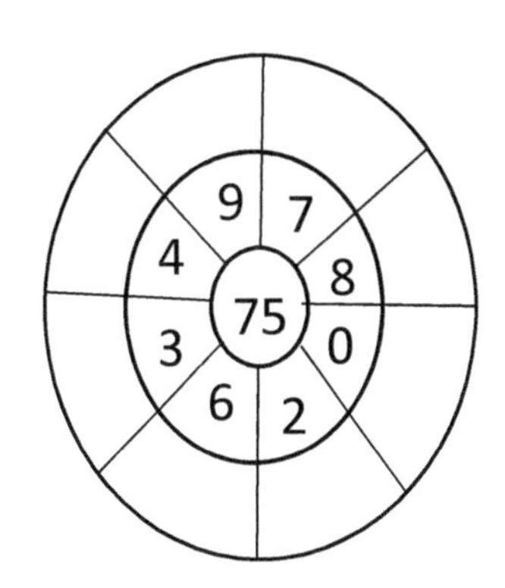

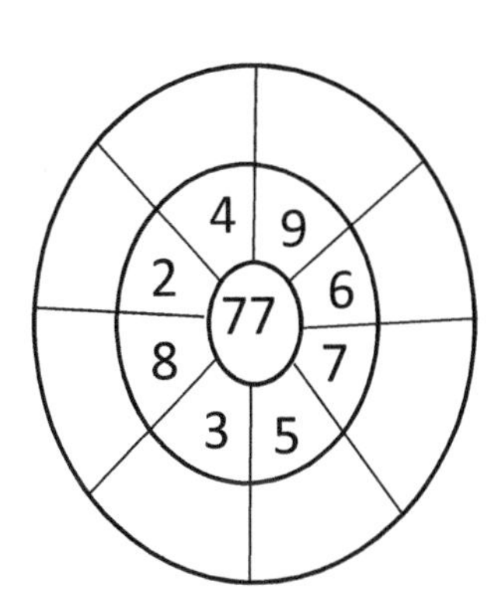

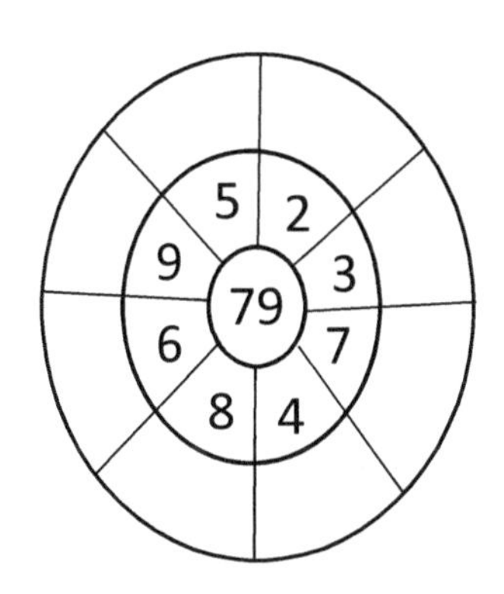

There are 76 peanuts in each box. How many peanuts are in 7 box?

______

Each block costs $5.00. How much do 79 blocks cost?

______

Write the answers in the boxes.

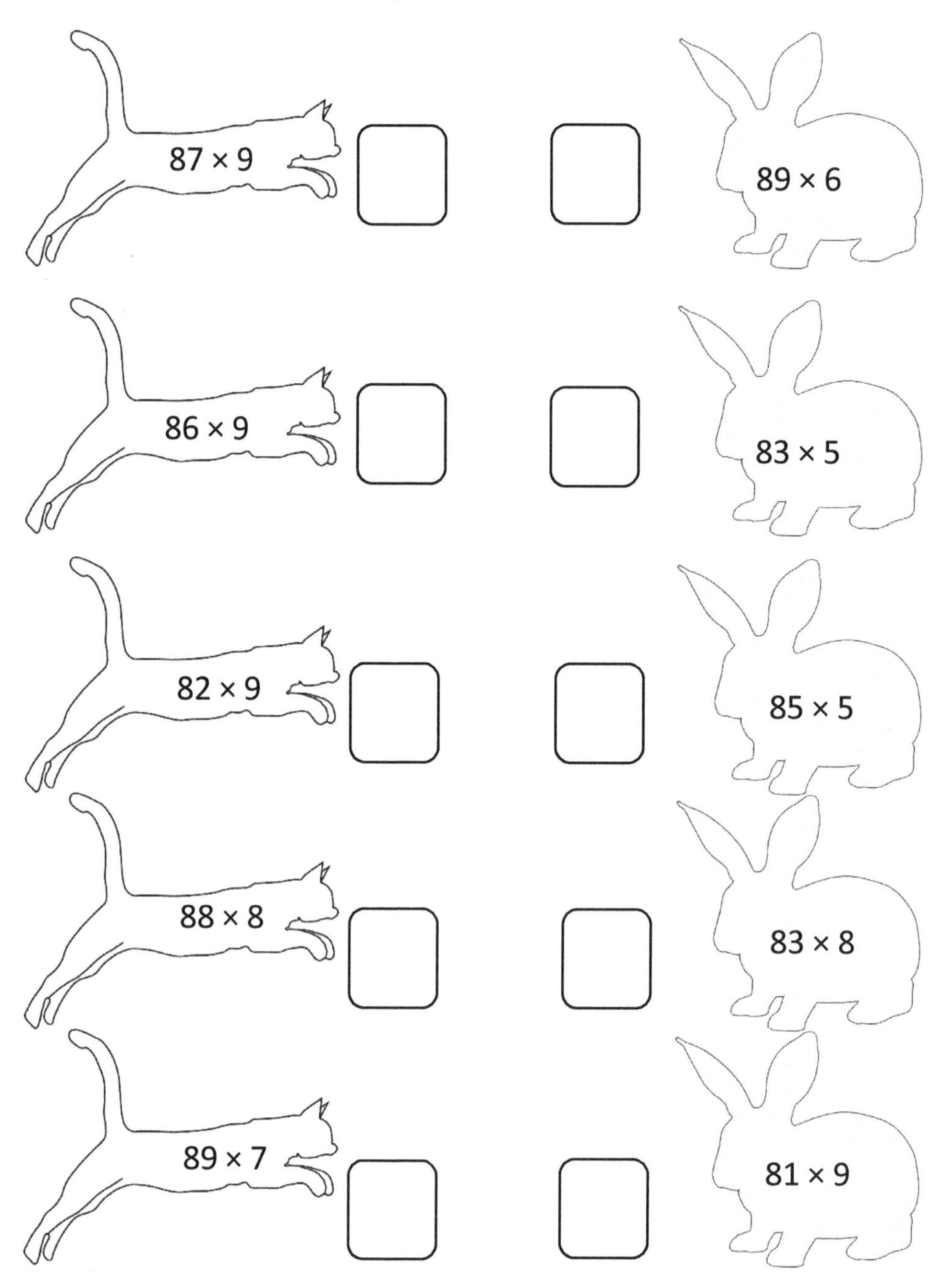

Find each missing number.

90 × ___ = 180

___ × 97 = 97

___ × 93 = 186

97 × ___ = 291

91 × ___ = 546

98 × ___ = 196

___ × 95 = 285

98 × 8 = ___

91 × ___ = 455

91 × ___ = 182

90 × ___ = 270

___ × 5 = 460

___ × 94 = 188

93 × ___ = 279

90 × ___ = 360

92 × ___ = 184

___ × 94 = 470

___ × 94 = 376

___ × 91 = 273

90 × 9 = ___

92 × ___ = 276

90 × ___ = 630

___ × 91 = 364

91 × 8 = ___

93 × ___ = 372

98 × ___ = 588

100 × 4 = ___

95 × 9 = ___

90 × 9 = ___

___ × 90 = 450

99 × 7 = ___

100 × 9 = ___

92 × ___ = 368

96 × 5 = ___

___ × 90 = 540

___ × 94 = 282

98 × 9 = ___

94 × ___ = 564

100 × 5 = ___

Complete.

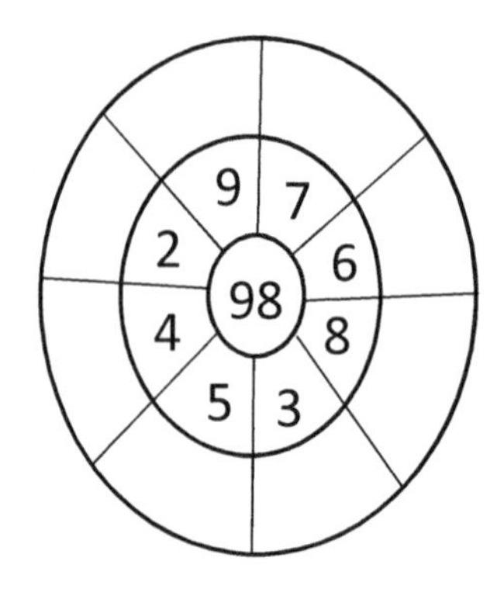

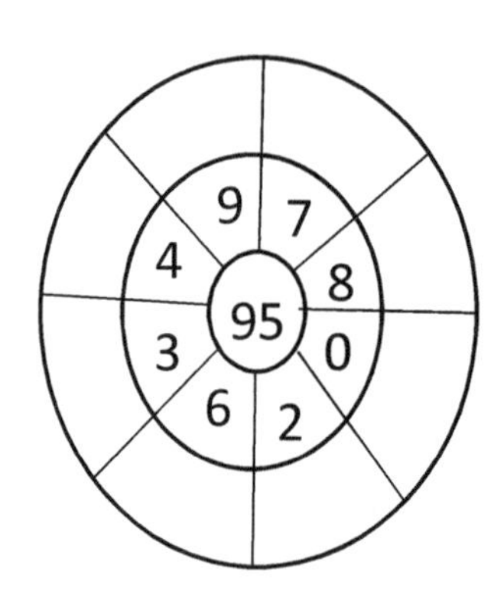

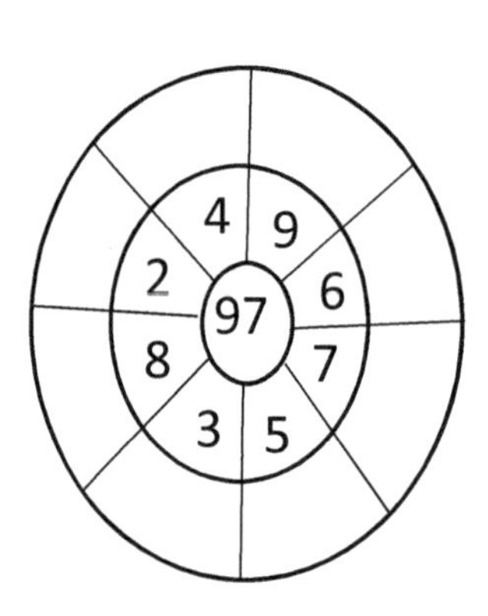

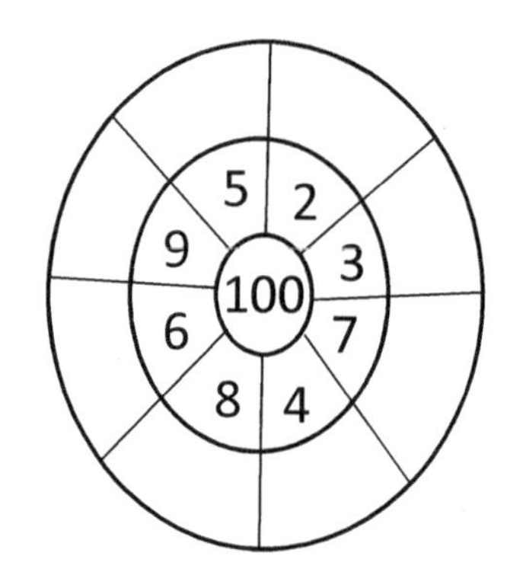

There are 95 Skittles in each box.
How many Skittles are in 8 boxes?

______

There are 96 peanuts in each box.
How many peanuts are in 6 boxes?

Write the answers in the boxes.

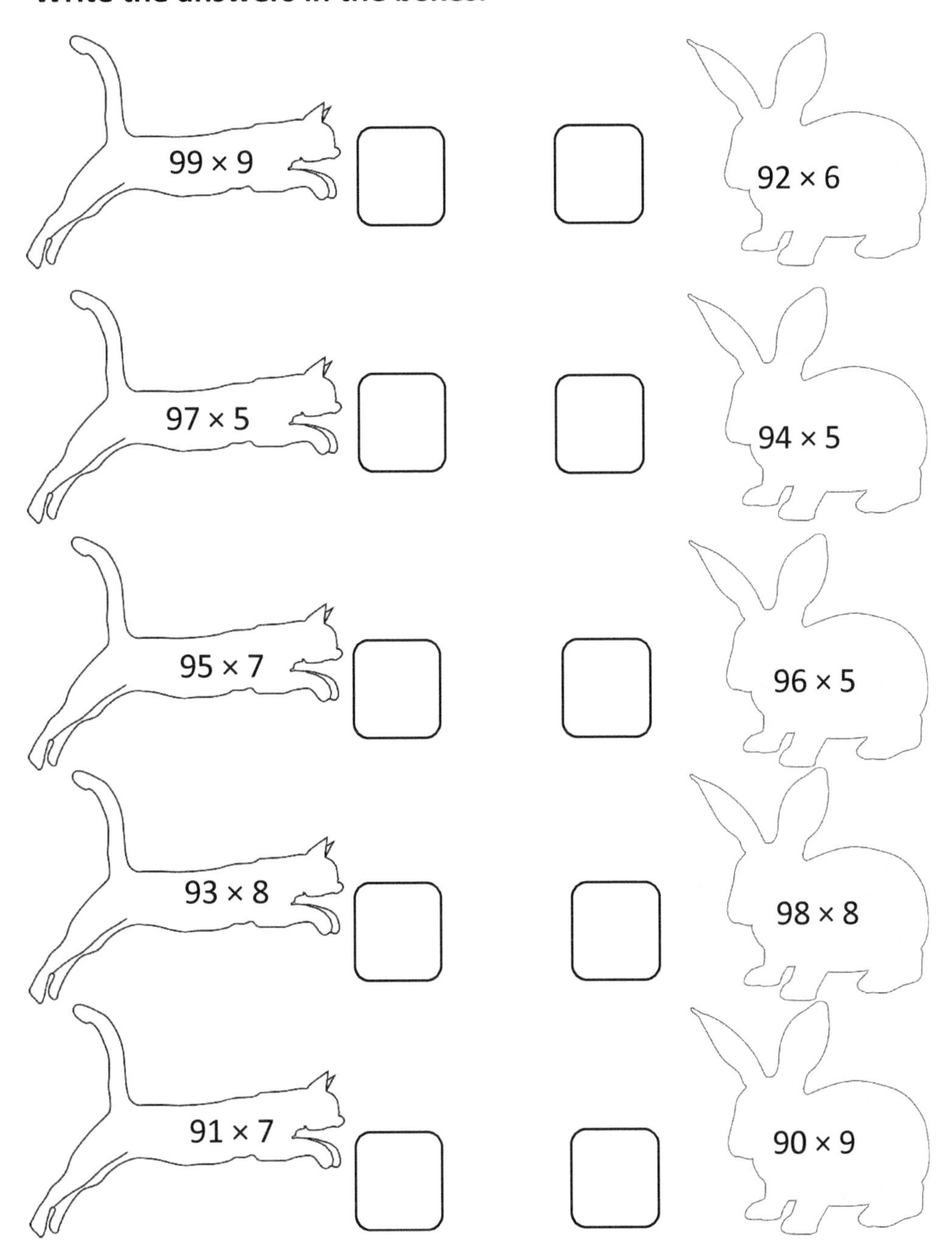

Multiplication two–digit number

Find each missing number.

12 × ___ = 72
___ × 5 = 55
___ × 3 = 18

11 × ___ = 55
11 × ___ = 132
11 × ___ = 11

___ × 10 = 110
___ × 4 = 44
12 × ___ = 24

12 × ___ = 36
10 × ___ = 60
___ × 4 = 36

___ × 9 = 108
7 × ___ = 70
11 × ___ = 66

12 × ___ = 84
___ × 11 = 88
___ × 6 = 48

___ × 1 = 77
12 × ___ = 96
12 × ___ = 132

11 × ___ = 22
___ × 11 = 99
11 × 0 = ___

10 × ___ = 30
11 × ___ = 121
12 × ___ = 144

11 × 3 = ___
11 × 10 = ___
___ × 6 = 60

10 × 2 = ___
12 × ___ = 60
12 × ___ = 120

11 × 4 = ___
___ × 11 = 15
___ × 10 = 20

11 × 7 = ___
12 × ___ = 12
12 × ___ = 0

Complete.

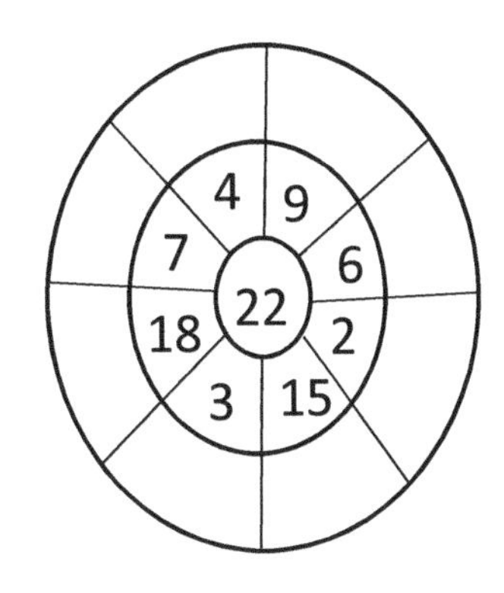

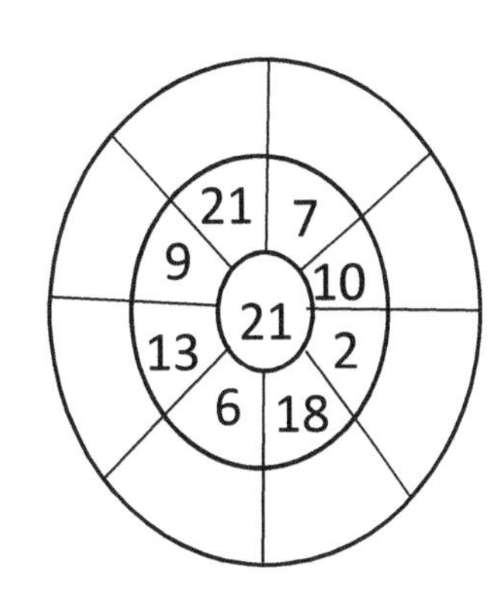

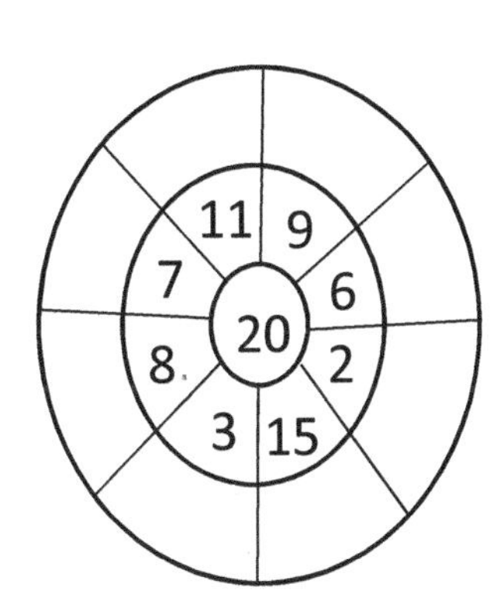

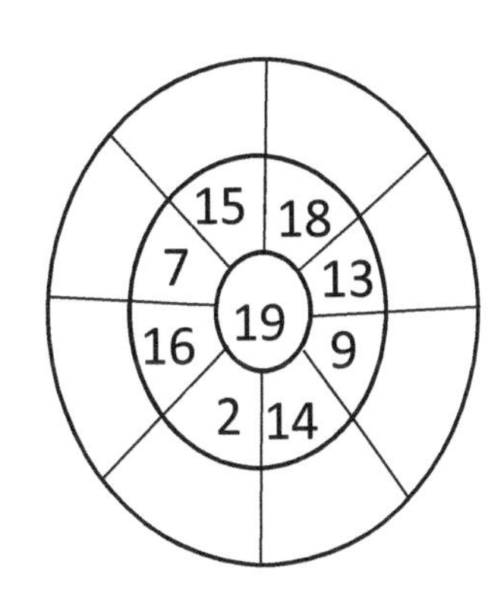

List the first ten multiples of each number.

13, ___, ___, ___, ___, ___, ___, ___, ___, ___

14, ___, ___, ___, ___, ___, ___, ___, ___, ___

15, ___, ___, ___, ___, ___, ___, ___, ___, ___

16, ___, ___, ___, ___, ___, ___, ___, ___, ___

17, ___, ___, ___, ___, ___, ___, ___, ___, ___

18, ___, ___, ___, ___, ___, ___, ___, ___, ___

$$\begin{array}{r} 20 \\ \times 11 \\ \hline \\ \hline \end{array}$$

$$\begin{array}{r} 18 \\ \times 13 \\ \hline \\ \hline \end{array}$$

$$\begin{array}{r} 23 \\ \times 19 \\ \hline \\ \hline \end{array}$$

$$\begin{array}{r} 21 \\ \times 17 \\ \hline \\ \hline \end{array}$$

$$\begin{array}{r} 12 \\ \times 18 \\ \hline \\ \hline \end{array}$$

$$\begin{array}{r} 18 \\ \times 14 \\ \hline \\ \hline \end{array}$$

$$\begin{array}{r} 19 \\ \times 19 \\ \hline \\ \hline \end{array}$$

$$\begin{array}{r} 22 \\ \times 15 \\ \hline \\ \hline \end{array}$$

$$\begin{array}{r} 19 \\ \times 17 \\ \hline \\ \hline \end{array}$$

$$\begin{array}{r} 20 \\ \times 16 \\ \hline \\ \hline \end{array}$$

$$\begin{array}{r} 17 \\ \times 15 \\ \hline \\ \hline \end{array}$$

$$\begin{array}{r} 21 \\ \times 13 \\ \hline \\ \hline \end{array}$$

$$\begin{array}{r} 24 \\ \times 19 \\ \hline \\ \hline \end{array}$$

$$\begin{array}{r} 25 \\ \times 17 \\ \hline \\ \hline \end{array}$$

$$\begin{array}{r} 26 \\ \times 20 \\ \hline \\ \hline \end{array}$$

Find each missing number.

21 × ___ = 420	___ × 25 = 275	19 × 23 = ___
18 × ___ = 270	14 × ___ = 364	21 × ___ = 483
___ × 12 = 168	29 × 24 = ___	27 × ___ = 324
19 × ___ = 399	13 × ___ = 260	20 × 24 = ___
___ × 17 = 238	27 × ___ = 702	29 × 21 = ___
15 × ___ = 195	___ × 23 = 345	___ × 26 = 286
___ × 11 = 286	22 × ___ = 418	18 × ___ = 324
17 × 28 = ___	___ × 29 = 145	14 ×20 = ___
25 × ___ = 475	22 × ___ = 198	19 × ___ = 228
28 × 13 = ___	12 × 27 = ___	___ × 16 = 256
27 × 21 = ___	12 × ___ = 228	23 × 23 = ___
19 × 24 = ___	___ × 28 = 644	28 × 19 = ___
26 × 17 = ___	23 × ___ = 529	22 × 16 = ___

Complete.

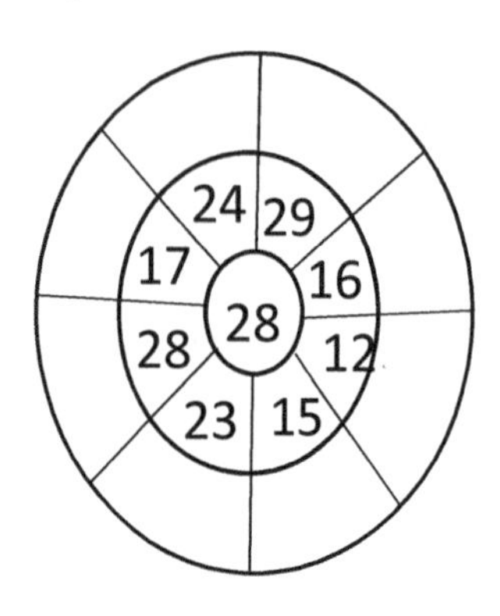

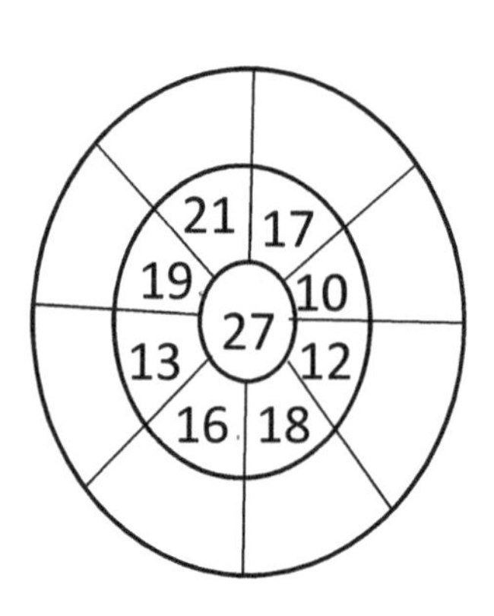

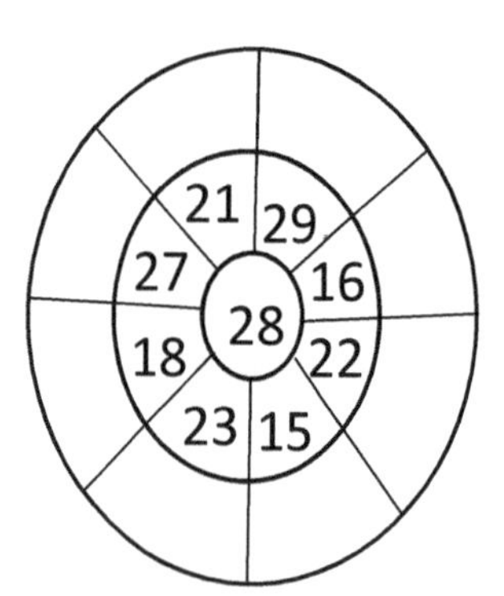

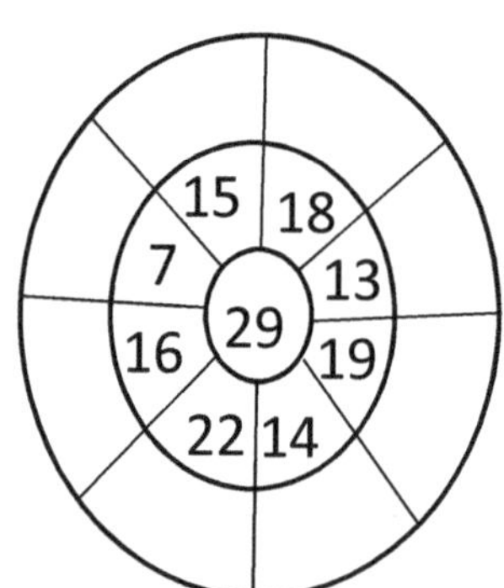

List the first ten multiples of each number.

20, ___, ___, ___, ___, ___, ___, ___, ___, ___

21, ___, ___, ___, ___, ___, ___, ___, ___, ___

22, ___, ___, ___, ___, ___, ___, ___, ___, ___

23, ___, ___, ___, ___, ___, ___, ___, ___, ___

24, ___, ___, ___, ___, ___, ___, ___, ___, ___

25, ___, ___, ___, ___, ___, ___, ___, ___, __

$$\begin{array}{r} 31 \\ \times 20 \\ \hline \end{array}$$

$$\begin{array}{r} 28 \\ \times 32 \\ \hline \end{array}$$

$$\begin{array}{r} 33 \\ \times 25 \\ \hline \end{array}$$

$$\begin{array}{r} 24 \\ \times 27 \\ \hline \end{array}$$

$$\begin{array}{r} 31 \\ \times 29 \\ \hline \end{array}$$

$$\begin{array}{r} 27 \\ \times 30 \\ \hline \end{array}$$

$$\begin{array}{r} 29 \\ \times 26 \\ \hline \end{array}$$

$$\begin{array}{r} 25 \\ \times 35 \\ \hline \end{array}$$

$$\begin{array}{r} 34 \\ \times 27 \\ \hline \end{array}$$

$$\begin{array}{r} 31 \\ \times 16 \\ \hline \end{array}$$

$$\begin{array}{r} 23 \\ \times 15 \\ \hline \end{array}$$

$$\begin{array}{r} 29 \\ \times 33 \\ \hline \end{array}$$

$$\begin{array}{r} 32 \\ \times 19 \\ \hline \end{array}$$

$$\begin{array}{r} 35 \\ \times 23 \\ \hline \end{array}$$

$$\begin{array}{r} 30 \\ \times 25 \\ \hline \end{array}$$

Find each missing number.

41 × 23 = ___	___ × 65 = 780	39 × 43 = ___
24 × ___ = 960	53 × ___ = 1060	71 × ___ = 1633
___ × 45 = 405	46 × 50 = ___	76 × ___ = 4180
29 × 43 = ___	68 × ___ = 1564	74 × 54 = ___
46 × 27 = ___	49 × ___ = 784	68 × 22 = ___
47 × ___ = 564	55 × 65 = ___	___ × 56 = 672
___ × 40 = 1680	62 × 49 = ___	78 × ___ = 858
29 × 48 = ___	56 × 71 = ___	23 ×60 = ___
25 × 46 = ___	78 × ___ = 1950	69 × 40 = ___
23 × ___ = 943	42 × 64 = ___	___ × 76 = 1140
49 × 23 = ___	39 × ___ = 1950	63 × 23 = ___
42 × 18 = ___	___ × 28 = 1400	58 × 29 = ___
34 × 40 = ___	57 × 77 = ___	72 × 16 = ___

Complete.

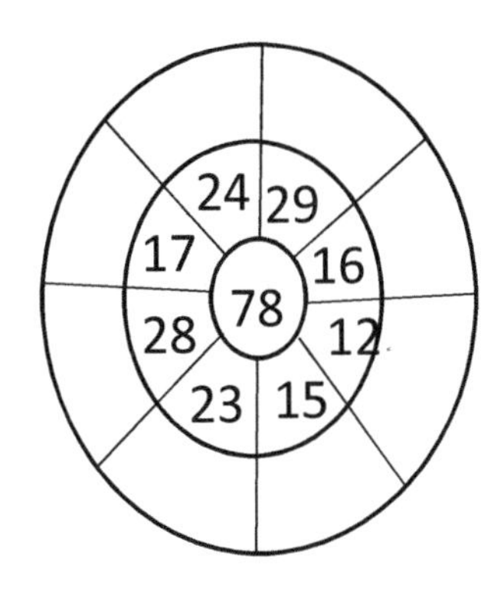

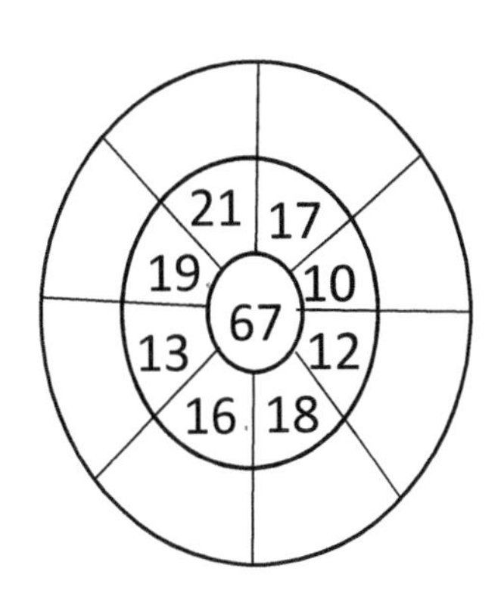

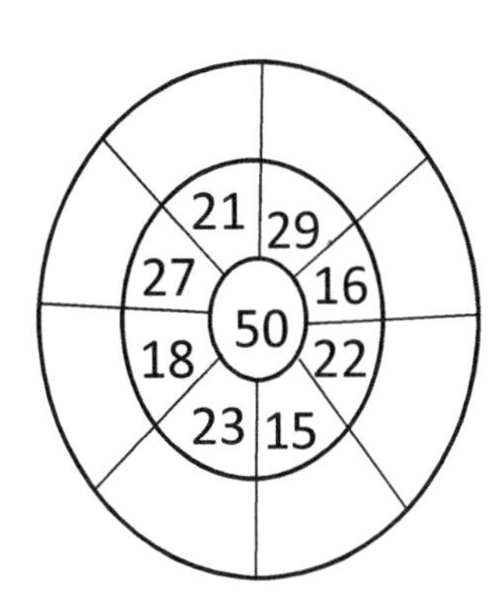

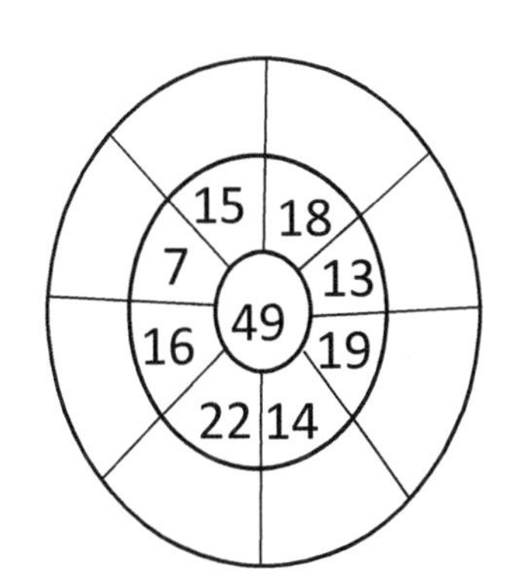

List the first ten multiples of each number.

40, ___, ___, ___, ___, ___, ___, ___, ___, ___

45, ___, ___, ___, ___, ___, ___, ___, ___, ___

50, ___, ___, ___, ___, ___, ___, ___, ___, ___

55, ___, ___, ___, ___, ___, ___, ___, ___, ___

60, ___, ___, ___, ___, ___, ___, ___, ___, ___

65, ___, ___, ___, ___, ___, ___, ___, ___, __

$$\begin{array}{r} 67 \\ \times 20 \\ \hline \end{array}$$

$$\begin{array}{r} 78 \\ \times 32 \\ \hline \end{array}$$

$$\begin{array}{r} 73 \\ \times 25 \\ \hline \end{array}$$

$$\begin{array}{r} 54 \\ \times 27 \\ \hline \end{array}$$

$$\begin{array}{r} 71 \\ \times 29 \\ \hline \end{array}$$

$$\begin{array}{r} 67 \\ \times 30 \\ \hline \end{array}$$

$$\begin{array}{r} 49 \\ \times 26 \\ \hline \end{array}$$

$$\begin{array}{r} 55 \\ \times 35 \\ \hline \end{array}$$

$$\begin{array}{r} 44 \\ \times 27 \\ \hline \end{array}$$

$$\begin{array}{r} 51 \\ \times 16 \\ \hline \end{array}$$

$$\begin{array}{r} 73 \\ \times 15 \\ \hline \end{array}$$

$$\begin{array}{r} 79 \\ \times 33 \\ \hline \end{array}$$

$$\begin{array}{r} 72 \\ \times 19 \\ \hline \end{array}$$

$$\begin{array}{r} 65 \\ \times 23 \\ \hline \end{array}$$

$$\begin{array}{r} 60 \\ \times 25 \\ \hline \end{array}$$

Find each missing number.

91 × 23 = ___	___ × 95 = 760	99 × 43 = ___
84 × ___ = 2016	84 × ___ = 2436	96 × ___ = 2415
___ × 85 = 4760	96 × 50 = ___	80 × ___ = 7200
99 × 43 = ___	79 × ___ = 6320	74 × 94 = ___
86 × 77 = ___	99 × ___ = 990	88 × 22 = ___
97 × ___ = 5238	95 × 65 = ___	___ × 60 = 3000
___ × 80 = 800	82 × 99 = ___	78 × ___ = 2028
90 × 38 = ___	96 × 61 = ___	97 ×60 = ___
87 × 46 = ___	88 × ___ = 1232	89 × 50 = ___
80 × ___ = 960	92 × 54 = ___	___ × 86 = 5590
82 × 80 = ___	79 × ___ = 1501	83 × 43 = ___
98 × 18 = ___	___ × 75 = 1875	78 × 99 = ___
81 × 50 = ___	97 × 77 = ___	76 × 96 = ___

Complete.

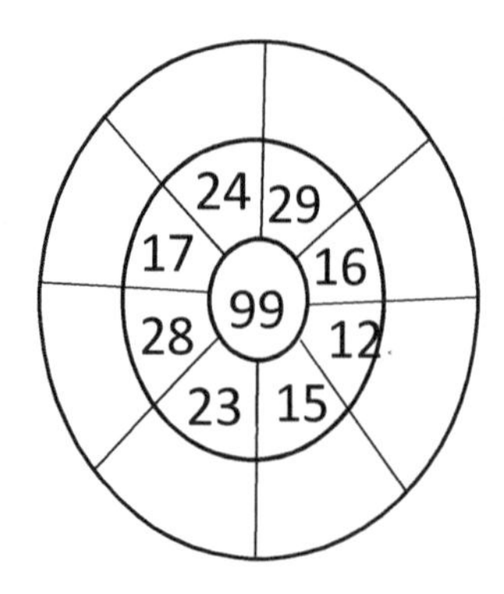

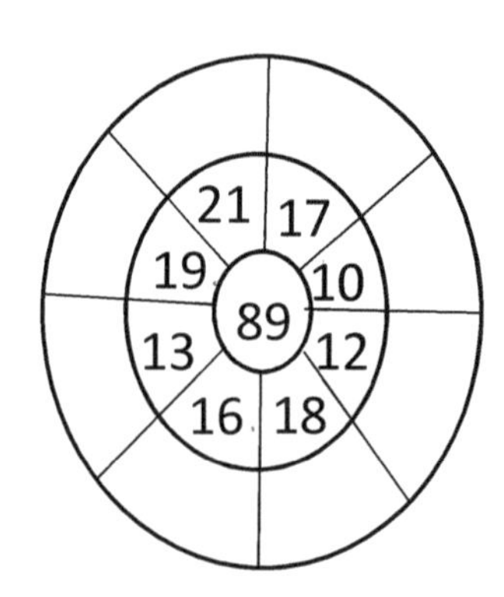

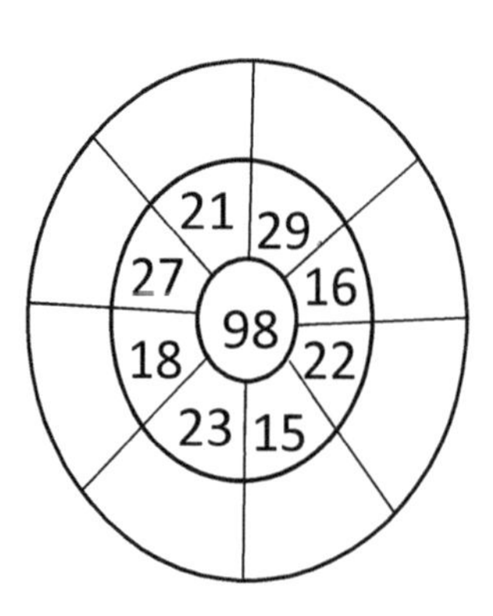

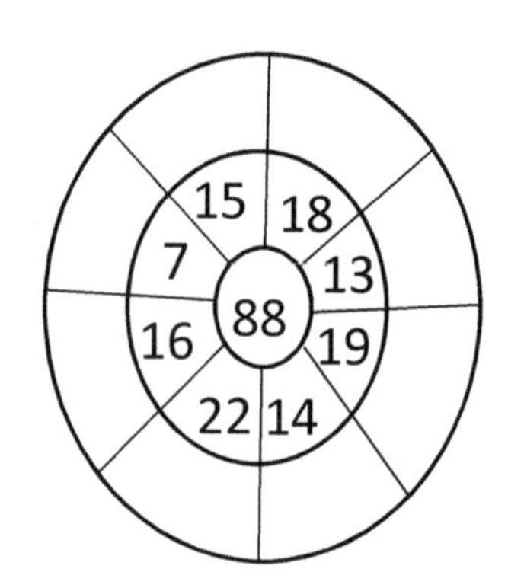

List the first ten multiples of each number.

70, ___, ___, ___, ___, ___, ___, ___, ___, ___

75, ___, ___, ___, ___, ___, ___, ___, ___, ___

80, ___, ___, ___, ___, ___, ___, ___, ___, ___

85, ___, ___, ___, ___, ___, ___, ___, ___, ___

90, ___, ___, ___, ___, ___, ___, ___, ___, ___

95, ___, ___, ___, ___, ___, ___, ___, ___, __

98×56	90×50	87×45
84×77	91×69	87×90
99×86	95×85	83×87
86×93	88×59	90×56
95×81	82×75	98×95

Multiplication three – digit number

Complete.

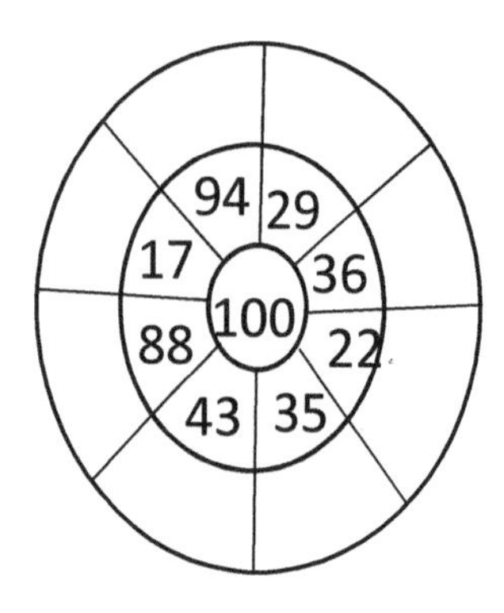

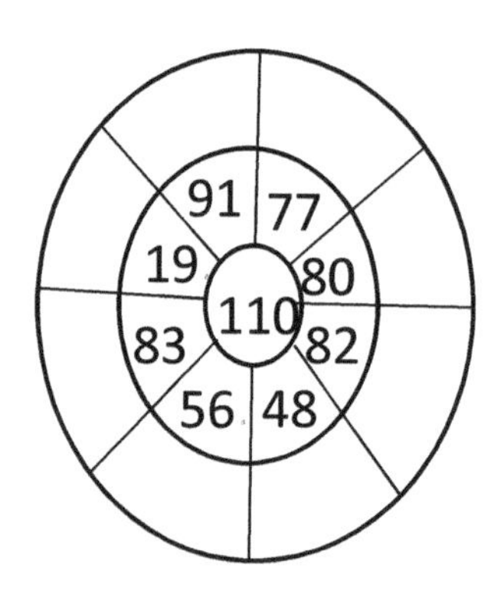

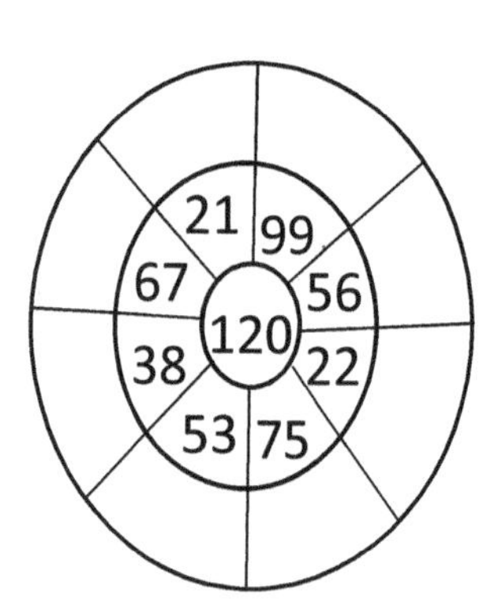

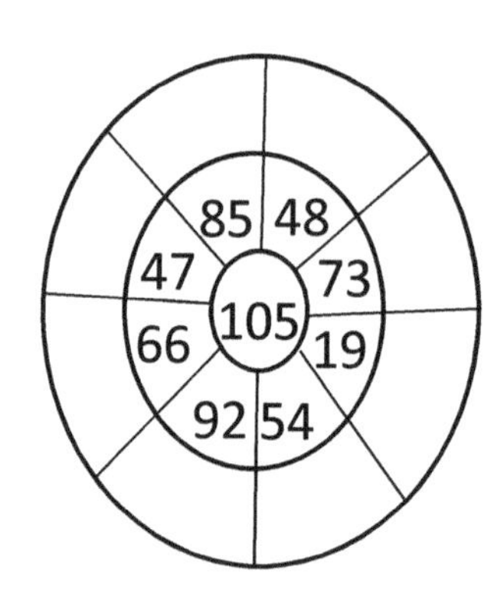

List the first ten multiples of each number.

100, ___, ___, ___, ___, ___, ___, ___, ___, ___

105, ___, ___, ___, ___, ___, ___, ___, ___, ___

110, ___, ___, ___, ___, ___, ___, ___, ___, ___

115, ___, ___, ___, ___, ___, ___, ___, ___, ___

120, ___, ___, ___, ___, ___, ___, ___, ___, ___

125, ___, ___, ___, ___, ___, ___, ___, ___, __

Find the answers.

$$\begin{array}{r} 120 \\ \times\ 56 \\ \hline \end{array}$$

$$\begin{array}{r} 190 \\ \times\ 40 \\ \hline \end{array}$$

$$\begin{array}{r} 187 \\ \times\ 55 \\ \hline \end{array}$$

$$\begin{array}{r} 854 \\ \times 77 \\ \hline \end{array}$$

$$\begin{array}{r} 931 \\ \times\ 69 \\ \hline \end{array}$$

$$\begin{array}{r} 817 \\ \times 40 \\ \hline \end{array}$$

$$\begin{array}{r} 199 \\ \times\ 86 \\ \hline \end{array}$$

$$\begin{array}{r} 955 \\ \times 85 \\ \hline \end{array}$$

$$\begin{array}{r} 83 \\ \times\ 87 \\ \hline \end{array}$$

$$\begin{array}{r} 856 \\ \times 33 \\ \hline \end{array}$$

$$\begin{array}{r} 188 \\ \times\ 99 \\ \hline \end{array}$$

$$\begin{array}{r} 690 \\ \times 36 \\ \hline \end{array}$$

$$\begin{array}{r} 951 \\ \times\ 81 \\ \hline \end{array}$$

$$\begin{array}{r} 982 \\ \times 65 \\ \hline \end{array}$$

$$\begin{array}{r} 798 \\ \times 95 \\ \hline \end{array}$$

Division

Division by 1, 2, 3 and 4

Write a fact for the following pictures.

☺ ☺ ☺ ☺ ☺

☺ ☺ ☺ ☺ ☺ 10 ÷ __ = __

☺ ☺ ☺

☺ ☺ ☺ 9 ÷ __ = __

☺ ☺ ☺

☺☺ ☺☺

☺☺ ☺☺ 12 ÷ __ = __

☺☺ ☺☺

☺☺ ☺☺ ☺☺ ☺☺ __ ÷ 2 = __

☺☺ ☺☺ ☺☺ ☺☺

☺☺☺ ☺☺☺

☺☺☺ ☺☺☺ __ ÷ __ = 4

Match.

$12 \div 4$	$21 \div 3$	$20 \div 4$	$18 \div 3$

$30 \div 3$	$9 \div 3$	$4 \div 2$	$14 \div 2$

If dividend is 24 and the quotient is 6, then what is the divisor?

______

Tip of the Day!

0 divided by any number equals 0.

For example, $0 \div 9 = 0$

Find each missing number.

27 ÷ ___ = 9 33 ÷ 3 = ___

___ ÷ 3 = 5 24 ÷ ___ = 8

10 ÷ 2 = ___ 18 ÷ ___ = 9

___ ÷ 2 = 8 ___ ÷ 2 = 1

___ ÷ 4 = 2 28 ÷ ___ = 7

24 ÷ ___ = 6 20 ÷ 4 = ___

3 x 9 = 27	27 ÷ 3 = 9
4 x 6 = 24	24 ÷ 4 = 9
3 x 7 = ___	___÷ 3 = ___
2 x 9 = ___	___ ÷ 2 = ___
3 x 6 = ___	___ ÷ 3 = ___

Write the answers in the boxes.

$3 \div 3$ ☐ ☐ $9 \div 3$

$15 \div 3$ ☐ ☐ $12 \div 3$

$16 \div 4$ ☐ ☐ $10 \div 5$

$8 \div 4$ ☐ ☐ $30 \div 3$

$24 \div 2$ ☐ ☐ $33 \div 3$

$\frac{20}{2} =$ ____

$\frac{30}{3} =$ ____

$\frac{27}{3} =$ ____

$\frac{12}{2} =$ ____

$\frac{16}{4} =$ ____

$\frac{24}{4} =$ ____

$\frac{20}{4} =$ ____

$\frac{18}{2} =$ ____

$\frac{16}{2} =$ ____

$\frac{21}{3} =$ ____

Find the quotient of 28 divided by 4. ______

Find the quotient of 24 divided by 3. ______

Division by 5 and 6

Write a fact for the following pictures.

☺☺☺☺☺ ☺☺☺☺☺

☺☺☺☺☺ ☺☺☺☺☺ 30 ÷ __ = __

☺☺☺☺☺ ☺☺☺☺☺

☺☺☺☺☺☺

☺☺☺☺☺☺ 18 ÷ __ = __

☺☺☺☺☺☺

☺☺☺☺☺ ☺☺☺☺☺

☺☺☺☺☺ ☺☺☺☺☺ __ ÷ __ = 4

☺☺☺☺☺☺

☺☺☺☺☺☺ __ ÷ __ = 5

☺☺☺☺☺☺

☺☺☺☺☺☺

☺☺☺☺☺☺

Match.

20 ÷ 5	36 ÷ 6	35 ÷ 5	10 ÷ 5

7

30 ÷ 5	15 ÷ 5	42 ÷ 6	18 ÷ 6

What multiplication fact can help you find 40 ÷ 5?

_____ × _____ = _____

Tip of the Day!

Check your answers by multiplying!

Just multiply the answer by the divisor.

For example, 15 ÷ 5 = 3 then 3 × 5 = 15!

Find each missing number.

___ ÷ 5 = 10

5 ÷ ___ = 1

60 ÷ ___ = 12

10 ÷ 5 = ___

___ ÷ 5 = 4

40 ÷ 5 = ___

48 ÷ ___ = 8

12 ÷ 6 = ___

___ ÷ 6 = 7

30 ÷ 6 = ___

24 ÷ 6 = ___

___ ÷ 6 = 11

5 x 4 = 20   20 ÷ 5 = 4

6 x 6 = ___   ___ ÷ 6 = ___

5 x 5 = ___   ___ ÷ 5 = ___

6 x 9 = ___   ___ ÷ 6 = ___

Write the answers in the boxes.

$5 \div 5$ = ☐

$15 \div 5$ = ☐

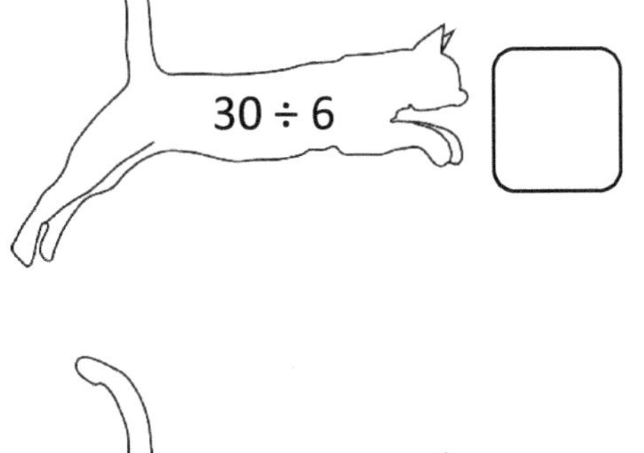

$30 \div 6$ = ☐

$42 \div 6$ = ☐

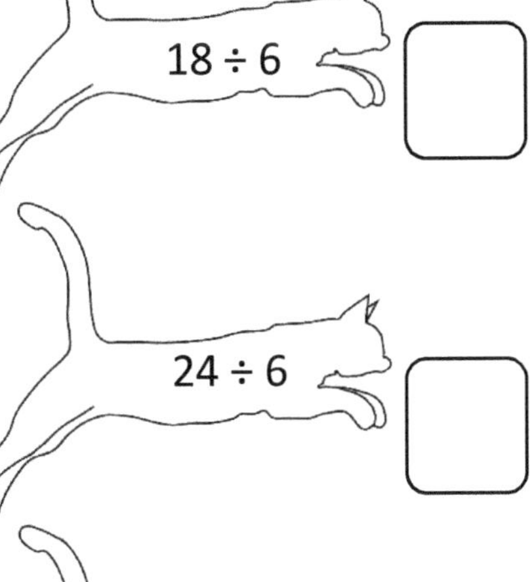

$18 \div 6$ = ☐

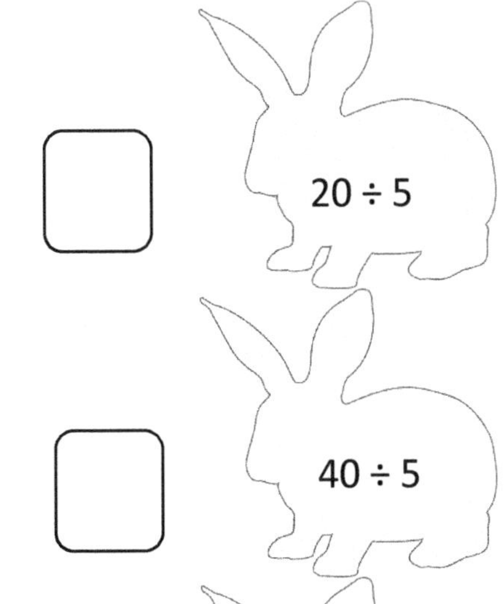

$20 \div 5$ = ☐

$24 \div 6$ = ☐

$40 \div 5$ = ☐

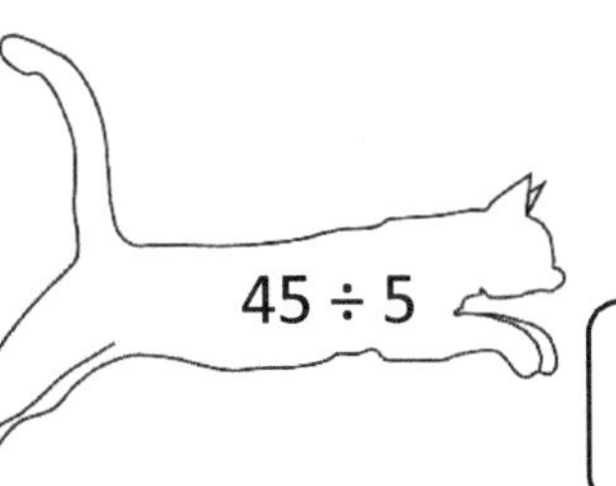

$45 \div 5$ = ☐

$48 \div 6$ = ☐

$\frac{48}{6} =$ ____

$\frac{40}{5} =$ ____

$\frac{50}{5} =$ ____

$\frac{60}{6} =$ ____

$\frac{36}{6} =$ ____

$\frac{12}{6} =$ ____

$\frac{10}{5} =$ ____

$\frac{45}{5} =$ ____

$\frac{42}{6} =$ ____

$\frac{15}{5} =$ ____

Ross has 54 marbles that she would like to give to her 9 friends. If she shares them equally, how many marbles will she give to each? _____ marbles

Division by 7 and 8

Write a fact for the following pictures.

☺☺☺☺☺☺☺
☺☺☺☺☺☺☺ __ ÷ __ = 3
☺☺☺☺☺☺☺

☺☺☺☺☺☺☺☺
☺☺☺☺☺☺☺☺ 32 ÷ __ = __
☺☺☺☺☺☺☺☺
☺☺☺☺☺☺☺☺

☺☺☺☺☺☺☺
☺☺☺☺☺☺☺ 28 ÷ __ = __
☺☺☺☺☺☺☺
☺☺☺☺☺☺☺

☺☺☺☺☺☺☺☺
☺☺☺☺☺☺☺☺ __ ÷ __ = 2

Match.

40 ÷ 8	42 ÷ 7	49 ÷ 7	48 ÷ 8

35 ÷ 7	21 ÷ 7	28 ÷ 7	32 ÷ 8

What multiplication fact can help you find 64 ÷ 8?

______ × ______ = ______

Tip of the Day!

Any number (except 0) when divided by itself equals 1.

For example, 9 ÷ 9 = 1 or 5 ÷ 5 = 1

Find each missing number.

42 ÷ ___ = 6

14 ÷ 7 = ___

___ ÷ 7 = 3

77 ÷ ___ = 11

28 ÷ ___ = 4

35 ÷ 7 = ___

40 ÷ ___ = 5

24 ÷ 8 = ___

___ ÷ 8 = 1

64 ÷ 8 = ___

16 ÷ 8 = ___

___ ÷ 8 = 9

6 x 7 = 42 42 ÷ 6 = 7

7 x 8 = ___ ___ ÷ 7 = ___

9 x 8 = ___ ___ ÷ 8 = ___

8 x 5 = ___ ___ ÷ 8 = ___

Write the answers in the boxes.

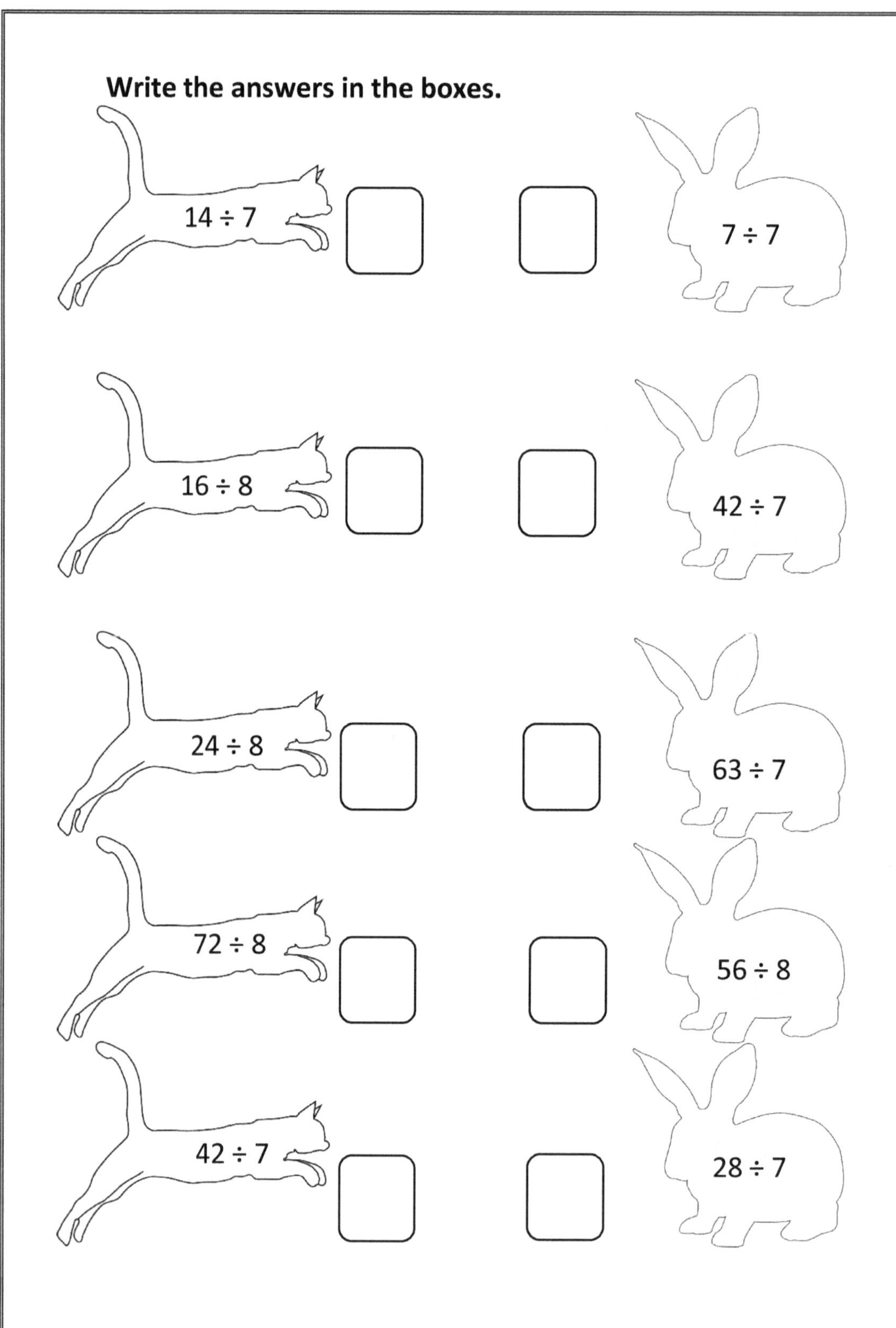

$\frac{64}{8} =$ ____

$\frac{56}{7} =$ ____

$\frac{42}{7} =$ ____

$\frac{70}{7} =$ ____

$\frac{72}{9} =$ ____

$\frac{64}{8} =$ ____

$\frac{21}{7} =$ ____

$\frac{48}{8} =$ ____

$\frac{49}{7} =$ ____

$\frac{80}{8} =$ ____

Mr. King has 64 books. He wants to put them in equal numbers on 8 bookshelves. How many books can he put on a bookshelf?

_____ books

Division by 9 and 10

Write a fact for the following pictures.

☺☺☺☺☺☺☺☺☺ ___ ÷ ___ = 1

☺☺☺☺☺☺☺☺☺
☺☺☺☺☺☺☺☺☺ ___ ÷ 9 = ___

☺☺☺☺☺☺☺☺☺☺
☺☺☺☺☺☺☺☺☺☺ 20 ÷ ___ = ___

☺ ☺ ☺ ☺
☺ ☺ ☺ ☺ ___ ÷ 10 = ___
☺ ☺ ☺ ☺
☺ ☺ ☺ ☺
☺ ☺ ☺ ☺
☺ ☺ ☺ ☺
☺ ☺ ☺ ☺
☺ ☺ ☺ ☺
☺ ☺ ☺ ☺
☺ ☺ ☺ ☺

Match.

$81 \div 9$	$27 \div 9$	$80 \div 10$	$60 \div 10$

$30 \div 10$	$36 \div 9$	$45 \div 9$	$40 \div 10$

What multiplication fact can help you find $72 \div 9$?

_____ × _____ = _____

Tip of the Day!

Any number divided by one equals that number.

For example, $9 \div 1 = 9$ or $7 \div 1 = 7$

Find each missing number.

72 ÷ 9 = ___

___ ÷ 9 = 0

___ ÷ 9 = 10

9 ÷ 9 = ___

108 ÷ 9 = ___

18 ÷ ___ = 2

___ ÷ 10 = 4

90 ÷ ___ = 9

60 ÷ ___ = 6

80 ÷ 10 = ___

___ ÷ 10 = 3

110 ÷ 10 = ___

9 x 7 = 63 | 63 ÷ 9 = 7

9 x 8 = ___ | ___÷ 9 = ___

10 x 5 = ___ | ___ ÷ 10 = ___

9 x 4 = ___ | ___ ÷ 9 = ___

Write the answers in the boxes.

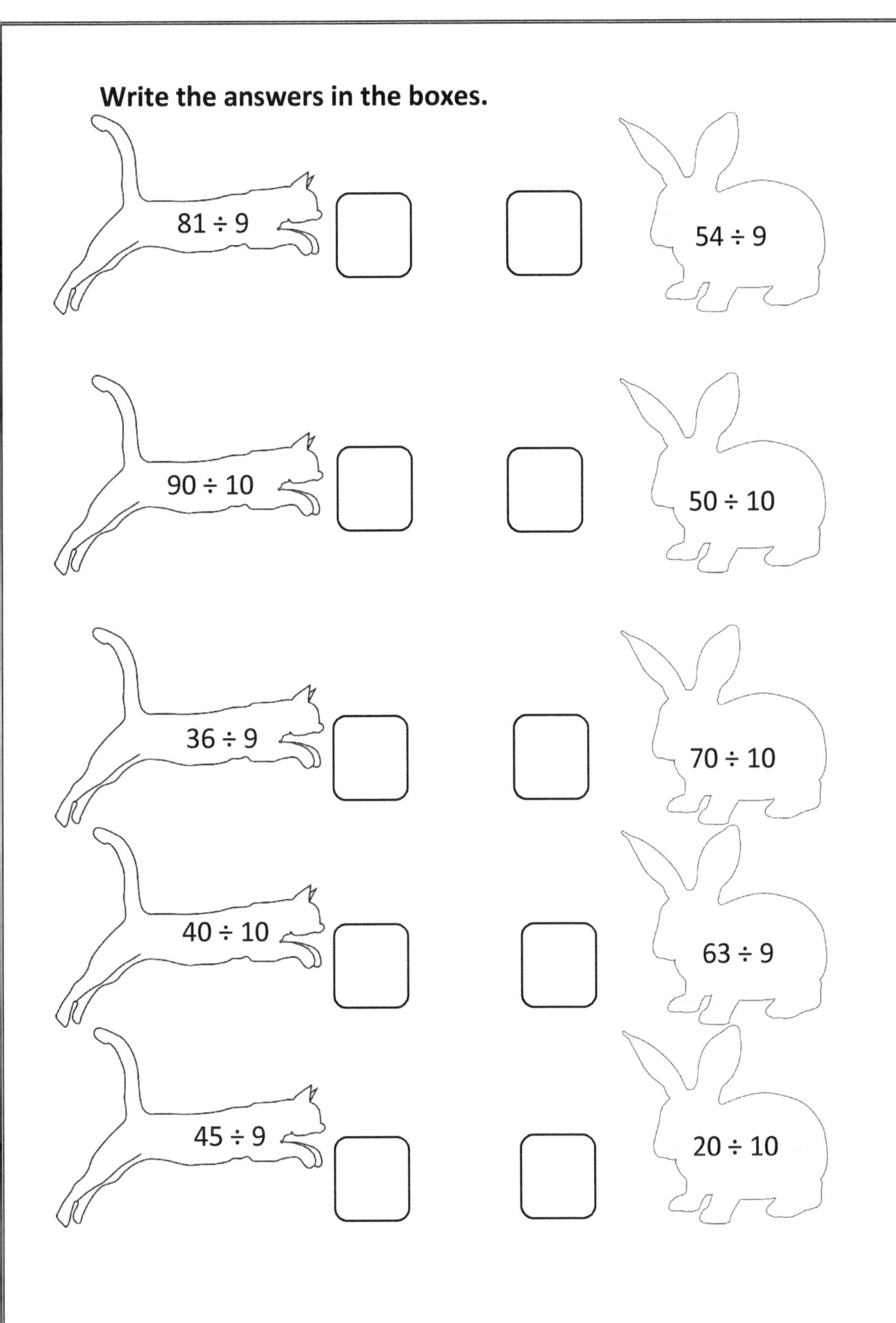

$\frac{63}{9} = \_\_\_\_$

$\frac{90}{9} = \_\_\_\_$

$\frac{36}{9} = \_\_\_\_$

$\frac{18}{9} = \_\_\_\_$

$\frac{9}{9} = \_\_\_\_$

$\frac{60}{10} = \_\_\_\_$

$\frac{10}{10} = \_\_\_\_$

$\frac{80}{10} = \_\_\_\_$

$\frac{81}{9} = \_\_\_\_$

$\frac{54}{9} = \_\_\_\_$

What multiplication fact can help you find 50 ÷ 10?

_____ × _____ = _____

Division by 11 and 12

Write a fact for the following pictures.

☺☺☺☺☺☺☺☺☺☺☺
☺☺☺☺☺☺☺☺☺☺☺
☺☺☺☺☺☺☺☺☺☺☺
☺☺☺☺☺☺☺☺☺☺☺

44 ÷ __ = __

☺ ☺ ☺ ☺ ☺
☺ ☺ ☺ ☺ ☺
☺ ☺ ☺ ☺ ☺
☺ ☺ ☺ ☺ ☺
☺ ☺ ☺ ☺ ☺
☺ ☺ ☺ ☺ ☺
☺ ☺ ☺ ☺ ☺
☺ ☺ ☺ ☺ ☺
☺ ☺ ☺ ☺ ☺
☺ ☺ ☺ ☺ ☺
☺ ☺ ☺ ☺ ☺

__ ÷ 11 = __

☺☺☺☺☺☺☺☺☺☺☺☺
☺☺☺☺☺☺☺☺☺☺☺☺
☺☺☺☺☺☺☺☺☺☺☺☺
☺☺☺☺☺☺☺☺☺☺☺☺
☺☺☺☺☺☺☺☺☺☺☺☺
☺☺☺☺☺☺☺☺☺☺☺☺

72 ÷ __ = __

Match.

60 ÷ 12	55 ÷ 11	96 ÷ 12	48 ÷ 12

33 ÷ 11	36 ÷ 12	77 ÷ 11	99 ÷ 11

What multiplication fact can help you

find 88 ÷ 11?

_____ × _____ = _____

Tip of the Day!

A fact family represents 4 related multiplication and division facts for a set of numbers. For example, this is the fact family for 3, 4, and 12.

3 × 4 = 12

4 × 3 = 12

12 ÷ 3 = 4

12 ÷ 4 = 3

Find each missing number.

___ ÷ 11 = 8

44 ÷ ___ = 4

99 ÷ ___ = 9

110 ÷ 11 = ___

___ ÷ 11 = 12

11 ÷ 11 = ___

24 ÷ ___ = 2

48 ÷ 12 = ___

___ ÷ 12 = 11

12 ÷ ___ = 1

144 ÷ ___ = 12

84 ÷ 12 = ___

11 x 5 = 55 55 ÷ 11 = 5

12 x 4 = ___ ___ ÷ 12 = ___

11 x 9 = ___ ___ ÷ 11 = ___

12 x 7 = ___ ___ ÷ 12 = ___

11 x 8 = ___ ___ ÷ 11 = ___

Write the answers in the boxes.

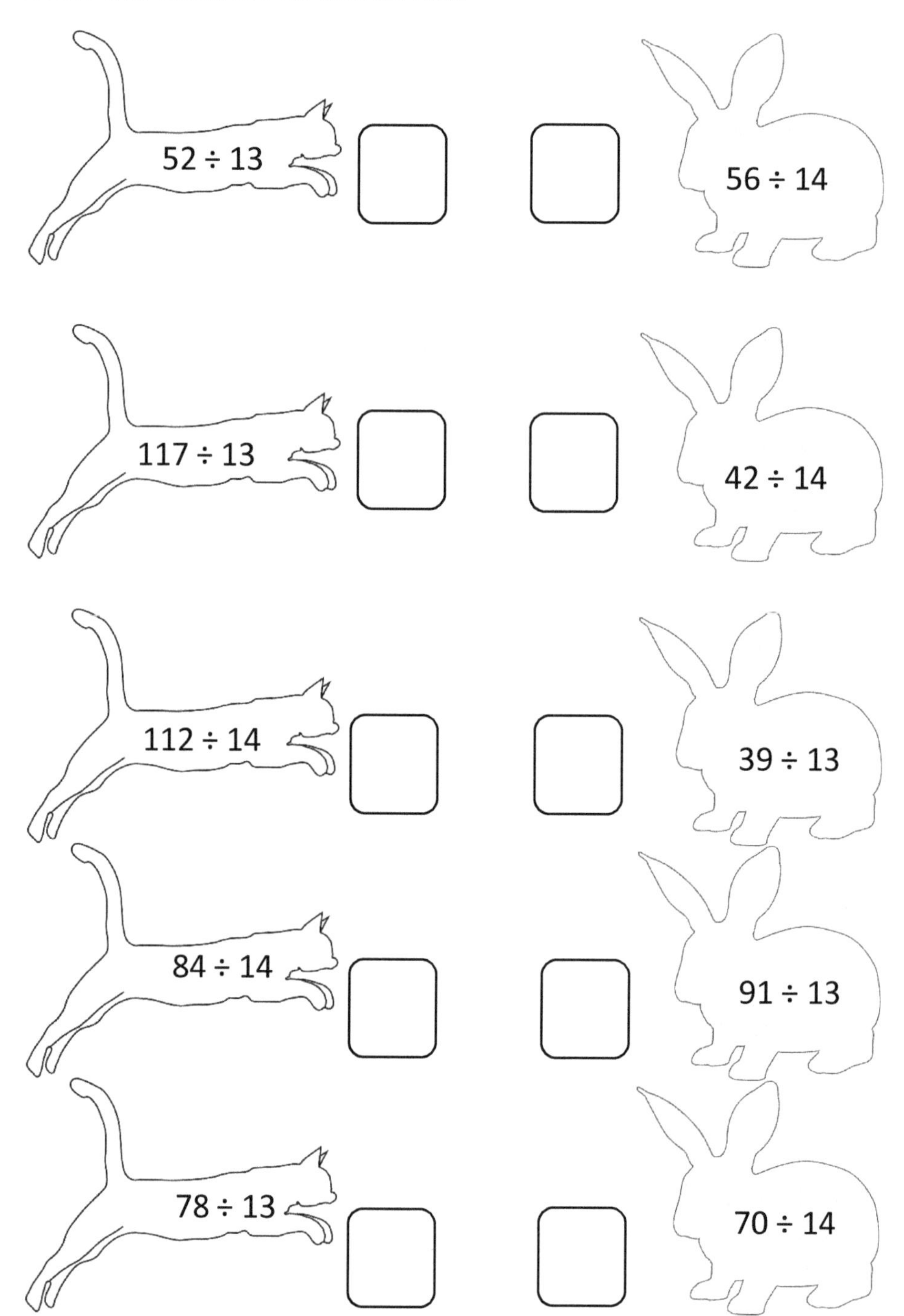

$\frac{72}{12} =$ ____

$\frac{48}{12} =$ ____

$\frac{121}{11} =$ ____

$\frac{144}{12} =$ ____

$\frac{36}{12} =$ ____

$\frac{88}{11} =$ ____

$\frac{120}{12} =$ ____

$\frac{99}{11} =$ ____

$\frac{132}{12} =$ ____

$\frac{96}{12} =$ ____

What multiplication fact can help you find 110 ÷ 11?

_____ × _____ = _____

"Effortless Math Education" Publications

Effortless Math Education authors' team strives to prepare and publish the best quality Mathematics learning resources to make learning Math easier for all. We hope that our publications help you or your student learn Math in an effective way.

We all in Effortless Math wish you good luck and successful studies!

Effortless Math Authors

CPSIA information can be obtained
at www.ICGtesting.com
Printed in the USA
BVHW011954150119
537897BV00007B/99/P

9 781986 356176